WITHDR

D0225930

THE
HISTORY OF
KUWAIT

ADVISORY BOARD

John T. Alexander
Professor of History and Russian and European Studies,
University of Kansas

Robert A. Divine
George W. Littlefield Professor in American History Emeritus,
University of Texas at Austin

John V. Lombardi
Professor of History,
University of Florida

A0002601415603

THE HISTORY OF KUWAIT

Michael S. Casey

The Greenwood Histories of the Modern Nations
Frank W. Thackeray and John E. Findling, Series Editors

Greenwood Press
Westport, Connecticut • London

KIRTLAND PUBLIC
LIBRARY

Library of Congress Cataloging-in-Publication Data

Casey, Michael S.
    The history of kuwait / Michael S. Casey.
        p. cm. — (The Greenwood histories of the modern nations, ISSN: 1096–2905)
    ISBN-13: 978–0–313–34073–4 (alk. paper)
1. Kuwait—History. I. Thackeray, Frank W. II. Findling, John E.
III. Title.
    DS247.K88C37 2007
    953.67—dc22   2007018368

British Library Cataloguing in Publication Data is available.

Copyright © 2007 by Michael S. Casey

All rights reserved. No portion of this book may be
reproduced, by any process or technique, without the
express written consent of the publisher.

Library of Congress Catalog Card Number: 2007018368
ISBN-13: 978–0–313–34073–4
ISSN: 1096–2905

First published in 2007

Greenwood Press, 88 Post Road West, Westport, CT 06881
An imprint of Greenwood Publishing Group, Inc.
www.greenwood.com

Printed in the United States of America

The paper used in this book complies with the
Permanent Paper Standard issued by the National
Information Standards Organization (Z39.48–1984).

10 9 8 7 6 5 4 3 2 1

Contents

Series Foreword *by Frank W. Thackeray and John E. Findling*   vii

Acknowledgments   ix

Timeline of Historical Events   xi

1   The Land and People of Kuwait   1

2   Desert Origins and Settlement (ca. 3000 B.C.E.–1756 C.E.)   15

3   Desert Sheikhdom (1756–1899)   29

4   British Protectorate (1899–1961)   47

5   Independence and Nationhood (1961–1990)   65

6   Invasion and Occupation (1990–1991)   85

7   Liberation (1991)   101

8   Reconstruction (1992–1999)   117

9   Kuwait Today (2000–)   129

Notable People in the History of Kuwait   143

Glossary   147

Bibliographic Essay   151

Index   155

Series Foreword

The *Greenwood Histories of the Modern Nations* series is intended to provide students and interested laypeople with up-to-date, concise, and analytical histories of many of the nations of the contemporary world. Not since the 1960s has there been a systematic attempt to publish a series of national histories, and, as editors, we believe that this series will prove to be a valuable contribution to our understanding of other countries in our increasingly interdependent world.

Over thirty years ago, at the end of the 1960s, the Cold War was an accepted reality of global politics, the process of decolonization was still in progress, the idea of a unified Europe with a single currency was unheard of, the United States was mired in a war in Vietnam, and the economic boom of Asia was still years in the future. Richard Nixon was president of the United States, Mao Tse-tung (not yet Mao Zedong) ruled China, Leonid Brezhnev guided the Soviet Union, and Harold Wilson was prime minister of the United Kingdom. Authoritarian dictators still ruled most of Latin America, the Middle East was reeling in the wake of the Six-Day War, and Shah Reza Pahlavi was at the height of his power in Iran. Clearly, the past 30 years have been witness to a great deal of historical change, and it is to this change that this series is primarily addressed.

With the help of a distinguished advisory board, we have selected nations whose political, economic, and social affairs mark them as among the most important in the waning years of the twentieth century, and for each nation we have found an author who is recognized as a specialist in the history of that nation. These authors have worked most cooperatively with us and with Greenwood Press to produce volumes that reflect current research on their nations and that are interesting and informative to their prospective readers.

The importance of a series such as this cannot be underestimated. As a superpower whose influence is felt all over the world, the United States can claim a "special" relationship with almost every other nation. Yet many Americans know very little about the histories of the nations with which the United States relates. How did they get to be the way they are? What kind of political systems have evolved there? What kind of influence do they have in their own region? What are the dominant political, religious, and cultural forces that move their leaders? These and many other questions are answered in the volumes of this series.

The authors who have contributed to this series have written comprehensive histories of their nations, dating back to prehistoric times in some cases. Each of them, however, has devoted a significant portion of the book to events of the last thirty years, because the modern era has contributed the most to contemporary issues that have an impact on U.S. policy. Authors have made an effort to be as up-to-date as possible so that readers can benefit from the most recent scholarship and a narrative that includes very recent events.

In addition to the historical narrative, each volume in this series contains an introductory overview of the country's geography, political institutions, economic structure, and cultural attributes. This is designed to give readers a picture of the nation as it exists in the contemporary world. Each volume also contains additional chapters that add interesting and useful detail to the historical narrative. One chapter is a thorough chronology of important historical events, making it easy for readers to follow the flow of a particular nation's history. Another chapter features biographical sketches of the nation's most important figures in order to humanize some of the individuals who have contributed to the historical development of their nation. Each volume also contains a comprehensive bibliography, so that those readers whose interest has been sparked may find out more about the nation and its history. Finally, there is a carefully prepared topic and person index.

Readers of these volumes will find them fascinating to read and useful in understanding the contemporary world and the nations that comprise it. As series editors, it is our hope that this series will contribute to a heightened sense of global understanding as we embark on a new century.

Frank W. Thackeray and John E. Findling
Indiana University Southeast

Acknowledgments

First, I would like to thank my editors, Kaitlin Ciarmiello and Sarah Colwell of Greenwood Press, for the opportunity to author this work and also for their patient and professional guidance along the way.

Next, I extend my lasting appreciation to my good Kuwaiti friends and former military colleagues, Ahmed and Marzoug. As my hosts, you made my sojourn in Kuwait enjoyable. As my mentors to all things Kuwaiti, you made my time there infinitely rewarding. It was an honor to know and work with you both. To me, you will always represent the heroic people of Kuwait.

Finally, but most importantly, I offer my humble and heartfelt gratitude to my family: to Alexandria, my mate for life, who soldiered on at home without complaint through war and overseas deployments; to Cameron, Cassandra, and Elaine, who represent the promising future; and to Colin, our Marine, who represents the honorable sacrifices made by so many servicemen and women so that we can sleep in peace at night.

Timeline of Historical Events

ca. 3000–2000 B.C.E.   Military and commercial activities by various Mesopotamian empires pass through Kuwait

ca. 2300 B.C.E.   Kuwait is part of the civilization centered on Dilmun in present-day Bahrain

ca. 600–300 B.C.E.   Greek trading post established on Kuwait's Faylakha Island, known to the Greeks as Icaros

610 C.E.   Prophet Mohamed founds Islam, which spreads rapidly

ca. 1613   Migrant fishing village established at Kuwait

ca. 1650   Drought forces Bedouin families, later known as the Bani Utub, to migrate from Najd in Central Arabia; the Al-Sabah family is among the immigrants

ca. 1672–1680   Sheikh Barrak bin Ghuraif of the Bani Khalid tribe builds a small fort at Kuwait

ca. 1710   The Bani Utub, including the Al-Sabah family, settle in Kuwait

1756	Sabah bin Jaber (Sabah I) elected sheikh of Kuwait, founds the Al-Sabah dynasty and rules until 1762; Kuwait is a vassal state to the Ottoman Empire
1762	Abdullah I becomes sheikh and rules until 1814
ca. 1766	Al-Khalifa and Al-Jalahima begin to depart Kuwait, leaving Al-Sabah family in control
1773–1775	Plague strikes Kuwait
1775	Kuwait's first contact with the British Empire through the British East India Company
ca. 1783	Kuwait's fleet defeats the Bani Kaab in a naval battle, fending off invasion
1793–1797	Series of unsuccessful Wahhabi invasions of Kuwait
1814	Jaber I becomes sheikh and rules until 1859
1859	Sabah II becomes sheikh and rules until 1866
1866	Abdullah II becomes sheikh and rules until 1892
1892	Mohamed becomes sheikh and rules until assassinated in 1896
1896	Mubarak (Mubarak the Great) assassinates his brother, becomes sheikh, and rules until 1915
1897	The Ottoman Empire recognizes Mubarak the Great as the provincial subgovernor of Kuwait
1899	January 23: Memorandum between Mubarak the Great and Great Britain recognizes Kuwait's sovereignty
1913	Anglo-Ottoman Convention
1914	Small desalinization plant built
1914–1918	First World War; Great Britain recognizes Kuwait's independence from the Ottoman Empire
1915	Jaber II becomes sheikh and rules until 1917
1916	The Great Arab Revolt against the Ottoman Empire
1917	Salem becomes sheikh and rules until 1921
1920	Ikhwan invasion and battle of Jahra ("Red Fort")
1921	Ahmad al Jaber becomes sheikh and rules until 1950

1922	Uqair Protocol; Neutral Zone established with Saudi Arabia
1934	Kuwait Oil Company receives oil concession, begins exploration
	The "Destructive Year"; rain destroys many of Kuwait's mud homes
1936	First exploratory oil well drilled in Kuwait
1938	Majlis Movement advocates for popular political representation in Kuwait's government
	First oil struck in Burgan field in Kuwait
1939–1945	Second World War; prevents development of Kuwaiti oil fields
1946	Kuwait's petroleum industry begins pumping oil and sells it overseas; oil revenues continue to grow annually; Kuwait begins to develop as a welfare state
1950	Abdullah al Salem (Abdullah III) becomes sheikh and rules until 1965
	A massive, modern desalinization plant is built to provide fresh water; other plants follow
1960	Kuwait National Petroleum Company (KNPC) founded
	OPEC forms; Kuwait is a founding member nation
1961	Kuwait Fund for Arab Economic Development (KFAED) created
	June 19: Kuwait becomes an independent emirate; Sheikh Abdullah III becomes Kuwait's first emir
	July 20: Despite an Iraqi protest, Kuwait joins the Arab League
1962	November 11: Kuwait's first constitution ratified by Emir Abdullah III
1963	January 23: Popular election for Kuwait's first National Assembly
	January 29: First National Assembly convenes
	May 14: Kuwait joins the United Nations
1965	Sabah III becomes emir and rules until 1977

1966	Kuwait and Saudi Arabia set borders, drop the Neutral Zone, and create the Divided Zone; agree to split oil revenues equally in the jointly held territory
1973	OPEC oil embargo causes steep increase in global prices; Kuwait's oil revenue spikes
1976	Kuwaiti government nationalizes the oil industry (for accounting purposes, retroactive to 1975)
1977	Jaber III becomes emir and rules until 2006
1979	Radical Shiite cleric Ayatollah Khomeini leads Iranian revolution, overthrows the Shah of Iran, and establishes an Islamic theocracy that threatens Sunni Kuwait
1980	Kuwait Petroleum Corporation (KPC) founded; oil industry restructured beginning in 1981
1980–1988	Iran-Iraq War; Kuwait supports Iraq
1981	Gulf Cooperation Council (GCC) organized
1982	Souk al-Manakh stock market crash
1983	Iran attacks Kuwaiti-flagged shipping and oil rigs in retaliation for Kuwait's support of Iraq; Iran encourages Shiite unrest and terrorist activities inside Kuwait
1984	GCC's Peninsula Shield defensive force established
1985	Thousands of foreign workers, primarily Shiites, are expelled from Kuwait to quell internal unrest
1987	May: In response to Iranian attacks, Kuwaiti oil tankers are reflagged and the U.S. Navy provides convoy protection in Arabian Gulf
1990	August 2: Iraq invades and occupies Kuwait, starting First Gulf War; Emir Jaber III takes exile in Saudi Arabia; United Nations Security Council Resolution 660 calls for immediate Iraqi withdrawal; U.S. forces soon deploy to Saudi Arabia to prevent Iraqi invasion; Operation Desert Shield begins
	August 8: Kuwait, called Kadhima by the Iraqis, is formally annexed as Iraq's 19th province
1991	January 17: Operation Desert Storm begins liberation of Kuwait

February 27: Kuwait liberated by the U.S.-led coalition

March 14: Martial law is in effect inside Kuwait; Jaber III returns from exile

October: Kuwait signs 10-year defense pact with the United States

2003   March 19: Operation Iraqi Freedom, later called the Second Gulf War, invades Iraq and soon topples Saddam Hussein

April 9: U.S. occupation of Iraq begins

2006   January 15: Saad becomes emir, rules briefly until, due to ill health, he abdicates and is simultaneously deposed by the National Assembly on January 24, 2006

January 29: Sabah IV becomes emir

April 4: Kuwaiti women vote for the first time in municipal elections

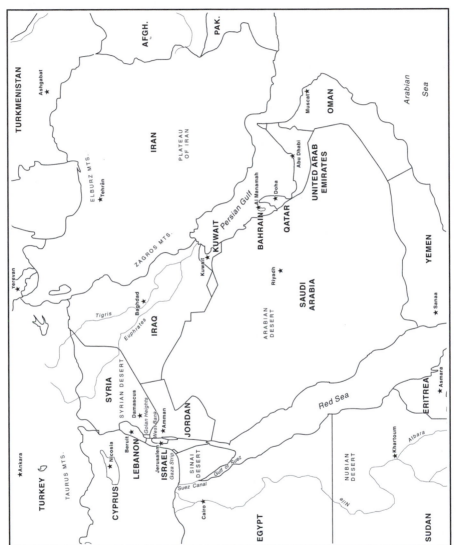

Map of the Middle East. Cartography by Mapcraft.com.

1

The Land and People
of Kuwait

Tucked into the most distant corner of the Arabian Gulf, the nation-state of Kuwait is a tiny but incredibly wealthy Arab kingdom that has been ruled for almost two hundred and fifty years by a single family, the Al-Sabah. In size, the *dawlat*, or state, of Kuwait is often compared to the state of New Jersey, but pure size is hardly an adequate measure of modern Kuwait's geostrategic importance regionally or throughout the world. In the not-too-distant past, the people of Kuwait were primarily desert nomads, but the long-term benefit of settling in an isolated and relatively benign location that met their modest needs must have been appealing, because once they arrived at Kuwait, they stayed, and remain to this day. Less than a century ago, the people of Kuwait were among this planet's poorest by almost any measure. Today, if such a thing could be calculated, the citizens of Kuwait collectively probably hold more economic power per capita than almost any other society in existence.

In a sense, Kuwait is synonymous with oil. Certainly one cannot understand modern-day Kuwait without first recognizing Kuwait's key niche in the oil industry, which drives the world's economies. Beginning in the twentieth century, Kuwait's vast petroleum reserves brought equally vast economic clout to this small desert country. Unfortunately, that same oil wealth also made Kuwait the financial envy of much of the world, especially of its large neighbors: Saudi Arabia, Iraq, and Iran. Oft overlooked, Kuwait became the center of the world's attention in 1990 after being invaded and occupied by Saddam Hussein's Iraqi armored forces. A military coalition led by the United States subsequently expelled the Iraqi invaders and quickly restored the land of Kuwait to its rightful owners. Beyond these facts, few people know much else about Kuwait or the Kuwaiti people.

Many people do not realize that, perhaps more than any other modern nation, Kuwait is a country of high contrasts. For centuries, Kuwait has served as a seagoing home for a desert people. Because it possesses only a minimal land area and the population of a medium-sized American metropolitan area, Kuwait is often disparagingly referred to as a mere city-state. Yet Kuwait packs the economic authority, and sometimes the political punch as well, of a heavyweight nation. Arguably the most independent of the Arabian Gulf nations, Kuwait spent most of the twentieth century as a protectorate of Great Britain before turning to the United States in recent decades for additional defense security. Thus, if one wants to truly understand Kuwait, timeworn stereotypes will no longer suffice. It is absolutely vital to study in detail the colorful distant past and the tragic recent history of the Kuwaiti people and their nation in order to gain true insight into their place in today's big picture.

Toward that end, this chapter serves as an introduction to the nation of Kuwait and to the Kuwaiti people as a whole. As such, it provides a thumbnail sketch of the geography, the economy, the people and their daily lives, the political structure of the government, and, especially, the national character of Kuwait the nation. Written accounts of Kuwait date back to the seventeenth century and generally refer to the area as Qurain, which comes from the Arabic word for high hill (*qarn*). On most early European maps, the name was typically spelled phonetically as Grane. Sometime between 1672 and 1680, Sheikh Barrak bin Ghuraif of the Bedouin tribe known as the Bani Khalid, which then ruled eastern Arabia, built a smallish fortress home on the spot. The Arabic word for fort is *kut*, a diminutive of which is *kuwait*, or "small fort." Since the late 1700s, the area has most usually been identified as Kuwait, though sometimes spelled alternatively as Kuwayt.

GEOGRAPHY

Kuwait's physical location is the first key to its importance in today's volatile world. Located in the heart of the Middle East, Kuwait is strategically positioned at the head, or northwest corner, of the Arabian Gulf. At just under seven thousand square miles, Kuwait is a little smaller than Connecticut or New Jersey. Kuwait has a land border of about one hundred and fifty miles with Iraq and another land border slightly longer with Saudi Arabia. With its many islands included, Kuwait's coastline, at almost three hundred miles, is substantial, and Kuwait Bay is one of the finest natural harbors in the entire

Map of Kuwait. Cartography by Bookcomp, Inc.

Arabian Gulf. With nine offshore islands of varying sizes, Kuwait claims a territorial sea 12 miles into the Arabian Gulf. Kuwait's land and ocean boundaries have always been a matter of contention, with armed conflict sometimes ensuing. In the aftermath of the two recent Gulf Wars, those borders are beginning to become finalized.

Tectonic forces are still actively reshaping the region around Kuwait. Kuwait lies on a portion of the Arabian Peninsula tectonic plate, which is being driven downward by nearby plates as the Red Sea expands. During the Jurassic and Cretaceous periods, similar tectonic plate movement caused folding in the Earth's layers, which trapped reservoirs of crude oil both onshore and offshore. The Arabian Gulf is fed by sedimentary deposits carried by river runoff, especially from the Tigris-Euphrates river system, causing the already-shallow sea to grow shallower over time. This warm water, almost an inland sea, is underlain by sedimentary deposits that have formed domes under which both water and oil are trapped. Generally, the oil sits between the impervious overhead cap, often limestone, and the brackish water on which the oil floats. Essentially the same situation occurs under land; oil is accessible using proven, relatively inexpensive drilling technologies. This ready access to petroleum makes the territory and offshore areas of Kuwait valuable real estate indeed.

The soil of Kuwait is alluvial; thus, it is sandy and high in minerals such as sodium, alkali, calcium, and sometimes gypsum. The reason these minerals are so common is because the high heat and minimal rainfall cause the little groundwater to carry the minerals toward the surface. The practical problem for Kuwaitis is that these high concentrations are detrimental to agriculture. Moreover, since the underground water is a leftover from a distant period in which rainfall was more prevalent, approximately thirty thousand to six thousand years ago, it represents a nonrenewable resource. This places a huge burden on the Kuwaiti government to ensure that this precious resource is managed wisely.

Although Kuwait lies very close to the Fertile Crescent, the natural advantages that that region enjoys are not shared with Kuwaitis. Kuwait lies in a floristic region known as Saharo-Sindian, which means the vegetation and wildlife found there are similar to the natural conditions of the area from Libya practically to Pakistan. As with many other countries in this region of arid land, vegetation and wildlife have been exploited and, in most cases, overused for centuries. Thus, the natural environment of Kuwait today is a pale representation of what it was just two or three centuries ago.

Only especially hardy plants and wildlife can survive in Kuwait's harsh climate. Kuwait has three separate ecosystems: desert, dunes, and salt marshes. Each ecosystem contains the kinds of grasses and shrubs expected in such conditions, and all of Kuwait's ecosystems show the unmistakable effects of overuse by humans and domesticated animals over the past three centuries. Herbage, when it does appear, rarely survives more than a few days before it is eaten by camels and other grazing animals. Thus, under the already-harsh conditions present in Kuwait, there have been few opportunities for lush vegetation to develop even when rain was present.

About fifty species of mammals are known to live in Kuwait. In physical size, the gazelle is the largest animal found in Kuwait, but it is considered an endangered species. Without gazelle on which to feed, the wildcats and canines are rarely ever seen today. In addition, almost three hundred species of birds migrate through Kuwait, but a much smaller number remains year-round. Finally, there are about forty species of reptiles, with a few poisonous snakes included, which can make travel off the beaten path exciting.

Like most of the other territories that lie along the Arabian Gulf, Kuwait's land area consists mostly of arid, sandy soil that is alluvial in origin. There are a few depressions, a ridgeline, and a handful of higher hills, but otherwise the country is level. Kuwait's isolated patches of higher, rocky terrain are limited in size and altitude. What high ground does exist generally lies in the west. From there, the land slopes down to reach sea level in the east. With most of the country barely above sea level, Kuwait's highest geographic point is only about three hundred meters. Less than 1 percent of the land area of Kuwait is arable, a limiting geographical factor that has had a significant effect on the subsequent development of the Kuwaiti people and their homeland. Kuwaitis must work hard for their daily rations. Confined to this essentially flat coastal plain, Kuwait lacks the depth of its neighbors. Therefore, Kuwait is tied to and dependent on the sea in a way that applies to few of its Arabian Gulf neighbors. In the past, the ocean actually fed the Kuwaitis. Today the sea is even more vital, since it is by sea that Kuwait transfers its petroleum and receives its vital sustenance.

The geography of Kuwait is of recent origin, relatively speaking. The country itself is covered by a bed of clay, silt, gravel, and sand that was deposited by a once-large, but no longer extant, river. This layer of sediment, several hundred meters thick in some spots, sits atop a large dome that consists of limestone. This massive rock formation in turn caps the reservoir of petroleum that provides Kuwait with its wealth and political influence.

Although Kuwait is sometimes noted as the only nation in the world without a lake, fresh water has been discovered underground on the west side of the country. A smaller aquifer was located deep underground to the south, as well, but the water it provides is extremely brackish and requires expensive distillation processing. These two aquifers, although insufficient for widespread agricultural irrigation, are nonetheless vital to adequately addressing Kuwait's drinking water needs and other commercial requirements. Prior to the discovery, much of Kuwait's water had to be imported. Extensive and expensive distillation plants now handle most of Kuwait's potable water needs, though a significant amount of fresh water must still be imported annually.

The weather of Kuwait is similar not only to its neighbors, but to almost every country across the Sahara geographical band. Kuwait is officially the fourth-hottest nation on Earth. Temperatures during the summer can easily exceed 120°F. Summers are long and oppressively hot; winters are short and relatively moist. Both temperature and rainfall can vary markedly year to year. The lowest recorded amount of precipitation was slightly less than one inch of rain. The highest annual rainfall was almost 14 inches. In fact, in late 1934, when torrential rain swamped the country and washed away many of Kuwait's mud-brick homes, the people referred to that entire year as Al-Sannah Al-Hadamah, Arabic for "the Year of Destruction."

During the summer, the daily high temperature averages 113°F. In winter, the daily low temperatures average 46°F. At any time of the year, but especially in June and July, a sandstorm driven by the northwest wind, known locally as a *shimal,* can create almost zero visibility conditions, which in turn hinders and sometimes precludes air traffic and even road travel. From October to April, light rain is normal, but the occasional heavy rainstorm can be a crippling problem for Kuwaitis, especially those who still live at the fringe of the desert; roads and homes are often damaged by flash flooding. Winter daily high temperatures are usually in the 70–80°F range. Springtime, which is cool and pleasant, is considered the finest season of the year, though this season also sees some rainfall. Total rainfall averages slightly more than five inches per year.

Kuwait City, the political capital and economic heart of the nation, is also the only major metropolitan area in the country. Several other significant population centers are found primarily up and down the coastline of the small country rather than inland. These larger towns include Al Ahmadi, Al Jahra, and Fahaheel. These population centers are connected by an extensive, modern network of highways. Along with Al Ahmadi, major seaports and high-tech ocean terminals include Ash Shu'aybah, Ash Shuwaykh, Doha, Mina Abd Allah, and Mina Su'ud. The industrial heart of the country is the Ash Shuwaykh district.

Offshore, nine islands add to the nation's limited land area, though most of these islands are either uninhabitable or insignificant in size. Faylakha Island is the most important historically because it contains several largely unexplored archaeological sites that date back thousands of years. Bubiyan Island, now connected to the mainland by a wide bridge, is the largest of the nine islands at around 333 square miles; since the Gulf War, however, this large island that was once home to thousands of Kuwaitis has been reserved exclusively for military purposes and serves as a bulwark against future Iraqi encroachment. Warbah Island, in the far north, is about 14 square miles in area.

The other coastal islands are Auhha, Kubbar, Miskan, Qaruh, Umm al-Maradim, and Umm Al-Naml. A few of the tiniest islands are only occasionally visited by local fishermen and serve mostly as a home to migrating birds. Of note, the ownership of several of these islands is disputed, as Iraq, Iran, and Saudi Arabia also contend for the potential prize of oil that might lie under these islands. Even today, the Kuwaiti Coast Guard and Naval Force must aggressively patrol these waters to prevent squatters from other nations, sometimes state sponsored, from staking their claims to a Kuwaiti islet.

Kuwait claims a 12-mile territorial limit, measured from the mainland and from the individual islands. This affords Kuwait a sea frontier of more than two thousand square miles. In the northern part of the country, especially lining Kuwait Bay, the waters are very shallow; in some areas they are little more than mud flats. To the south, waters are deeper and the bottoms are sandy. This is where some of the better recreational beaches are located, but also where the massive shipping ports and offshore terminals have been erected to handle the gigantic petroleum tankers that move in and out of Kuwait daily.

ECONOMY

The Kuwaiti dinar, the local currency, was created at independence in 1961 to replace the Indian rupee, which had been the coin of the realm. The dinar is issued by the Central Bank of Kuwait and now, almost every year, is rated as one of the highest-valued monetary units in the world. The strength of Kuwait's currency is a clear reflection of Kuwait's entire economy. The solid foundation on which both are based is petroleum.

Kuwait controls approximately 10 percent of the world's known oil reserves. Proven oil reserves are slightly less than 100 million barrels, and proven natural gas reserves are 1.5 trillion cubic meters. Estimates of Kuwait's holdings, rather than proven reserves, run even higher. Not surprisingly, Kuwait's economy is entirely focused on the petroleum industry. Oil makes up more than 60 percent of Kuwait's gross domestic product (GDP). In addition to the United States, Kuwaiti oil is purchased primarily by Japan, South Korea, Singapore, and Taiwan. Of note, all are major allies and trading partners of the United States. Thus, it is considered vital to both the American economy and U.S. national security that the flow of petroleum from Kuwait not be disrupted by regional instability or terrorism. This political fact is critical in understanding the United States' recent military and diplomatic efforts to liberate and defend the little nation of Kuwait.

Other than petroleum and natural gas, the only natural resources found in significant quantities in Kuwait are fish and shrimp, but even these once-thriving local industries are now relatively small in scale. Kuwait's natural pearling industry once led the world, and brought with it incredible wealth for Kuwaiti businessmen, but the development of cultured pearls in Japan shattered that dominance prior to the Second World War.

Before the oil boom of the mid-1900s, Kuwait's fishing industry was adequate for providing enough food for the small population. The skyrocketing population, driven by development of the oil industry, and, lately, ecological damage to the fishing grounds of the Arabian Gulf caused by the Iraqi military have severely depleted the availability of seafood. Most food for the people of Kuwait now comes from outside the small country, though a small but growing portion of those imported foodstuffs is processed locally, which has led to a growing industrial sector. Besides food processing, other Kuwaiti industries include petrochemicals, cement, fertilizers, and ship building and repair. These local industries also have the highest potential for growth in the future.

Almost 40 percent of Kuwait's GDP is in services, and less than 1 percent is connected to local agriculture. Kuwait is self-sufficient when it comes to fish, but other produce is extremely limited. Despite irrigation, the land and climate have always hindered farming, which remains insignificant economically. Except for seafood, Kuwait must import almost all other foodstuffs required to meet the growing population's needs. Other major imports include vehicles and repair parts, clothing, and construction materials, especially wood. Kuwait lacks the resources and the industrial capacity to meet these needs domestically, and no society can continue for long without them. The primary providers of these essential materials are the United States, Germany, Japan, the United Kingdom, Saudi Arabia, Italy, France, and China. It is also possible that the post–Saddam Hussein government of Iraq will become a solid trading partner with Kuwait, but the ongoing insurgency in Iraq has hindered much positive development in that direction.

Kuwait's citizens enjoy some of the finest telecommunications services in the entire Middle East. Largely rebuilt or modernized since the Gulf War, Kuwait's telephone system is first rate. The country is served by numerous television and radio stations. Several modern satellite links and a fiber-optic cable tie the country to neighbors and key allies in the region. Kuwait also boasts one of the highest levels of Internet use anywhere in the Muslim world, and the Kuwaitis' computer savvy makes them highly competitive in today's fast-moving, high-tech business and financial environments.

PEOPLE

Practically all Kuwaiti citizens are ethnically Arab by birth, meaning they can trace their origins back to the Arabian Peninsula prior to the advent of Islam. The official language of the country is Arabic, though English is widely understood, especially in the major business and population centers. Arabic belongs to the Hamito-Semitic family of languages, which is related to Hebrew, Aramaic, and Ethiopian, among others. Spoken Arabic is colloquial in nature. The spoken dialect of Kuwait is essentially Arabian Peninsular—in other words, Arabic as spoken in Saudi Arabia, but Kuwaiti Arabic is significantly different from the dialects spoken in, say, Syria, Egypt, or Algeria.

Written Arabic is the *lingua sacra*, or "sacred language," of Islam, because the revelations made to Mohamed were delivered and recorded in Arabic. Largely because of the language's religious significance, written Arabic is similar across the Arabic world, which further helps foster a sense of sameness and brotherhood among Arabic-speaking peoples. This sense of Arab oneness also encourages pan-Arabism, a political initiative to throw off arbitrary territorial borders and live as one great Arab nation. Pan-Arabism regularly strikes a chord in and among Arabs, and the movement continues to disturb the social and political fabric of modern-day Kuwait.

Almost all of Kuwait's citizenry follow the religion of Islam. While many noncitizens within Kuwait are also Muslims, those from other areas, such as South Asia, generally bring with them a host of other religious beliefs. While Kuwait does not engage in the kinds of aggressive measures that some other Muslim nations employ to limit the exercise of faiths other than Islam, Kuwait is still home to very few Christians or Jews. As a Muslim, the typical Kuwaiti believes that God (Allah) revealed himself directly to the prophet Mohamed, as recorded in the Qur'an, Islam's holy book.

Within Islam, Muslims are divided into Sunnis and Shiites. One key distinction between the two involves authority in the absence of Mohamed. Sunni Muslims believe that, following the death of Mohamed, temporal and religious leaders—caliphs and imams, respectively—could be elected by the community to their leadership posts. Shiite Muslims, however, maintain that only direct descendants of Mohamed can fill these highest positions of authority. In Kuwait, Sunnis greatly outnumber Shiites by at least three to one, though this ratio has never been accurately determined. This still-strong Shiite presence in Kuwait can be affected by what happens in Shiite Iran, just across the Arabian Gulf.

Partly as a result of the negative effects of the Iraqi occupation on older Kuwaitis and partly as a result of a baby boom since the Gulf War, Kuwait's population is rather young. The median age of the population is in the mid-twenties. All Kuwaiti citizens, girls as well as boys, receive compulsory free education through high school. If a citizen chooses to pursue a college degree, he or she can do so for free, either in Kuwait or outside the country. The literacy rate in Kuwait, for males and females alike, exceeds 80 percent, which is well above the norm found among Muslim nations. Supported by a comprehensive national health care program, life expectancies for Kuwaiti men and women are in the upper seventies and continue to rise slowly.

Compared with conditions in the West, the cultural restrictions placed on the personal lives of Kuwaiti women remain numerous and substantial, but movement is definitely in the direction of more social and political freedoms, and the hope of full civil rights for Kuwaiti women remains alive and the objective attainable. When compared with women in many other Muslim countries, the women of Kuwait enjoy remarkable latitude culturally. In recent years, the role of women in Kuwaiti society and politics has continued to expand, and Kuwait is a definite trendsetter in the Muslim world in this regard.

Only a few generations ago, most Kuwaitis were nomadic camel herders, fishermen, or pearl divers. Today, only about half of all Kuwaitis work on a daily basis. The majority of those Kuwaitis who do work are employed by the national government. Almost all Kuwaitis are city dwellers who reside in Kuwait City or one of the other several large towns, such as Al Jahrah and

Al Ahmadi, which serve as suburbs for the capital. Kuwait's population saw a huge dip during the Iraqi occupation and the subsequent Gulf War but has rebounded strongly since that time. The continually rising population now stands at almost 3 million people. Of those people, however, less than half are actually Kuwaiti citizens. The rest are almost all temporary or guest workers.

These noncitizen employees, well over a million in number and constituting about 80 percent of Kuwait's labor pool, perform virtually all the manual labor as well as filling the many necessary service occupations. Some are European or American technicians, but most are unskilled laborers who come primarily from Asia and across the Arab world. A subset of these guest workers is the *bidun*. The word means "without"—in this case, without a sovereign nation to call one's own. While often of Palestinian origin, these stateless Arab workers can also be expatriates from Iraq, Egypt, Iran, or Syria; in any case, they are technically in the country only temporarily, which makes their economic and political position within Kuwait very precarious.

As political and social turmoil occurs in the Arab world, it is often transferred to Kuwaiti society through these bidun. As Kuwaiti and international political leaders readily comprehend, Kuwait's entire economic infrastructure would rapidly collapse were it not for these foreign workers. Moreover, any problem for or disruption of these foreign workers, such as Arab nationalism or Islamic radicalism, has an immediate negative effect on Kuwait's fragile economy and, through it, on the economies of the nations that rely on Kuwait for petroleum. Economic, and therefore political, stability in and around Kuwait is vitally important to the United States and to Kuwait's trading partners and allies, which makes the country's matters of prime interest in Washington, DC, and other major capitals in both the East and the West.

Viewed from the outside, the people inside Kuwait appear to be broken into only these two obvious categories: Kuwaitis and non-Kuwaitis. Close internal observation of Kuwaitis, however, makes apparent several other key dividing lines among the Kuwaiti population. Sunnis constitute the majority of Kuwaitis, but the significant Shiite sector is sometimes influenced by outsiders—historically the Iranians, who sometimes seek advantage by fomenting domestic discord inside Kuwait.

Kuwait is a welfare state. The country essentially has no citizens below the poverty line, though domestic workers and the families of foreign workers sometimes endure a relatively meager existence. Living above the poverty line, however, is not the same thing as enjoying social and economic equality. Despite the historic efforts and recent initiatives of Kuwait's rulers, there is a large gap in socioeconomic status between most Kuwaitis and those few at the very top of society. That division has been further exacerbated in the last decade as a new schism has evolved along gender lines. As a Muslim society, Kuwait continues to grapple with the complex issue of civil rights for women.

Some forward steps have been observed in recent years, but other advancements have been rescinded, at least temporarily. Of note, despite these social and political problems, Kuwait remains at the leading edge of political and social modernization among Arab nations.

A final partition of the Kuwaiti population was recently caused by the Iraqi invasion. Those Kuwaitis who stayed behind and suffered under, or even resisted, Saddam Hussein's legions continue to struggle over reconciliation with those Kuwaitis and temporary workers who collaborated with the Iraqi forces and with those who fled altogether for the duration of the war. The fact that the royal family spent the entire occupation and liberation in exile outside the country has colored political developments in the war's aftermath.

POLITICAL STRUCTURE

Kuwait's governmental structure is a form of constitutional monarchy. Specifically, since independence, the tiny nation has been a hereditary emirate: a nation-state ruled by an emir, or prince, who accedes to the throne because of blood ties. Kuwait's ruling dynasty comes from the Al-Sabah family, which helped found the country in the middle of the eighteenth century and, first as sheikhs, now as emirs, has ruled it ever since. During this long period of Al-Sabah rule, Kuwait has vacillated politically between quasi-independence, being a part of the Ottoman Empire, and being a protectorate of the British Empire. For centuries, Kuwait's rulers have had to find a balance between independence and security, and the designs of hostile neighbors have often caused Kuwait to seek protection where it could be had. Upon receiving official independence from Great Britain in 1961, a new constitution delineated the political structure of the new nation—a political structure that has continued to slowly evolve over time.

Kuwait's emir is the formal head of state and, along with the prime minister who is named by the emir, oversees the executive branch of government. The crown prince is the heir apparent, the Al-Sabah male next in line to be emir, and often serves as prime minister, as well. Al-Sabah family members also fill many of the key spots in the cabinet and elsewhere in the government. A cabinet or council of appointed ministers provides advice to the emir and the prime minister. The popularly elected legislative body is the National Assembly, or the Majlis al-Umma. A High Court of Appeal heads the judicial branch of government, a multitiered system that handles everything from traffic court to appeals of death sentences. While Kuwait possesses a civil law system that is secular in nature, civil laws governing personal behavior for both men and women are based on the Shariah, the body of Islamic law. Though the Kuwaiti government is highly centralized, there are five internal administrative subdivisions or governorates that essentially serve as county governments.

The age of majority for Kuwaitis is 21. Until very recently, suffrage was restricted to adult males whose families have resided in Kuwait since 1920 or to those naturalized citizens who have lived in Kuwait for more than 30 years. Since the typical temporary worker remains in Kuwait only three to five years, this substantial residency requirement essentially disenfranchises virtually all guest workers, regardless of how long they or their ancestors live and work in the country. The question of full voting rights for women, as well as practical access to those rights, has been at the top of Kuwait's political agenda for several years. While there are no true political parties in the American or European sense, the interests of the Kuwaiti people are represented in various other ways in the political process.

Kuwaiti national defense is in the hands of the military branches of Land Force, Naval Force, and Air Force, which includes air defense forces. The National Guard augments these standing services. There are both compulsory and voluntary service options, but most Kuwaitis receive deferments for education or other purposes. Non-Kuwaitis, then, make up a sizable proportion of the armed forces, though senior officers are always Kuwaiti citizens. Kuwait also serves as a secure rear area, staging point, and port of embarkation/debarkation for U.S. and coalition military forces operating in Iraq and, potentially, throughout the Arabian Gulf region.

While Kuwait continues to play an active role in the complicated and contentious politics of the Middle East and throughout the Arab world, the First Gulf War has heightened awareness of the need for protection from neighbors with aspirations for Kuwait's oil wealth. The role of Kuwait's protector is now served by the United States, though Great Britain continues to maintain a diplomatic and military presence in and around Kuwait. Some of the major international organizations of which Kuwait is a member nation include the Gulf Cooperation Council (GCC), the International Atomic Energy Agency (IAEA), INTERPOL, the League of Arab States (LAS, commonly the "Arab League"), the Non-aligned Movement, the Organization of the Islamic Conference, the Organization of Petroleum Exporting Countries (OPEC), the United Nations (UN), the World Health Organization (WHO), and the World Trade Organization (WTO).

NATIONAL CHARACTER

It has sometimes been disparagingly suggested that Kuwait is not a country but simply a "corporation with a flag." This common prejudice suggests that the Kuwaitis have no national identity as a people, only a business interest in their so-called nation. While there are definitely some Kuwaitis for whom this is true, as a generalization it is far from the truth. No one who visited Kuwait in the immediate aftermath of the Gulf War would believe such a negative opinion. Not every Kuwaiti acted heroically during the war, no more than would every single citizen of any other nation, but the Kuwaiti people as a whole endured the nearly unendurable in order to survive the brutal occupation of the Iraqi army. Afterward, the survivors, virtually every one of whom suffered grievous personal and financial loss, chose to rebuild rather than to relocate to a more secure home somewhere else, in spite of a vengeful Saddam Hussein still in power across the border. To do so took more than a business interest in an economic enterprise; it took a sense of national identity, a characteristic not universally present throughout the modern Arab world. The people of Kuwait survived more hardship in a shorter period of time than practically any modern Arab people have been forced to experience. Of note, the Kuwaitis came out of that "trial by fire" stronger than ever as a people and a nation.

Interestingly, following the Gulf War, one Western observer compared the Kuwaitis to the Americans in 1812 just after Washington, DC, the new nation's capital city, had been sacked and burned by British troops; every last Kuwaiti was "mad as hell and not going to take it anymore." Despite horrific personal suffering and economic loss, the Kuwaitis were determined that neither their homeland nor their homes would ever again fall under the sway of a brutal foreign invader. In the face of vociferous disapproval from most of the Muslim world, Kuwait's stalwart support of subsequent efforts to initially contain and disarm, then eventually to defeat Saddam Hussein and rebuild Iraq serves as ample proof of their national determination. The First Gulf War was a defining moment for the people and the nation of Kuwait. Those once-nomadic people and their new country are stronger and more prosperous now than ever before. The reasons behind Kuwait's courageous "renaissance" after being conquered by Iraq are found in the study of Kuwaiti history.

2

Desert Origins and Settlement (ca. 3000 B.C.E.–1756 C.E.)

Kuwait is a small slice of the area of the world sometimes referred to as the "cradle of civilization." It is not known for sure how far back into prehistory to situate civilization in Kuwait, but it is clear that the area was home to a series of different peoples over the millennia. Some of those migrants came to conduct trade with the many imperial cities of ancient Iraq and Iran. Other migrants came for opportunities for prosperity offered by the pearling industry, which was centered on the Arabian Gulf for centuries. Some, like the family groups of Bedouin nomads who created the Kuwait we see today, would be driven from their homes by harsh weather, stopping where they did because of the respite that the grazing lands of Kuwait provided to their herds of camels, goats, and sheep. Except for those Bedouin families, however, none of these peoples came to stay. In this chapter, the early iterations of and influences on civilization in ancient Kuwait are considered.

ANCIENT INHABITANTS (ca. 3000–300 B.C.E.)

It is likely that some areas of present-day Kuwait have never served as a home to humans; other parts, in particular Faylakha Island, have provided shelter or sanctuary to a long list of travelers, traders, and troops. Directly offshore in Kuwait Bay, Faylakha Island is an obvious stopping point for those

sailing the upper reaches of the Arabian Gulf. Numerous archaeological artifacts can be found on Faylakha Island that can be dated as far back as the third
millennium B.C.E., though proof of human habitation begins to fade away
again sometime around 1000 B.C.E.

Putting early life on Faylakha Island into historical context requires knowledge of the ancient kingdoms of Mesopotamia and Iran, but few documents
exist to shed light on ancient Kuwait. What little is known of those ancient empires comes largely from the deciphering of clay tablets, composed in cuneiform, or wedge-shaped writing, which was invented in ancient Mesopotamia.
To date, unfortunately, written records do not afford a comprehensive record
of life specifically on Faylakha Island. Thousands of clay tablets are extant but
not yet deciphered, however, so there is much to learn. Unlike parchment and
papyrus, clay tablets do not significantly degrade over time, so it is possible
that much more can be learned about Faylakha Island and its possible position
in the trading empires in and around ancient Mesopotamia.

Today's Arabian Gulf island nation of Bahrain, located not far from Kuwait,
was once home to the ancient civilization of Dilmun. Commercial and military outposts of Dilmun's civilization were spread around the periphery of
the Arabian Gulf. One of those distant stations was established on Faylakha
Island around 2300 B.C.E. It is likely that subsequent merchants on Faylakha
Island traded actively with the series of empires that were preeminent in ancient Mesopotamia and Iran, possibly even incorporated into one or more of
those early empires. If so, it is even possible that Faylakha Island was once ad-
ministered under the famous code of Hammurabi, Mesopotamia's law-giving
king. It is fairly certain that the trading post on Faylakha Island was linked in
some fashion with the mercantile center of Susa and the cities of the kingdom
of Uruk. It is also probable that at least a few of Kuwait's other islands were
inhabited during this period; some later relics have been found on Umm al-
Naml Island, but archaeological excavation still continues.

As part of the steady Hellenizing march of the army of Alexander the
Great, Greek sailors and commercial interests later established a small trading
colony on Faylakha Island. These Greeks left behind engraved stone tablets
that have helped archaeologists study the history of the island during this era.
Alexander's Greeks, who would not stay long, referred to their new island
home as Icaros. Several reasons have been suggested to explain the choice
of name for the island. One possibility is that Faylakha Island's shape was
reminiscent of the island of Icaros in the Aegean Sea, an island well known
to the Greek mariners. The Aegean Icaros was the burial site of the mythical
Icaros, who, along with his father, Daedalus, manufactured feathery wings
to escape from prison. In exuberance following his new freedom, the fool-
ish Icaros flew too close to the sun and melted the wax cementing his wings,
causing him to plunge to his death on the island below. Alternatively, and just

as logically, it has been suggested that the Greeks chose the name Icaros because the oppressive summertime heat of Kuwait hinted at what it would be like to approach the blazing sun. An ancient Greek temple marks the site, and archaeological excavation is ongoing at several other locations on Faylakha Island. Until a written record is discovered, it is doubtful if the question about the island's naming will ever be resolved.

Following the Hellenization of Faylakha Island and most of the Fertile Crescent by Alexander's armies, Greek became the primary language of the commercial class, so it was probably also the language of the merchants on Faylakha Island. Thus, the Greek cultural artifacts found in Kuwait do not necessarily indicate they were left behind by ethnic Greeks. It is quite possible that Greek-speaking Arabs or Persians might well have deposited some of the numerous archaeological treasures in Kuwait over the centuries.

After Alexander's untimely death, control of Faylakha Island likely fell to the Seleucids, the dynasty that inherited those parts of Alexander's conquests based in Persia. Since the rest of Mesopotamia enjoyed almost two hundred years of peace and prosperity that accompanied this Hellenization, it is likely that conditions on Faylakha Island were also amenable. How the trading post on Faylakha Island fared under the subsequent Parthian and Sassanid imperial regimes is still to be determined. Given that the Sassanids had influence as far away as Rome, it is highly likely that they also had some effect on nearby Faylakha Island. Faylakha Island's importance should not be overstated, however. While close to major sea lines and landlines of communications, it was nonetheless off the beaten path, and probably only rarely received much attention from its imperial overseers, regardless of the empire they represented. Later, however, with the emergence of Islam, this area of the Arabian Gulf would begin to grow in importance.

DESERT NOMADS (300 B.C.E.–ca. 1650 C.E.)

The large plateau located in the very heart of the Arabian Peninsula is known as the Najd. This region of the central Arabian highlands has been the home of a nomadic people of Arabic origin called the Baduwin or, more commonly in the West, Bedouin. In general usage, the word Arab applies to the people who lived on the Arabian Peninsula prior to the arrival of Islam. The name Bedouin is more restrictive and descriptive, as it signifies an Arab of the desert. This is an apt term, because the Najd is one of the most imposing deserts on Earth. In earlier centuries, a number of civilizations had attempted to establish a foothold in the Arabian region, most often at its edges, but by this time the graves of those early inhabitants were covered by sand. It is not an accident that a large part of the peninsula's interior is known as the Empty Quarter, or Rub al Kali.

Little is known about central Arabia prior to the coming of Islam, and it is likely to stay that way unless or until something is discovered in an archaeological exploration. Until then, the lack of written records precludes in-depth knowledge. What can be said is that the people of the region were nomadic or seminomadic, they were organized tribally, and their economy revolved around rearing livestock, with a low level of agriculture and small handicrafts. For centuries, the Bedouin of the interior had raided the caravans that moved around and through the Arabian region carrying riches such as spices and silks from as far away as China. Determined military efforts from the powers that be, whether Persian, Roman, or Ethiopian, however, kept the piracy to an acceptable level, and this thievery never conveyed vast wealth on the Bedouin.

Meanwhile, the location that is now Kuwait, while always on the far periphery of Central Arabia, still held a strategic position along the straight line that connected Central Arabia with Mesopotamia and Persia. Thus, even though permanent settlements in Kuwait were few and far between chronologically, it was not uncommon for military forces to move through the area while on campaign. In 529 c.e., two Arab armies engaged each other in battle in the area of Wara, inside present-day Kuwait. Another major battle was recorded in 623 c.e. That year, a Persian army was defeated by an Arab cavalry force in the Kazima area of modern Kuwait.

The true nomadic pastoralism of the Bedouin was not so much a choice as a survival strategy. Because they lived in an environment where vegetation covered less than 10 percent of the surface area, it was not possible to let the seasons dictate the tribe's foraging. Since it was only a matter of weeks before grazing herds devoured the available pasturage, the need to move on was compelling. To the extent that there was a sense of land ownership of these habitual grazing spots, it was communal, indeed tribal, in nature. Upon arrival in Kuwait, this tribal situation would alter slightly, but in the Najd, there was no other way for the Bedouin to exist.

Teamwork was the other indispensable requirement for survival in the Arabian Desert. The very nature of the environment forced families to work together and confined most interaction to trusted members. Herds and waterholes needed to be protected from outsiders, and the tribal nature of Bedouin life was established. The structure was fairly straightforward. Among the Bedouin of this period, individual families grouped together to make up a household. Households then grouped into a clan, and clans grouped into a tribe. Most Arab clans took their name from a common ancestor, some tribes tracing their lineage to biblical times. The family heritage of Mohamed the prophet, to name just one, is reported in three disputed versions: in the first, he is related to Adnan, Ishmael's son; in the second version he is related to Abraham; and in the third, Mohamed's line goes all the way back to Adam.

Along with the ancestor's name went the appellation "sons of" or "people of." The Bani Khalid, for example, are essentially the sons or people of Khalid.

The nomads who settled Kuwait were known as the Bani Utub. In early records, this name has been written with wild fluctuations of spelling: Attaba, Atib, Atub, Otab, Otub, Ottoobee, Utba, and Uttoobee. This is not unusual. Since the Arabic alphabet lacks several English vowels, the spelling of Arabic words often varies. This text will adhere to Utub, which appears to be the standard spelling in documents written by Arab chroniclers. Spelling aside, the origins of the name are not definite. Unlike most group names, this one reflects the clan's involvement in a significant historical incident, but there is still some debate about the event being referenced. The name's traditional explanation comes from the migration to Kuwait itself.

The very act of migrating out of the Najd set this particular group apart from its former neighbors and clansmen. The migratory change of status also resulted in a new name to classify these hopeful settlers: the Bani Utub, or "people who wandered or moved." A second, less authoritative explanation of the group's name, based on the Arabic word for threshold, *atiba,* will be discussed in the next chapter. Regardless of the group's ultimate origin, this reorientation of traditional clan and family relationships created a new subset of the existing Amarat section of the Anizah tribe. This new grouping would essentially rewrite the historical connections between the migrants and the rest of the people of the Arabian Peninsula.

The Bedouin of the Najd consist of a host of hereditary tribes, most of which can trace their heritage back for centuries. A Bedouin man, regardless of his social standing within his own local community, looked with disdain on non-Bedouin. Every Bedouin man could take great pride in his lineage: he was an Arab al Ariba, or an "Arab of the Arabs"—a proud descendant of Yarab, father of all the Arabs. To the Bedouin, all other Arabs are Arab al Musta Ariba, "Arabs who became Arabs." Within these two major groups, superior and inferior tribes exist. The superior tribes are considered sharif because of their aristocratic heritage based on the pure blood that ties them directly to the time of Mohamed. The remaining tribes, which constitute the vast majority, are nonsharif tribes.

Another way to classify Arabs, an approach that the Bedouin employed when considering outsiders, is determined by where one lives. The Badia, or Bedouin, as was noted, are nomads who live in the desert in black tents and travel constantly with their herds of camels, sheep, and goats. The Arabs of the village, however, are known as Al Hadhar, townspeople who live in permanent homes of mud bricks or stone. An Arabic villager is known to the Bedouin as a Hadhari.

While it is likely that Bedouin daily life has remained unchanged for centuries, there is no way to know for certain, because these were essentially prehistoric times. Oral history was proudly passed on to each succeeding generation, but few written records were kept. Indeed, the Bedouin refer to pre-Islamic times as the Aiyam al Juhl, or Days of Ignorance—meaning not only ignorance of the One True God, Allah, but also ignorance of history in general. Historical events were simply not recorded. In the centuries before the arrival of Islam, most of the region's people believed in many gods; even today, the Bedouin still tread lightly to avoid disturbing the *jinun,* or evil spirits (genies), which some still believe live under the sands.

Islam

Mohamed was born into the Quraysh tribe of Mecca in approximately 570 c.e. Probably in 610 c.e., Mohamed had a vision of the Archangel Gabriel; Mohamed soon became a prophet and began to spread the word, and the monotheistic practices, of Islam. The Qur'an (alternately Koran) is the sacred book of the Muslims, or followers of Islam, because it contains the revelations of God (Allah) to Mohamed. Of note, since Arabic was the language through which, it is believed, God transmitted his message to Mohamed, Arabic is the language of revelation for Muslims everywhere. This connection between religion and Arab identity would eventually feed movements like the fundamentalist Wahhabi rising inside Arabia and Arab nationalism.

The new religion of Islam was quickly adopted by some Arab tribes; for others who were slow to convert, the new Muslims were not averse to using the sword to spread Islam's message and authority. This new religion quickly covered almost the entire Arabian Peninsula and thereby replaced the animistic practices of the early Bedouin. Controversy over who should succeed Mohamed as caliph *(khalifa)* would later divide Muslims into Sunnis and Shiites; almost all Bedouin adopted the Sunni stance that caliphs could be elected rather than chosen based solely on blood relation to Mohamed, as the Shiites maintained.

The arrival of Islam had an immediate and profound impact on the Bedouin. Islam did not merely govern the relationship between an individual and God, it also proscribed the relationships in and among the entire community. The religious law of Islam, Shariah, governed the interactions between Muslim men and women, and Muslims with non-Muslims. The extent to which Islam created new relationships among the Bedouin or merely codified existing relationships is not entirely clear today. That Islam made those interpersonal relationships concrete and unbending is indisputable. One aspect of desert life that did not change under Islam was the tribal orientation of the Bedouin. Another unaffected aspect was male domination of Bedouin society; indeed, Islam actually reinforced these two social facets. Significantly, Islam had been the religion of almost all Bedouin for one thousand years before the migration to Kuwait would begin. The first Kuwaitis no doubt harbored many doubts about their uncertain future, but none whatsoever about their religious convictions.

Within this socioreligious framework, relations were grouped by a shared common clan name and fit somewhere into a broader tribal structure. When capitalized and placed before a name, the Arabic word *al-*, meaning "the," identifies a tribe or family—similar to "The Smiths" or "The Joneses" in English. One example is the Al-Sabah, the Bedouin family that helped found Kuwait and has ruled it ever since. The traditional home of the Al-Sabah family was Hadar, in the Aflaj district of central Arabia. The Al-Sabah were a sept or subset of the Dahamsat section of the Amarat tribe. The Amarat tribe was a major component of the Anizah, an aristocratic Muslim group that held sharif status.

To the Arabs, sharif status signified a noble or honorable lineage, a matter of extreme pride to every member of the community. The male head of a tribe or house was the sheikh. Within the tribe, people identified most closely with their family; kinship was the ultimate tie binding the society. At least until a Bedouin made a name for himself, he was generally identified as the "son of so-and-so" *(Ibn)*. Females were known as "daughter of so-and-so" *(Bint)*, but could expect to later be known as "mother of so-and-so" *(Umm)*.

Though the sharing of a tribal name was a source of pride to all, there was by no means equality among the many individual families that made up a tribe. Social strata within each community were well defined and readily apparent to all community members. The socioeconomic status of a Bedouin family was easily recognized by counting its camels or by observing its mobile home. The actual wealth of a family was measured in camels, which constituted a savings account with four legs. To be considered a herd, a group of 70 camels was required. Camels have always held a special place in Bedouin affairs. For centuries, camels were considered the single most reliable way to measure wealth. For example, early in the twentieth century, before oil profits changed everything, all Bedouin recognized the Anizah tribe as the wealthiest of them all. The Anizah, of sharif heritage, had widely spread across Saudi Arabia, Iraq, and Syria. The fighting strength of the tribe was estimated at thirty-seven thousand males of military age, and collective tribal wealth totaled approximately 1 million camels.

To the Bedouin, one's house and one's tent were the same—*bait* in Arabic. Inside, the black Bedouin tents were partitioned between male and female, as well as between family and guest. Fires burning *jalla*, dried camel manure, were used to heat Arab coffee, *qahwa*, which played so prominently in the community's social life. The size of a Bedouin family's home displayed the family's collective wealth. A typical family lived in a house of one pole, *bait abu amud* or simply *gutba*. As the wealth of the family grew, so did the size of its tent and, accordingly, its social standing. Moving up in the world meant moving into a tent of two poles *(bait abu amudain)*, then three *(abu thalath amdan)*, and even four poles *(bait abu arba'a amdan)*. Over time, because the practice was so common, some Bedouin coined special words to identify a house of two *(gutubain)*, three *(m'thaulidh)*, and even four poles *(m'rauba)*.

Beyond its social aspects, however, the life of the Bedouin was centered on the camel. To the Bedouin, a camel was never simply just a camel. It might be a pack camel *(jamal)* that carried the family's household goods from location to location. It might be a camel kept to provide milk to be used in cooking *(naga)*, or it might be a riding camel *(dhalul)*. Each herd of camels required constant attention. The animal disease of mange was a terrifying malady that could quickly cost an entire herd if left unchecked. Good pasturage *(khad)*, the kind needed to avoid the ravages of mange, usually consisted of *nussi*, or desert grass, but might include the shrubbery the camels preferred *(arfaj)*. As quickly as a Bedouin scout could locate satisfactory pastureland and the herd was moved, it was time to look for the next grassy spot. Bedouin were nomads by necessity: every 10 days to 2 weeks, a camel herd would devour the nearby pasturage, making a move a must. The process of packing, making a one-day journey, and reestablishing camp was known as *shidda*. While the camels did not need to carry their own water, the Bedouin had to lug their own drinking and cooking water in containers made of goat or camel skin.

MIGRATION (ca. 1650–ca. 1710)

Probably not later than 1613, a small fishing village was established in what is now Kuwait. The modest collection of tents and huts was known as Qurain, from *qarn*, the Arabic word for hill. The few European sailors who plied the Arabian Gulf were aware of the village, listing it as Grane on maps drawn in the middle of the seventeenth century. The fishermen and their families of Qurain were members of the Bani Khalid tribe, which controlled eastern Arabia and the coastline from Qatar practically to Basrah. Technically, the sheikhs of the Bani Khalid were the first rulers of Kuwait, but there is little evidence that many of them ever even visited the locale, let alone lived there for any length of time.

Perhaps in 1672—or perhaps in 1680, since both dates were recorded—Barrak bin Ghuraif, while sheikh of the Bani Khalid, decided to build a residence in Qurain (in the present-day Kuwait City residential neighborhood of Wattiya). Tribal tradition suggests this was a summer home, located in a more amenable area than the sheikh's previous summer abode. It is also possible that the site was chosen for military purposes. The sheikh was certainly interested in protecting his domain from incursions out of Basrah, and he would have liked to bring Basrah itself into his sheikhdom had the opportunity arisen. Whatever his reasons, Sheikh Barrak decided to also make his home into a small fort, or *kut*. While the area was soon referred to locally as Kuwait, the diminutive Arabic word for small fort, there was as yet no thriving seaport settlement to stand behind the name. This new name would not appear in print until a Dutch seafarer noted Kuwait on a nautical chart drawn in 1765. The small fort and rude huts surrounding it would still be around when the Bani Utub, the first true Kuwaitis, would travel from afar to make the site their new home.

Beginning in the late 1600s, a lingering drought struck the central Arabian Peninsula, making further heavy use of the already-sparse farming areas almost impossible. The lack of rainfall also severely limited the availability of grazing land for Bedouin herds of camels and sheep. Insufficient rainfall has always been a fact of life for these hardy desert nomads, and they were not quick to succumb to this natural obstacle. It is with avowed purpose that, even today, the Bedouin use the word *rahma* to mean both rain and mercy, because when there is sufficient rain, it is a sign of God's mercy.

Conditions in Hadar, in the Aflaj region of central Arabia, where the Al-Sabah family raised its tents, were especially harsh. Some members of the Al-Sabah and Al-Khalifa families, kinsmen from the Amarat tribe, packed up and moved to Qatar, likely adapting to the sea and becoming involved in the small-scale pearling operations going on there at the time. After being driven out by the governor, or *mutasallim*, of Bahrain, some of these same families moved on to the area around Basrah, where they reportedly made their living as caravan raiders and pirates, preying on the small vessels that sailed up and down the Shatt al-Arab River. Before too long, Basrah's governor drove the migrants away from the Ottoman province. Eventually, this group settled in and around the region still primarily known as Qurain. Upon their arrival, there was already the small fishing and pearling village at that location. The nearby area was under the local sheikh, a member of the Bani Khalid who continued to rule eastern Arabia. The new arrivals were allowed to settle in the location, and the mounted forces of the Bani Khalid continued to keep the peace in the region.

By approximately 1710, back in the Najd, the situation had become dire; the area could no longer support the local population, even at subsistence levels. Additional local Bedouin families, including the remainder of the Al-Sabah, determined to move, as well, seeking better prospects for their herds and themselves. These families included the aforementioned Al-Sabah and the Al-Khalifa. In their travels, the migrants were joined by other desperate Bedouin families, the most important of which were the Al-Jalahima (which today are known as the Al-Nisf).

While there are no surviving written records, it can be safely assumed that, in the Bedouin manner, a council, or *majlis*, was held, at which the heads of these important families laid out the advantages of moving, while other elders certainly noted the risks that were being courted by the community. Those Bedouin with the courage to challenge the unknown would become the first Kuwaitis, though they did not know it at the time. The Bani Utub collected their herds and said their goodbyes to family and friends. Then these Bedouin migrants, which included members of the Al-Sabah family, moved off into the unknown.

The migrating families first headed in the direction of the dry river bed, or *wadi*, at Duwasir, where they hoped to find both water and more promising grazing opportunities. Unfortunately for the migrants, conditions at Wadi Duwasir were untenable, as well, so the Bani Utub packed their tents again and moved on. This process was repeated numerous times, with occasional changes of direction as they went. As the migration continued, other small groups of hopeful settlers joined or detached from the original migrating travelers.

When this group of migrants arrived on the coast of the Arabian Gulf, it settled at Zubara on the Qatar peninsula. By this point, members from several other major Bedouin families had already joined the Al-Sabah. These new families included the Al-Shamlan, the Al-Saleh, and the Al-Zayid. Their original family name having come from the Arabic word for more, the Al-Zayid were noteworthy among the earliest settlers for possessing more camels and sheep than the other migrating families. (Today the family goes by the name Al-Ghanim.) All these early settlers would eventually make their individual and collective marks on Kuwaiti history. In the short term, however, conditions were as bleak as they had been in the Najd.

Some of these Bani Utub families remained in and around Qatar for as long as 60 years. Others, unwilling to wait for conditions to improve, drove their herds and flocks north, to Kuwait. Some of those who remained in Qatar adopted the sea as a way of life. They, too, would later migrate to Kuwait, but for them, the journey would be by sea. All these Bedouin groups, originally from the Najd region of Central Arabia, and each with an Al-Sabah contingent, finally made their way to Kuwait. Oral tradition among the Al-Sabah maintains that the first of their line to actually reside in Kuwait settled there in 1613, but there is no other evidence to substantiate such an early arrival. More likely, the first Al-Sabah arrived by 1710, and the last large contingent of the family arrived no later than 1756.

SETTLEMENT (ca. 1710–1756)

The exact date of arrival in Kuwait is unknown. It was likely 1710, but some oral reports suggest it might have been 1713 or even as late as 1716. In any case, by the time these migrants had arrived in Kuwait, they were already calling themselves the Bani Utub, a name that is still heard today. Some of these Bani Utub settlers even began to refer to their new home as "Najd by the sea," though the name probably denotes more fond hope than actual similarity to their original homeland. The term is infrequently used today, though it is occasionally encountered in traditional Kuwaiti songs and poetry. Despite their nostalgia for the old, nomadic ways, the Kuwaitis soon began to sink roots into the sandy soil of their new home.

A composite group of Arabs, the Arabdar, or "Arabs of the homeland" *(dar)*, soon developed. No longer nomadic but not yet settled, this group centered its ramblings on the new settlement, where trade goods and seafood were usually available. In the summer, these seminomads lived in or near town but moved about seeking better pasturage during winter months. Since their travels were circumscribed by time, they never got far from the homeland of Kuwait. The next half step toward a settled lifestyle followed soon for many. While the true Bedouin stuck to camel breeding, within the Hadhar and Arabdar of Kuwait various occupational specialties developed. These specialists included obviously indispensable workers such as shepherds, farmers, and blacksmiths.

An underclass of outcasts was already in existence in Kuwait by this time, known among the Bedouin as the Sulubba. Not actually members of any tribe, Sulubba were blood descendants of camp followers of Christian Crusaders, which caused them to be looked down on by the Bedouin. In Kuwait's growing economy, many Sulubba served as hunters and desert guides. Others mended pots and pans for Kuwaiti housewives. Sulubba were not allowed to live inside the town's walls, so they set up their camp just outside the gate.

In conjunction with this occupational specialization, not long after arrival in the area, the first Kuwaitis studied and categorized the region into four groups based on the arability of the soil: *harra* is good, arable soil; *daim* are larger depressions in the ground that collect some rainwater in certain times of the year; *hazam* is stony ground; and *sabkhah* is saline swampland. This initial hydrographic survey led to the establishment of smaller crop-tending developments around the few pieces of arable land. Crude agricultural implements available to Kuwait's farmers included a wooden plow *(ifdan)*, an iron hoe *(sakhin)*, and a wooden rake *(masah)*. Of these, the sakhin was probably the most useful, since it aided in the construction of the small but indispensable channels used to irrigate the land surrounding the local wells. The locations of most other encampments were determined by the need for grazing for Bedouin camels, sheep, and goats.

The shrub arfaj is preferred by camels and lies along Kuwait's coastal plain. Further inland, desert grass, or nussi, can be found to sustain the herds. *Hamdh* bushes are a type of saline-laden brushwood. These woody plants serve the same purpose as a salt lick and, thus, help keep the animals healthy. Until the early twentieth century, when block salt could be provided to each herd, the Bedouin needed to periodically relocate their camel herds to a new location where fresher hamdh bushes could be found.

Wells in the region of Kuwait were usually around 12–25 feet deep during this period. As the water table fell over the centuries, those seeking water have repeatedly been forced to dig ever deeper. A water lift is known locally as an *arjiyah*. From the well, the brackish water is collected and lifted in animal skins. Donkeys are used to provide the lifting power. The water then flows through a channel, or *saqiyah*, to reach the nearby field under cultivation.

During these same years, 1710–1756, the Bani Utub newcomers slowly took over the entire settlement from the Bani Khalid. In their climb to the top, the Bani Utub were led by three prominent families: the Al-Sabah, the Al-Khalifa, and the Al-Jalahima. For their part, the Bani Khalid controlled the port and maintained the peace, retaining their focus on the desert rather than the nearby seaways. The Bani Khalid oversaw the caravans to Baghdad and Syria, but they also kept their eyes on Basrah and the rest of the Arabian Gulf. Once the Wahhabis began to surge out of the Najd, holding back the Wahhabi tide became the preoccupation of Bani Khalid rulers. A battle for succession among hopeful Bani Khalid contenders sprung up in 1722, following the death of Sheikh Sadun. The internal power struggle further distracted the Bani Khalid from the growing commercial center of Kuwait.

Recognizing the potential afloat, and also realizing that this was the only way to gain preeminence, the Bani Utub took up the trades required for success in seagoing enterprises. They learned how to build and sail ships, how to make rope and sails, and how to fish and dive for pearls; most valuable of their new skills, however, was commercial in nature. Many of the Bedouin migrants became traders, and the wisest of these invested in vessels of their own, doubling the commercial risk but also doubling the profit potential.

The commercial network that these new merchants inherited and quickly expanded had numerous facets to it. Kuwaiti exports included horses, ghee, and pearls. The export of horses served the British army in India, which needed a constant supply of mounts for its various campaigns across the Indian subcontinent. The high-bred Arabian horses themselves were provided by the Bedouin; the Kuwaitis merely served as middlemen in the transfer. The export of ghee, or clarified butter, was based on the ready availability of dairy products provided by Bedouin herds.

Again, Kuwaiti merchants had only to meet the Bedouin at the city's gates to receive their goods, then merely load those goods onto Kuwaiti vessels for transshipment to their ultimate destination. Even the pearls were relatively easy to acquire, since Kuwait was not far from some of the richest pearling banks in the Arabian Gulf, which were located near Bahrain. Kuwaiti merchants worked collaboratively to build and crew sailing dhows that could spend the summer months in the pearling trade.

Imports included wood, rice, cotton, spices, sugar, coffee, tobacco, fruits, wheat, dates, fish, and, tragically, sometimes even human slaves. Not surprisingly for a growing settlement and bustling harbor, the availability of wood for building was of prime importance. Teak wood from India was the most prized, but it was not always available. Since Kuwait had no wood of its own, Kuwaiti vessels rarely returned home without some shipbuilding materials stowed in their holds. Sail-making materials were equally valuable. Many of the other imported commodities not only served the Kuwaitis themselves, but were resold to the Bedouin for even higher profits. In the winter, the same Kuwaiti vessels that had sailed for pearls now made the rounds of available seaports, buying and trading as they went.

Within this bustling commercial and political context, in only a few decades, Kuwaiti merchants were able to build personal and family wealth that dwarfed what they had accumulated as nomads. The Al-Sabah family—which not only engaged in trade like the other Bani Utub, but also oversaw the collection of taxes from port operations—became the richest and most powerful of all. That the Al-Sabah were uniquely positioned to reap the benefits of these valuable opportunities probably came as a bit of a surprise. As early as 1716 by one account, the sheikhs of the Al-Sabah, Al-Khalifa, and Al-Jalahima families had negotiated a power-sharing scheme along the following lines: the Al-Khalifa would control trade, the Al-Jalahima would control pearling and fishing, and the Al-Sabah would control the local government and military affairs.

What was not fully appreciated by these early sheikhs was that administration of government included collection of taxes on all desert caravans and inbound sea traffic, with a portion at least potentially available for diversion into family coffers. This administrative power also brought with it the ability to negotiate trade agreements with nearby communities at terms favorable to Al-Sabah commercial interests. In these matters, the sheikh of the Al-Sabah also took pains to seek counsel from other leading merchant families; by building consensus on most matters, and adopting win-win trading strategies, he was able to co-opt most of the other leading families.

The earliest documented foray into foreign affairs by the new settlers of Kuwait came in 1730. The Portuguese were making aggressive military inroads into the Arabian Gulf with the intention of cornering the commercial opportunities. One of Oman's religious leaders requested all possible assistance from friendly settlements all along the southern Arabian Gulf. Kuwait responded by sending two vessels loaded with munitions. While the Portuguese naval threat would never actually lead to an invasion of Kuwait, this marks the first instance of Kuwaiti awareness that mutual defense might be required in the future.

One of Kuwait's next documented experiences in diplomacy had even more far-reaching consequences. To be able to enjoy prosperity, Kuwait was driven by a need to pacify the local Ottoman governor in the nearby seaport of Basrah, at the mouth of the Shatt al Arab (River of the Arabs). The new community in Kuwait could not have hoped to last very long if the Ottomans perceived Kuwait as a threat militarily or commercially. As long as it was seen as a backwater, Kuwait was of minimal interest to the Ottomans, and it was the task of Kuwait's first ambassador to the Ottoman Empire to ensure continued imperial disinterest. A council consisting of senior members of the main families was again seated to determine the best candidate for this key position. The man ultimately elected to this important post was Sabah bin Jaber, senior member of the Al-Sabah family. Age, wisdom, and bravery were all vital qualities, but the characteristic that earned Sabah the job as ambassador was his obvious luck (*hadh*)—to the Bedouin an indispensable ingredient of solid leadership.

Kuwait's timing, and that of Sheikh Sabah, was fortuitous because the Ottoman Empire was in a period of strategic decline. Ottoman diplomatic and military efforts were largely directed toward holding off the Russians and the Austrians, with whom the Ottomans would fight a series of wars in the 1770s, 1780s, and 1790s, and at the hands of whom the Ottomans ultimately suffered costly defeats. At the fringes of the Ottoman Empire, small parts of the empire that had once been under positive imperial control were beginning to successfully establish themselves as locally autonomous states in their own right. Thus, the people of Kuwait, under the Al-Sabah family, established their new home at the most favorable possible time. By most accounts the year was 1756 when Kuwaitis elected Sabah as their new sheikh. The Al-Sabah dynasty had officially begun.

3

Desert Sheikhdom
(1756–1899)

It is commonly agreed that Sabah bin Jaber, the head of his family, was elected sheikh of the settlement of Kuwait, the first in the family to be so recognized. There is some doubt over the exact date of his election, as both 1752 and 1756 have been recorded. There is no question, however, that Sheikh Sabah's credentials for the post were solid, and this new position was in line with the power- and profit-sharing deal struck decades before by Kuwait's leading families. Sabah I's succession to the sheikhdom was certainly supported by the leading commercial interests in the thriving port city. Al-Sabah family tutelage of market conditions and foreign relations with the nearby Ottomans had resulted in profits all around, and there was no reason to expect anything less from Sabah I.

Thus, while Sabah I enjoyed wide support, he also understood that he was, at least in part, answerable to the top commercial families in the performance of his administrative responsibilities. The protocol of *shura* (consultation) with Kuwait's leading families and merchants became the hallmark of Al-Sabah rule, then and now. That he was elected to the post set Sabah I apart from almost every other ruler in the region, rulers who had come to power by seizing it from others by force. Every subsequent Kuwaiti leader would follow in the tradition of Sabah I in that he would rule cautiously, seek political support domestically, and rely on diplomacy to the maximum extent possible internationally.

As the new sheikh, Sabah I handled the local administration of justice and the collection of taxes and tariffs. To help him in this role, Sabah I, like any Muslim ruler, could always look to the Qur'an and Shariah law for guidance. *Salifa*, or custom, was equally important in resolving differences in Bedouin tradition, however, and it appears that Kuwait's sheikhs were especially good at following custom and avoiding discord. Traditional Kuwaiti accounts of the time specifically note that Shariah law was not always followed. Sabah I was also assisted by the help of a *qadi*, or judge, to administer the town and its visitors. Kuwait's first qadi was Ibn Fayruz, whose tenure in the post roughly coincided with Sabah I's reign.

Sabah I continued in his role as chief diplomatic officer for the settlement, and he stayed in almost constant touch with the Ottoman Empire and with nearby cities and tribal leaders. Probably in 1760, he oversaw construction of the first defensive wall to completely encircle the town. In 1762, however, not long into his tenure, Sabah I died. After soliciting input from Kuwait's leading families and wealthy merchants, and ensuring adequate consensus among interested parties, a group of senior Al-Sabah family members selected Abdullah, Sabah's youngest son, to replace his father in the top post. This arrangement of selecting the next sheikh set a precedent that is still followed today. Abdullah I maintained the policies of his father, which resulted in continued economic benefits for the community as a whole.

As Kuwait began to prosper in the late 1760s under Al-Sabah sheikhs, the former backwater port developed into an increasingly important stop on the circuit of both trading vessels and passing caravans. Camel caravans from southern Arabia that had once ignored Kuwait began to stop there on their trips to and from Syria and Lebanon. The wells of the Kuwaiti village at Jahra provided much better drinking water when compared with other locations available along the major caravan route. Caravans consisted of merchants and their goods; armed guards to protect those goods; guides to lead the caravan through the territories of Bedouin groups along the way; camels, donkeys, and mules to carry the goods; tribute to be paid for free passage along the way; and sometimes European travelers, whose records of these caravans are quite informative.

Large caravans traveled slowly, usually around seven hours daily, and took from one and a half to two and a half months to reach Aleppo. Smaller, lighter caravans covered the same ground in less than one month. Twice annually, the largest caravan traveled between Aleppo and the Basrah-Kuwait region. Smaller caravans from the south and west traveled to Kuwait to join the larger caravan on its way to Syria. Documents survive from as early as the 1750s that record caravans of as many as five thousand camels, more than one thousand men, and hundreds of armed guards. Smaller, speedier caravans might have only a few hundred camels and other beasts, and perhaps a handful of European travelers. Because additional camels were needed in Aleppo to carry Syrian goods into North Africa, some caravans sped along with unladen camels. The smallest and lightest caravans could complete the journey in as few as 14 days. While every caravan varied widely in size and scope, and its profits were by no means confined to Kuwait, every time a caravan completed its rounds, the merchants of Kuwait grew wealthier.

There were alternatives to caravans from the upper Arabian Gulf. Ships could always travel between India and Europe by rounding Africa, but the trip was long, expensive, and subject to disruption by hostile naval forces and by pirates. A second major caravan route sat at the top of the Red Sea. East-bound ships deposited trade goods at Suez. From there, the goods moved to Alexandria by camel caravan, where they could be loaded onto a ship again for transshipment to Europe. This was a very safe route, but in 1779, Ottoman officials prohibited Christian merchants from doing business in Suez. These circumstances made the caravans from Kuwait/Basrah to Aleppo a safe alternative for European merchants.

The cost of travel included payments to Bedouin chieftains along the way, but that could not be avoided. Additionally, a high tariff was almost always collected in Ottoman Basrah, which cut into the merchants' profits. In Kuwait, however, the sheikhs sometimes collected only 2 percent on goods shipped through their harbor, and sometimes there was no tariff collected at all. More and more merchants looked to Kuwait for business. From 1756 to 1763, the British did everything in their power to prevent the French from using the waterways and caravan routes from the Gulf; this probably cost Kuwait some business, but not so much that it showed. Kuwait was about to come into its own as an ocean terminal and commercial center.

At the same time that the camel caravan trade grew in size and scope, Arab-owned vessels that had once served only Basrah now made Kuwait a regular port of call. Moreover, new vessels financed by wealthy Kuwaiti families began to conduct a circular trade, to the benefit of all. Kuwaiti-built sailing ships participated in pearling in the summer months. In the wintertime, those same vessels and crews sailed as far as India and Madagascar, retuning with valuable cargoes of wood, spices, and slaves. Wood for building Kuwaiti ships was imported from India. Kuwaiti vessels traveled to Basrah to pick up dates, then visited ports along the Persian Gulf, and then proceeded to Zanzibar and to Karachi, Pakistan. When the vessels returned to Kuwait about seven months later, they would be carrying spices, cloth, mangrove logs, and rice. The logs were needed to provide timber for the roofs of houses. Nomadic Bedouin groups that had rarely visited soon began to return to Kuwait's markets year after year.

Prosperity also brought unwanted attention, however. Outsiders looked to Kuwait with envy. Moreover, the once-iron-clad authority of the Bani Khalid was beginning to wane region-wide. The height of their power in the region had been in the early eighteenth century, when they controlled much of the eastern Arabian Peninsula out as far as Kuwait and Qatar. Internal squabbles and outside threats distracted Bani Khalid leaders from protecting Kuwait. By the 1750s, the Bani Khalid were practically overwhelmed dealing with the new challenge posed by the rise of the radically fundamentalist Wahhabis in Central Arabia. Kuwait's inhabitants would have to tend to their own physical defense.

THREAT OF INVASION

While written records do not exist to confirm such popular accounts, local legends, passed on by oral tradition from generation to generation, shed light on these turbulent early years in the development of Kuwait. For example, Kuwaiti legends tell of perhaps the first armed conflict faced by the new settlers. Nearby, across the Arabian Gulf, lived the Al-Nassar family. The Al-Nassar were an Arab people of the Bani Kaab tribe, which had taken up residence in the Arabistan region of Persia (now Iran). The Bani Kaab traced their line to a sharif tribe originally from Central Arabia, essentially making them former neighbors of the Bani Utub. Just as the new Kuwaiti Bedouin had migrated, the Bani Kaab had done so years before, making their new capital in Dawraq, a city east of Basrah. Over time, many of the families of this tribe had intermarried with Persians, who were largely Shiite Muslims. A strong sea power, the Bani Kaab sometimes dared to attack British ships. The Bani Kaab fought both for and against the Persians and the Ottomans, choosing whichever side offered the greatest advantage to the tribe, while also posing a threat to the smaller semiautonomous communities in the upper Arabian Gulf. Probably in the 1760s, the Bani Kaab openly turned to piracy and considered among their favorite prey the pearling and trading vessels of Kuwait and Bahrain.

Probably in 1766, shortly after succeeding his father Sabah I as sheikh, Abdullah I had his leadership skills put to the test, and the future of the Al-Sabah dynasty was placed in serious jeopardy. A senior member of the Al-Nassar family sought the hand in marriage of an Al-Sabah woman named Mariam, and a dispute soon arose. To the Al-Nassar, their blood was still pure, but to the Bani Utub, the intermarriage with Persians made all Bani Kaab blood impure. The fiercely proud Al-Sabah quickly rejected the suitor's offer, and the deeply insulted Al-Nassar sent a small fleet of ships to Kuwait to take the woman by force. The people of Kuwait were about to face the first serious attack on their new country.

Not all of Kuwait's inhabitants were eager to face the Bani Kaab assault. Many settlers from the Al-Khalifa and Al-Jalahima families packed their tents and headed for Qatar. For some this departure was caused by fear of Bani Kaab invasion. For others, the Al-Nassar invasion represented the failed diplomacy of Al-Sabah leadership, which had at times reverted to tribute to buy off the Bani Kaab. The Al-Khalifa were not in favor of continued tribute. Moreover, this outside threat came at a time when Kuwait's Al-Khalifa were questioning why they had awarded preeminence to the Al-Sabah in the first place. They clearly were not happy that Al-Sabah sheikhs had become strong enough to name their own sons as their successors. A contemporary European account states the Al-Khalifa left because they didn't want to share their profits with the Al-Sabah. In any case, the Al-Khalifa believed they were a family equally qualified to rule, but it clearly was not destined to be rule of Kuwait.

All these reasons were enough to cause most, and possibly all, of Kuwait's Al-Khalifa to bag their possessions and move on, beginning as early as 1766. From Kuwait, the Al-Khalifa moved on to Zubara, then to Bahrain; soon after arrival, they conquered the island and their descendants rule Bahrain to this day. Evidently, despite this rift, no grudges were held by either family. During a later period, when the Al-Khalifa were temporarily deposed, the Al-Sabah sent Kuwaiti forces to help them regain their holdings. The Al-Sabah and the Al-Khalifa have maintained good political and economic relations ever since.

The departure of the Al-Khalifa and Al-Jalahima cemented Al-Sabah authority over the settlement, but they still had to deal with the warring Al-Nassar, who continued to prey on Kuwaiti vessels and threatened actual invasion. The Al-Sabah were determined to dig in and fight for their newfound political autonomy. History only records that the Al-Sabah were able to repeatedly repel or deter the Bani Kaab invasion of their territory.

Local legend offers more colorful elaboration. According to tradition, Sheikh Abdullah gathered his most trusted lieutenants to his home, and each man was directed to stand in the doorway of the sheikh's house. In turn, each man swore an oath to die before letting an enemy cross the home's threshold, or *atiba,* which would violate the honor of the Al-Sabah. Because of this oath, some say, this original group of stalwart Kuwaiti defenders became known as the Bani Atib, "People of the Threshold," providing a very different explanation for the origin of the group's mysterious name.

Mariam, the lady in dispute, heavily armed herself and helped muster the Bedouin of the area to fight off the Al-Nassar attackers. Her cousin Salim, probably also of the Al-Sabah, led a Kuwaiti war party, dressed as fishermen, in a midnight assault on the Al-Nassar invasion fleet, attacking one ship at a time. After sneaking aboard and killing or capturing the crew, the attackers silently paddled to the next anchored ship in line and repeated their attack, taking five Al-Nassar vessels in all.

Next, Salim, against the wishes of Sheikh Abdullah, assembled a motley flotilla of Kuwaiti vessels. Salim led the sortie against the now-demoralized Al-Nassar invaders. With timely help from a windy storm, the attacking vessels from Arabistan were driven off, and Kuwait survived the first serious attempt on its independence and survival. It would not be the last attempt by an outsider to conquer Kuwait. Regardless of whether details have been added or embellished in these traditional folk tales, the critical contribution to the survival of Kuwait made by Mariam and Salim, among other early heroes, is indisputable. For martial inspiration, modern Kuwaiti troops still use one of only two *nakhwa,* or war cries. Depending on their specific family and tribal background, Kuwaiti soldiers shout *Awlad Salim* ("Children of Salim") or *Ana ikhu Mariam* ("I am the brother of Mariam") before engaging in battle.

Whether or not these legends are true, what is clear is that Sheikh Abdullah saw to Kuwait's defense; in particular, no expense was spared in arming and expanding the Kuwaiti fleet in the face of the Bani Kaab threat. By 1779, the Kuwaiti fleet was strong enough to deter Bani Kaab assault. War broke out again in 1780, primarily as a result of Bani Kaab piracy. By 1783, when the Bani Kaab sued for peace following the naval battle of Riqqah, the naval strength of Sheikh Abdullah I allowed him to demand and receive tribute from the Bani Kaab. That strength would be indispensable when Kuwait faced its next big threat: the Wahhabis, who would storm out of the Arabian Desert.

While tribal affiliation had always been important, and remains so today, Kuwait's sense of national identity was already beginning to develop at this early stage in its history. As the formerly nomadic settlers remained in one place season after season and continued to sink "roots" in Kuwait's soil year after year, their tie to the land strengthened considerably. The more these settlers viewed Kuwait as home, the more they viewed themselves as Kuwaitis. As the sense of a Kuwaiti identity grew, the perceived differences with other peoples, even Bedouin, slowly set the Kuwaitis further apart from neighbors and other Arabs. Subsequently, some visitors found this characteristic quaint, and others found it peculiar; its existence, however, would prove critical in Kuwait's ability to survive Iraqi invasion and occupation in the modern era.

Interestingly, Kuwaitis of this time also developed an outward-looking orientation to the world around them; this was equally a function of external threat and the related tradition of their seagoing trade. Continuing threats from the Ottomans, the Persians, the Bani Kaab, the Qawasim, and the Wahhabis forced Kuwait's sheikhs to keep an eye on the horizon for approaching danger. The commercial and military advantages of maintaining strong positive relations with sometimes-competing outside powers, in particular the Ottomans and the British, encouraged the Kuwaitis to constantly position and reposition according to the prevailing political winds. Isolation was not a viable foreign policy; the Al-Sabah sheikhs, whether they liked it or not, were forced to interact with their world.

This developing Kuwaiti worldview is unique; many other peoples in the region have historically looked inward. While there are advantages and disadvantages to each worldview, the Kuwaitis have almost always been able to capitalize on the advantages financially and politically. Moreover, this mindset is just one more way in which the Kuwaitis differ from other Arab countries. The more the people identified with Kuwait, the more legitimacy and authority accrued for the Al-Sabah sheikh. Soon Kuwait's geographically anchored rulers were far more powerful than they would have been had they remained nomadic desert sheikhs. The authority of the Al-Sabah sheiks was always tempered, however, by the realization that Kuwait's merchants could always pack and leave for another port along the Arabian Gulf. Almost invariably, whenever unpopular Al-Sabah policies met with threats of leaving by wealthy merchant families, the sheikh quickly moderated his position and sometimes even reversed course completely.

Every Al-Sabah sheikh understood that other sheikhs and emirs would gladly welcome Kuwaiti merchants, and the money they carried—a move that would not only weaken Kuwait but proportionately strengthen Kuwait's economic competitors. Moreover, once the Al-Khalifa and Al-Jalahima were gone, the Al-Sabah concluded that it was better to have any disgruntled merchant in Kuwait, where he could be watched and countered, than in exile nearby, where he might foment trouble. For all these reasons, an economic system of checks and balances soon developed almost unconsciously and has functioned effectively, to varying degrees, ever since.

Under Abdullah I, Kuwait thrived commercially. That business boomed for Kuwait is somewhat surprising, since Basrah was the major seaport in the upper Arabian Gulf. Generally speaking, whenever business was bad for Basrah, it was good for Kuwait, and between 1750 and 1850, business was especially bad for Basrah. The city experienced a host of problems that often encouraged and sometimes compelled seagoing traffic to utilize Kuwait instead of Basrah. Plague struck Basrah in 1773. The Persians and the Arabs aligned with them laid siege to Basrah in 1775, disrupting commerce. When the Persians and their allies conquered Basrah, several key merchants from there moved to Kuwait to reestablish their businesses. Internal Ottoman squabbles or incompetence hindered Basrah's administration as a seaport, and a high tariff in Basrah encouraged shipowners to sail instead through Kuwait to avoid the tax. The British East India Company had even established a factory-fort at Basrah, which should have been a business advantage, but conditions became so bad in Basrah that the company moved its factory to Kuwait for the period 1793–1795.

CONTACT WITH THE BRITISH EMPIRE

In the mid-1770s, the Kuwaitis had their first significant exposure to the British Empire. In 1776, the British East India Company established several new factory/trading posts along the Arabian Gulf. When it came to the Arabian Gulf, Great Britain was less interested in gaining control than enforcing stability. The sea lines of communications from Great Britain's invaluable imperial holdings in India to the Red Sea and, later, the Suez Canal were of paramount importance in British strategic calculations. British goals, then, were twofold. First, Great Britain sought to ensure that an inimical foreign power could not use the Arabian Gulf as a base for threatening those lines of communications. Second, it was critical that local powers in the region never gain enough military strength to threaten those British lines of communications on their own.

During this period, British mail and diplomatic dispatches to and from the Orient were regularly carried through the Arabian Gulf via the port at Basrah. At the time, the British East India Company was struggling through the empire-building process, and a reliable flow of mail was imperative to British success in and around India. In 1775, plague again struck Basrah, and Persian forces along with Arab allies took advantage of the port's weakness to launch their own assault on the city. Plague had also hit Kuwait in 1773. Although many died, the town was plague free by the time Basrah was engulfed a second time by plague. To keep the mail moving, the British East India Company made overtures directly to the sheikh, who responded with interest. Shortly thereafter, British mail was routed through the port of Kuwait until 1779, when Basrah once more became available to the British colonial enterprises.

This stay in Kuwait afforded the British a unique opportunity to consider future relations with Kuwait. In 1776, the British considered stationing an agent, for political and commercial purposes, in Kuwait. Since none was available, however, they decided to utilize British naval officers whenever Royal Navy or company ships put into Kuwait's harbor. Correspondence of the British East India Company from 1776 makes specific mention of the importance to British interests that Kuwait remain independent of regional powers such as the Persians.

As had his father before him, Sheikh Abdullah I struggled to maintain a policy of scrupulous neutrality. When war broke out between Great Britain and France in the late 1770s, however, Abdullah I was hard pressed to stay uncommitted to one side or the other. Until recently, France had maintained its own factory-fort in Persia, directly across the Arabian Gulf. It was equally important to the French as to the British that the critical lines of communications from Europe to India remain open for their own purposes, but closed to their adversary.

Sheikh Abdullah regularly allowed messengers and mail from both belligerent parties to covertly transit his territory, until an incident occurred in 1779 that forced his hand. At that time, the factor of Britain's East India Company in Basrah became aware that a French officer was in Kuwait on his way to India with important military dispatches. Acting on his own authority, the factor left in person to petition Sheikh Abdullah I, whom he knew well from the time he had been stationed in Kuwait, to turn the Frenchman over to the British. Abdullah I was initially unwilling to do so, since in Arab tradition, once hospitality was given, it could not be rescinded arbitrarily without a loss of honor. Once Abdullah I could be convinced that the French officer was a debtor avoiding his debts, however—which may or may not have been the case—the sheikh allowed the British to seize the French dispatches and take the officer into custody.

The circumstances of this decidedly unneutral incident provided Abdullah I with some measure of face saving, and it also showed his goodwill toward the British. As hostilities continued between France and Great Britain, both sides began to attack each other's shipping in and around the Arabian Gulf. To protect the mail, both sides took to using Arab vessels, often Kuwaiti, to carry their mail without worry of being stopped. Soon Abdullah I was back in the good graces of the French as well as the British. (When a similar situation arose in 1793 and Abdullah I again turned a French messenger over to British authorities, little notice was taken.)

WAHHABI THREAT

A new threat soon appeared on the horizon. The Islamic fundamentalist Wahhabis were a major land power by this time. Though held in check by the Bani Khalid for several decades, new Wahhabi offensives coincided with Bani Khalid internal squabbles. In 1793, the Wahhabis attacked Kuwait directly. Kuwaiti forces that met the Wahhabis outside the city walls were decisively defeated. The Wahhabis took the field and large quantities of spoils of war, but left without attacking the walled city proper.

In 1794, the Wahhabis returned to Kuwait with as many as four thousand troops and two thousand camels. This time Abdullah I decided to garrison the walls and hope for the best. It is possible he understood that he would receive military support from the British East India Company, which currently had its factory in Kuwait. Britain's position was neutrality, especially when it appeared that the Wahhabis would be victorious. For some reason, however, the factor in Kuwait decided on his own initiative to intervene. Several naval guns were carried ashore from company vessels. These few cannon were sufficient to deter an all-out Wahhabi assault on the city. For his part, the factor neglected to inform his superiors of his actions on behalf of Sheikh Abdullah I.

In 1795, the Wahhabis, whose total ground force numbered around fifty thousand troops, completely overran al-Hasa, the capital of the Bani Khalid, and essentially ended the war. Surviving Bani Khalid members flocked to the sanctuary of Kuwait, where Abdullah I offered them asylum. In 1796, the Ottomans used Basrah to launch an attack against the troublesome Wahhabis.

Abdullah I provided two hundred Kuwaiti boats to help provision the Ottoman army. Both of these actions further infuriated the Wahhabis, who returned in 1797 to try again to take the city. Abdullah I's forces fought outside the city and were again defeated, but as before, the Wahhabis were sufficiently weakened that they could not hope to take the city. Through these several decades of threats from the Wahhabis, there is no evidence that Kuwait ever paid tribute.

That Abdullah I was able to stand strong in the face of this considerable threat no doubt increased his stature in the eyes of Arabs and of the British. Interestingly, in 1803, the Wahhabis requested help from Abdullah I, who sent his fleet to participate in a show of force to pacify Musqat. The Wahhabis eventually became so troublesome that the Ottoman governor of Egypt actively campaigned against them. In 1811, the Ottomans recaptured the Muslim holy cities of Mecca and Medina from the Wahhabis. In 1818, the Ottomans destroyed the Wahhabi capital of Dariyya outside present-day Riyadh. Until the Wahhabis were able to recover from these setbacks, they would no longer be a threat to Kuwait.

In the early nineteenth century, the Qawasim, pirates as far as the British were concerned, operated out of present-day United Arab Emirates (UAE), right at the mouth of the Arabian Gulf. In addition to running slaves, the Qawasim stopped passing vessels to demand payment for safe passage. Already a threat to Kuwaiti vessels, the Qawasim eventually began to prey on British vessels. British diplomats attempted to pacify the sultan of Oman, to whom the Qawasim ultimately answered. When diplomacy failed to resolve the violent depredations, the Royal Navy was compelled to intervene in the region. In 1805, Sheikh Abdullah I made an offer of his fleet to help the British subdue the Qawasim. The British did not accept, for some unknown reason, but the offer no doubt further improved Kuwait's standing with the British Empire.

It took Britain more than 10 years, from 1809–1820, to completely subdue the Qawasim pirates, making it a costly undertaking. During that time, the Qawasim, who had adopted Wahhabism, remained a substantial seaborne threat to Kuwait. In 1810–11, the Qawasim threatened to blockade or invade Kuwait. Though Kuwait's earlier wall had fallen into disrepair and, in spots, had been outgrown, the Kuwaitis quickly threw up a new wall around their expanding town. The Qawasim were ultimately deterred by the heavily walled city with perhaps as many as seven thousand defenders and a large, well-armed fleet second in size only to that of Musqat itself.

Eventually, the British Royal Navy was able to neutralize the pirates' strongholds at Ras al Khaymah, Ajman, and Sharjah, and then continued to track down the remaining pirate vessels that dispersed to smaller ports around the Arabian Gulf. With the Qawasim pirates temporarily under control, Great Britain needed to consider the best next step. Not wishing to again let a similar situation develop in their absence, the British determined to maintain a small presence in the Arabian Gulf to stay on top of regional developments and to deter the slave trade.

Sheikh Abdullah I enjoyed a lengthy rule, to 1814, when he was succeeded by Jaber I. By this time, the Al-Sabah were firmly in control of Kuwait, as long as business was good and the wealthy merchants of the town could be kept appeased. That was the primary task of Jaber I. The burgeoning transit trade, whether carried by vessels or camels, continued to prosper. The exploding market, however, was in natural pearls. Pearls were a valuable commodity for which there was no commercially available alternative at the time.

ECONOMIC DEVELOPMENT

The end of the Napoleonic Wars in Europe led to a *Pax Britannia* in Europe, America, and elsewhere—Kuwait included. As the Industrial Revolution kicked into high gear in Western Europe, the disposable income that it created fed a demand for luxury goods, a demand that had not been seen for centuries. The Kuwaiti pearling fleet, based in Kuwait's fine natural harbor, and with the nearby pearling banks of the central Arabian Gulf, was in an ideal position to take advantage of the lucrative possibilities. Soon the majority of Kuwait's citizens were involved, directly or indirectly, in the pearl trade. Kuwait's merchant class quickly specialized in pearls.

These same astute merchants were generally also the shipowners, and they took the lion's share of the profits, with a hefty slice for the Al-Sabah. Ship captains were next in line, followed by crewmen. Pearl divers, who assumed the daily risks involved in the dangerous end of the business, received their cuts, as well. Additionally, shipwrights soon built yards along Kuwait's waterfront, rope makers built their vital rope works nearby, and water haulers shuttled with their lighters to and from the Shatt al Arab in Basrah carrying the freshwater needed for the growing settlement and the ships' crews.

By midcentury, hundreds of Kuwaiti vessels, both large and small, were making the trip to the pearl banks each summer. As long as the demand remained sky-high, Kuwait benefited. In midcentury, following the opening of the Suez Canal, the once-thriving East-West trade through the Arabian Gulf began to dwindle. The slave trade continued to pump money into ports nearer to the Arabian Gulf's mouth, but those profits eventually trickled to Kuwait, as well. Until European nations, especially Great Britain, put the slavers out of business, there seemed to be enough profit to support a growing middle class of shopkeepers and tradesmen in Kuwait.

Unlike Musqat, which thrived on slavery, Kuwait never made slaving a prime aspect of its trade. Sometimes slaves were brought ashore in Kuwait for sale or, more likely, for transshipment by desert caravan to northern or western locations. Occasionally, Kuwaiti shipowners opted for the quick profits of a slave run, at the risk of losing their vessel to a British cruiser attempting to prevent the trade. While the details of Kuwaiti involvement in the slave trade are unknown, it is clear that the British, who used a heavy hand to stamp out the practice whenever they could, rarely raised even an eyebrow at Kuwait's marginal participation in the illicit trade.

Around the Arabian Gulf, Britain invariably used diplomacy when it looked like the cheapest way in which to proceed. Seeking out friendly and compliant, or at least financially motivated, rulers along the gulf, Great Britain signed a series of diplomatic agreements that traded British pounds for peace and stability in the region. These truces were so prevalent that an entire area along the gulf became known as the "trucial coast." This area extended from Oman to Bahrain and was ruled by the Al-Khalifa, fellow travelers to the Al-Sabah. Although Kuwait was not a member of this group of nations formally connected to Great Britain, the Kuwaitis made every effort to remain on good terms with the British whenever possible.

The political options open to Kuwait's sheikhs were pretty clear to all. Kuwaitis had only to watch what was happening in other nearby sheikhdoms and emirates. As early as 1835, both Dubai and Bahrain had ceded some of their sovereign authority to the British Empire in return for steady financial support and military protection on an as-needed basis. In return, Great Britain oversaw foreign policy for each emirate. This also helped ensure that foreign powers did not pluck these smaller territories piecemeal when the opportunity arose. In 1882, the British employed the same strategy with the small sheikdoms that collectively constitute present-day UAE. Kuwait would eventually acquiesce in 1899 and Qatar in 1916.

Throughout the nineteenth century, Great Britain made it a top strategic priority to dissuade the Ottomans from employing military measures to dominate Kuwait and other Arabian Gulf emirates. At the same time, Great Britain attempted to protect the emirates from each other, and especially from outside threats. The outside threats with which the region's sheikhs were most concerned included the Al-Saud of Arabia. The Wahhabi legions of the Saudis were both a direct and immediate threat to Bahrain and Oman and would develop into a direct threat to Qatar and Kuwait in the early 1900s. Because of historical claims to areas such as Bahrain, the Persians of Iran were always considered possibly hostile.

While Al-Sabah sheikhs observed the benefits of British protection, they were also aware of the pitfalls. For example, the Al-Sabah were also watching when Great Britain used the death of Oman's ruler, Said ibn Sultan, to divide the ruling family's property into two separate kingdoms, Oman and Musqat, and set up the conditions under which Oman's East African "empire" of Zanzibar would slip away. It is highly likely that Kuwait's sheikhs sought to avoid opening the door to any such British intervention, while doing everything in their power to maximize the commercial opportunities made possible by British hegemony.

While the circle of wealth continued to expand beyond the Al-Sabah and the merchants, it is important to emphasize that most of Kuwait's citizens—the men who provided the unskilled labor, and the women and children who relied on those men for their sustenance—generally lived in abject poverty. Mud houses, often roofed with rushes when wood was unavailable or prohibitively expensive, were cramped. Water carried from nearby wells was generally available, but sometimes too brackish for human consumption. Protein in the diet came mostly from fish.

Fortunately for the common people of Kuwait, the Al-Sabah, when compared with ruling families elsewhere, were relatively generous with their wealth, providing gifts of food and other commodities. This was, in part, a result of Islamic teachings that encouraged charity to the poor. Their motives were not purely altruistic, however; the practice gave Kuwait's rulers more daily control over the population, which soon came to rely on handouts and which could not afford to let popular discontent cause those handouts to cease. Under these conditions, it is not at all surprising that modern-day Kuwait would develop into the largest welfare state on the planet. In 1814, Abdullah I had been succeeded by his son, Jaber I, who ruled for an especially extended period, until 1859. Sheikh Sabah II succeeded Jaber I in 1859 and ruled until his own death in 1866. Though his reign was shorter, Sabah II was still only the fourth ruler in over a century of Al-Sabah control of Kuwait. The stability that this afforded Kuwait was enjoyed by all Kuwaitis, but especially the merchant class. As Kuwait thrived, however, the Ottoman Empire starved for funds.

CLOSER OTTOMAN TIES

In 1866, Abdullah II became sheikh of Kuwait and determined to forge a closer relationship with the Ottoman Empire. His reasons for doing so are not certain. It might have been fear of the British. It might have been in anticipation of possible rewards. It might have been the personal charisma of the new Ottoman governor of Baghdad, Midhat Pasha. Midhat Pasha enacted a number of administrative measures that improved the military and financial position of the Ottomans around the Arabian Gulf. His next objective was to restore Ottoman control over al-Hasa and the other territories of Arabia lost to the Al-Saud family and their Wahhabi legions in 1795. The British were very concerned about Kuwait's role in this expedition. From past experience, they had reason to expect Kuwaiti neutrality. Moreover, in 1841, Kuwait's Sheikh Jaber I had allowed his son to represent him by signing a naval truce. That truce was effective for only one year, however, so its precepts were certainly not in effect three decades later. The British were painfully aware that Kuwait had not been a signatory to the 1820 General Treaty of Peace, signed by the region's other sheikhs, nor had Kuwait signed the 1861 Maritime Treaty.

Thus, the British could only look on aghast as hundreds of Kuwaiti cavalrymen under Abdullah II's brother Mubarak joined the Ottoman troops, and the entire Kuwaiti fleet put to sea with Sheikh Abdullah II personally in command. Bombardment by the Kuwaiti fleet was instrumental in capturing the city of al-Qatif. This was especially galling to the British, since the Ottoman warships refrained from firing on the city so as to avoid breaking their own maritime agreement with Great Britain. Once the expedition turned inland, Kuwait's fleet could not be of much assistance. Eventually the campaign ground to a halt on its way to Riyadh.

In 1871, the attention of every Kuwaiti, from Abdullah II down to the lowliest seaman on Kuwait's bustling waterfront, was drawn to a maritime disaster of the first order. That year a huge storm far off in the Indian Ocean created waves that swamped and sank many, perhaps even hundreds, of Kuwait's valuable pearling vessels. Ships were lost, divers were lost, and harvested pearls were lost. While the economic consequences were painful, they were also short lived. There was too much money to be made in pearls for Kuwaitis not to rebuild the fleet and sail off again in search of pearls. The rebound was rapid, and Kuwait's economy again boomed. By 1886, Kuwait minted its first coins in copper due to insufficient quantities of Indian rupees, which normally exchanged hands.

Partly as a reward for the friendship of Sheikh Abdullah II, and partly in an attempt to cement his subordinate relationship, the Ottomans formally recognized Abdullah II as *qaimaqam,* or provincial subgovernor, in 1871 when Midhat Pasha passed through Kuwait. On paper, this meant Abdullah II was responsible to the governor in Basrah for the efficient administration of Kuwait. This documented instance of dependence on the Ottomans would later become one of Iraq's primary rationales for insisting that Kuwait was historically part of Iraq. The Ottoman Empire did not receive anything more than this nominal dominion over Kuwait, but at the time, Ottoman officials were satisfied with what they had accomplished.

For his part, Abdullah II also appeared satisfied with the new arrangement, as the situation remained unchanged throughout his rule, which lasted until 1892. He was still dependent on the Ottomans for water. As Kuwait grew, the amount of water provided by the wells at Jahra inside Kuwait was woefully inadequate to fill demand. Kuwait's drinking water had to be carried by boat from the Shatt al Arab, where the vessels were loaded. If the governor of Basrah closed the tap, Kuwait would be in dire straits. Moreover, the Al-Sabah had invested in parcels of agricultural land near Basrah, land that was well within the Ottoman domain. The sheikh could fully expect those lands to be confiscated should he ever run seriously afoul of Ottoman authorities in the future. Under Abdullah II, the Ottoman flag was often seen flying from Kuwaiti vessels and sometimes actually flew over Kuwait City itself on ceremonial occasions.

Besides Midhat Pasha, other reformers attempted to improve conditions around the Ottoman Empire. In the mid- to late-1800s, the Ottomans took fairly drastic administrative, legal, and educational measures to reform the systems already in place around their shrinking empire; collectively, these new procedures were known as the *tanzimat*. While the tanzimat did foster modernization in a number of locations around the empire, especially where land holding was still medieval in nature, the effect on Kuwait was marginal. Al-Sabah control was too strong, and Kuwait's sheikhs were able to avoid being further drawn into the imperial bureaucracy. Even under Abdullah II, Ottoman troops, administrators, and tax collectors were never physically stationed in Kuwait.

Beyond the tanzimat, the Ottomans also attempted to appease European powers in order to preclude Western intervention in Ottoman affairs or Ottoman lands. Generally, these efforts revolved around protection of European Christians within the empire's boundaries, but major European powers such as France, Russia, and especially Great Britain always reserved the right to intervene on behalf of perceived dangers. As Great Britain's commercial ties to Kuwait grew stronger over time, Ottoman administrators were increasingly loath to act decisively against the sheikhs for fear of catalyzing a British intervention.

Throughout the late 1800s, the Ottomans had desperately strived to catch up with Europe. Internal Ottoman confusion, such as that caused by the abortive constitutional reforms in the period 1876–1878, created conditions under which even well-meaning Ottoman bureaucrats lacked the guidance necessary to administer the slippery economic and political affairs of Kuwait. Educational and political reforms, however, were only partially implemented; ultimately, most were unsuccessful. When European banks took over the bankrupt Ottoman finances in 1881, any hope for progress was dashed. An unintended consequence of these attempts at reform, however, was a heightened political awareness throughout the Ottoman Empire. Internally to the Ottoman Empire, this heightened awareness would foster nationalism and encourage protests and calls for political reform.

In Kuwait, however, the Al-Sabah sheikhs were always especially careful to allow only those improvements that could be kept under positive control and not get out of hand. The country's conservative rulers ensured that the sheikhdom remained firmly based on conservative principles. A revolutionary zeal for revamping Kuwait was to be avoided at all costs. While the bureaucrats of the Ottoman Empire tried to gain more control over local affairs in the area, and especially over the collection of taxes and tariffs, Kuwait was routinely viewed by the Ottomans as of minimal importance in the overall imperial scheme.

Kuwait was not very important to the British Empire either, as long as other imperial powers did not show significant interest in changing the status quo. A stated British interest was in limiting the influence enjoyed by the Ottomans, as well as other European powers in the region. Great Britain included France, Russia, and Germany on the short list of countries to watch. As the Ottoman need for funds became more acute, Kuwait was increasingly pressured to support the empire financially, which in turn made the British all the more uncomfortable.

ASSASSINATION OF MOHAMED

Abdullah II died in 1892 and was replaced by Mohamed. Mohamed, reportedly of weak character, was not an effective ruler. He attempted to share authority with two of his brothers, Jarrah and Mubarak. Mohamed and Jarrah collaborated to run the financial affairs of Kuwait. Mubarak was relegated to keeping the peace among the Bedouin, placing him outside the city walls and farther from the seat of power. At the same time, a wealthy Kuwaiti merchant, originally from Iraq, became an unexpected participant in Kuwait's destiny. Yusuf ibn Abdullah al-Ibrahim was a distant relative of Kuwait's rulers and confidante of Basrah's Ottoman governor. Mubarak might have been ambitious in his own right, or he might have feared that Mohamed intended to do away with him. It is even possible that Yusuf was conspiring to get Kuwait for himself, forcing Mubarak to act. In any case, early one morning in the summer of 1896, Mubarak, his sons Jaber and Salem, and several loyal retainers entered the palace. Mubarak shot and killed Mohamed. When Jaber's weapon failed to fire, his servants stepped in and murdered Jarrah, his uncle. With his brothers assassinated, Mubarak immediately declared himself ruler of Kuwait.

Yusuf immediately traveled to Basrah, where he might petition the Ottoman governor to intercede on his behalf. Yusuf also convinced the sons of the murdered brothers, Mohamed and Jarrah, to join him, strengthening his claim to Kuwait. Local Ottoman authorities were sympathetic to Yusuf and the other claimants. In July 1897, Yusuf, along with Basrah's governor, threatened Kuwait by sea, and Mubarak formally requested the British to position a gunboat off the Kuwaiti coast. The British refused, not willing to upset the Ottomans. Perhaps not wishing war themselves, even with Kuwait, the local Ottoman forces withdrew. Simultaneously, Mubarak contacted the Ottoman governor in Baghdad and the Grand Mufti in Istanbul to gain their support for him to become the qaimaqam, the post his father, Abdullah II, had held. To gain their support, Mubarak had to convince them that the widespread rumors of Great Britain being behind the coup were false. With the help of lavish gifts to these and other Ottoman officials, Mubarak was eventually able to receive their official approval in December 1897.

DEFENSE PACT WITH THE BRITISH EMPIRE

Yusuf, however, would continue to plot and scheme for several years to depose Mubarak militarily. In 1898, when another Yusuf-instigated attack seemed likely, Mubarak again requested British protection, and the British again denied the request. Late that year, however, the British became aware of Russian initiatives toward a deal with the Ottomans to build a railroad spur from Baghdad to Kuwait. The scheme, headed by a Russian entrepreneur named Count Kapnist, was not likely to succeed, but the British were not about to chance it. The British government contacted its resident political agent in the Arabian Gulf, Lieutenant Colonel M. C. Meade, who operated out of Busheyr in Persia (Iran). Meade was directed to expeditiously formalize an agreement with Mubarak to prevent the Ottomans from gaining more sway over Kuwait. Meade was also ordered to keep the hoped-for deal a secret, to avoid aggravating the Ottomans or the Russians.

In January 1899, during a personal hunting trip rather than a formal diplomatic session, Meade and Mubarak agreed to and signed a bond rather than a formal treaty between sovereign states. The agreement obligated Mubarak and his successors to not receive the representatives of any "Power or Government" without the prior approval of the British government. This essentially gave Britain complete control of Kuwait's foreign policy. Nowhere in this original bond was any mention made of British obligations to protect Kuwait from outside threats.

Mubarak was initially reluctant to sign the document without additional assurances from Meade that British protection would be forthcoming. Meade responded with a personal note, again not a formal treaty or otherwise binding document, which assured Mubarak that as long as he followed the letter of the bond, he could expect the "good offices of the British government" on Kuwait's behalf. Meade's note also added that a payment of fifteen thousand Indian rupees, or about fifteen hundred British pounds, would be forthcoming as the first annual installment of British financial assistance. Finally, Meade's note swore Mubarak to secrecy about the deal. Mubarak was convinced and signed the bond. Reportedly, two of Mubarak's brothers were in attendance, and when the sheikh asked them both to countersign the bond, each refused. Afterward, Mubarak apparently asked Meade if the agreement extended to Mubarak's extensive agricultural holdings outside Basrah (clearly part of the Ottoman domain). Meade, evidently on his own initiative, expressed the opinion that these lands were *probably* included in the agreement. Having led his land and people into partnership with Great Britain, Sheikh Mubarak Al-Sabah, soon to be widely known as "Mubarak al-Kabir" or "Mubarak the Great," was ready to lead Kuwait into the twentieth century.

4

British Protectorate
(1899–1961)

At the turn of the twentieth century, a growing Kuwait City and its immediate environs held around fifty thousand settled inhabitants. As a rule, these people lived as they had always lived. Relative to their nomadic kinfolk, their everyday life was stable, and Al-Sabah rule was generally benign. On the other hand, except for the major merchant families, few Kuwaitis were growing rich. Indeed, most Kuwaitis worked as hard as ever to earn a living. That conditions in Kuwait were better than elsewhere in the region, relatively speaking, is proved by the increasing immigration to Kuwait from around the Arabian Gulf's southern shores, as well as from the hinterlands of the Arabian Peninsula. Efficient administration of government by the Al-Sabah and thriving commerce were widely attractive.

As before, the common Kuwaitis still lived in mud homes, the floors of which were covered with rushes gathered and exported from nearby marshes in Iraq. Wood and stone remained prohibitively expensive for all but the very wealthy. European visitors to Kuwait around this time noted the quaint Kuwaiti habit of sleeping on the flat roofs of their homes to avoid the stifling nighttime heat of summer. In approximately 1905, a new source of water was found inside the country, but the primary source of drinking and cooking water remained the Shatt al Arab. While the need for water created work for Kuwaiti water carriers, it also meant that Kuwait was desperately dependent on the goodwill of Ottoman governors in Basrah who controlled the flow of water to Kuwait.

Kuwaiti fishing boats still did double duty as trade-carrying vessels, and Kuwaiti merchants continued to show steady profits that exceeded the norm in other Arabian Gulf emirates. The wealth with which the Industrial Revolution had rewarded the United States and Western Europe also brought a demand for luxury items—a demand that Kuwait, fortuitously located near some of the world's richest natural pearl banks, was eager to fill. Even though the pearling season ran from only mid-May until mid-September, those four months promised enough profit to keep the Kuwaiti fleet afloat all year, allowing pearling vessels to carry cargo the rest of the year.

After 1900, when British naval authority had all but eliminated slave running as a profitable activity for merchant vessels, the profits from pearling became all the more attractive. In 1906 Kuwait was known to have possessed 461 boats that employed over nine thousand men in the pearl trade. Along with the families they supported, these pearl fishermen represented about a third of Kuwait's population at the time. Over the course of the next several decades, the pearl trade in Kuwait would continue to expand. At its height, the pearl trade employed as many as fifteen thousand Kuwaitis as crew members and divers on at least seven hundred vessels, both large and small. Again, factoring in their dependents, this meant that almost half of all Kuwaitis were, to varying degrees, dependent on the continuation of pearling profits. Two developments, both outside the control of Kuwait, would dramatically change the situation for the worse: the global depression of the 1920s and the marketing of cultured pearls by the Japanese at about the same time.

Cultured pearls were not a new invention. The Dutch had first bred a cultured pearl in the 1700s but made no attempt to profit from the knowledge. In the late 1800s, both the Japanese and the Australians discovered an effective process for producing cultured pearls, but neither process was yet as financially efficient as it needed to be in order to be competitive. In the 1920s, however, when a Japanese entrepreneur introduced a streamlined process for making cultured pearls, the effect on Kuwait's hugely successful natural pearl industry was both predictable and devastating.

The bottom fell out of the natural pearl market, and with it came the collapse of Kuwait's pearl-based economy. The result was that, almost overnight, Kuwait became as desperately poor as anyplace on the planet. The people of Kuwait were forced to rely on Great Britain more than ever. Within a few years, however, a new discovery would force another change on Kuwait, one that most poor Kuwaitis would conclude was for the betterment of all. In 1936, the first oil well would be sunk by a jointly held British and American petroleum company in the rich oil field of Burgan, Kuwait.

AL-SABAH FAMILY DYNASTICS

As the century began, it was by no means certain that the Al-Sabah would still rule Kuwait a few decades hence. The assassination that had empowered Mubarak the Great also set a dangerous precedent for other would-be sheikhs, Al-Sabah or otherwise. It was clear that the old manner of accession, from father to son in the direct Al-Sabah line, had outlived its usefulness. On the death of Mubarak the Great in 1915, a new method of selecting the sheikh was adopted: the sheikhdom would alternate between the two branches of Mubarak's family, from his son, Jaber, to his other son, Salem, and then back and forth. All but Mubarak's branch of the family were thus excluded from ruling as sheikh, though there were still many opportunities for advancement in the government, and also accretion of wealth, for all members of the Al-Sabah family. This private family arrangement would subsequently be made an official part of the country's constitution upon independence.

As it was, when Mubarak the Great died in 1915, he was replaced by his son Jaber. When Jaber, in turn, died shortly thereafter in 1917, he was replaced by Salem, who ruled briefly, as well, only until 1921. On Salem's death, Ahmad would assume the throne and rule until his own death in 1950, a period of dynastic stability that came at just the right moment in Kuwait's tumultuous twentieth century. The Kuwait that Mubarak passed along to his heirs was quite different from the one he had "inherited," but only in regard to its relationships with the Ottomans and the British. The Kuwaiti people, however, did not notice any difference whatsoever in their daily lives.

In comparison, the Kuwait that Sheikh Ahmad left behind in 1950 was vastly different from the Kuwait he had ruled first in 1921. The engine of that change was petroleum, but Sheikh Ahmad deserves much credit for how he planned for and oversaw the subsequent transformation of Kuwait. In 1950, Abdullah assumed authority over the sheikhdom, and he would rule until 1965. The Kuwait that he received from Ahmad was practically ready for independence, and it was Abdullah's task, and honor, to lead Kuwait into a bright, independent future. The remainder of this chapter discusses subsequent developments that bridged Mubarak the Great's Kuwait of 1899 to Sheikh Abdullah's Kuwait of 1961.

RELATIONS WITH THE BRITISH EMPIRE

The treaty that Mubarak the Great hammered out with the British imperial government would continue in effect all the way to Kuwait's full independence in 1961. The treaty afforded Great Britain a substantial degree of control over Kuwait's economic and international prospects, and the British attempted to add to their power in Kuwait at every opportunity. In 1909, the

KIRTLAND PUBLIC
LIBRARY

British obtained Sheikh Mubarak's agreement that he would make no oil exploration concessions to anyone without prior approval from Great Britain. In doing so, Britain was signaling the growing unease with which it viewed the expansive foreign policies of a resurgent German Empire.

After the Suez Canal was finally opened in 1869, the British were sent into a near panic at unsubstantiated rumors that the Ottomans would ever consider collaborating with any other major European power to build a railway to Kuwait. Although that situation never fully materialized, the British remained especially attentive to Ottoman interaction with any rival European powers. Soon the Germans, whose regional power was beginning to spread globally, began to show interest in the Middle East region. British alarm at German designs on the Middle East grew apace. A Berlin-to-Istanbul railroad was one thing, and serious enough at that, but diplomatic talk of extending that same railroad all the way to Basrah was a great fright to Britain's statesmen.

The burgeoning German Empire strongly considered how to most efficiently develop Basrah into a major seaport that would receive goods from throughout the Near East. In Basrah, the German theory held, those sought-after Oriental goods would arrive by sea but would be quickly cross-loaded onto railcars for rapid transit to the heart of Europe, for further distribution by German merchants. Vast profits would accrue to Germany, while British seaborne trade through the Suez Canal would become marginalized. German engineers discovered, however, that the heavy silting caused by the Tigris-Euphrates river system would severely hamper Basrah's potential as a major seaport. Expensive dredging would become a never-ending drain on their plans for Basrah. Once German diplomats began to look for less expensive alternatives, they quickly spotted the protected natural harbor of Kuwait near at hand. When Great Britain concluded that an economic alliance between the Ottoman Empire and the German Empire could have such dire financial consequences for Britain's commercial interests, it became of prime interest for the British to acquire Kuwait in some form for the British Empire instead.

German plans had already made their way onto paper, and German engineers were dispatched to complete the final surveys necessary before any construction could begin. The Berlin-Baghdad-Basrah railroad line was actually planned to terminate at Ras al Kadhima, the point projecting into Kuwait Bay from the north. The reason for shifting the terminal to Kuwait was apparent to the German engineers on the ground in the region. The Germans knew that making the necessary improvements to the existing port facilities at Basrah would be cost-prohibitive due to the never-ending expense of dredging required to allow large ships to access the channel. The Shatt al Arab, much like the Mississippi and every other major river, deposits tons of silt each year to feed an ever-expanding delta. German engineers had sought out a less expensive solution to the costly alternative of dredging, and Kuwait Bay, the deepest open-water port on the Arabian side of the Gulf, was the perfect alternative. In 1912, Ottoman functionaries discretely pressured Sheikh Mubarak to approve the German railway development plans, at that time known as the "Taurus System."

While economic considerations remained foremost, it was not lost on German strategic planners that a new coaling station in Kuwait would also open up the entire Arabian Gulf to the Imperial German Navy. The British admiralty was absolutely terrified at the prospect, as it was already pulling warships from around the globe to concentrate on defending home waters from the expanding fleet of German battleships nearby in the North Sea. Maintaining a strong naval presence in the Arabian Gulf would be almost impossible under the circumstances. To forestall such unacceptable eventualities, the British sought to strike their own deal—in this case with the Ottomans themselves.

Anglo-Ottoman Convention

In 1913, perhaps wishing to appease the Turks in the hope that this would keep the Germans out of the Arabian Gulf, the British formally negotiated and approved the Anglo-Ottoman Convention. Sheikh Mubarak was displeased, since the convention partially ceded his hard-won autonomy from the Ottoman Empire while marking the limits to the defense that the British Empire would provide to him. The convention, to which Kuwait was by no means a signatory, specifically referred to Kuwait as an autonomous *caza* (district or subprovince) of the Ottoman Empire, and reduced Kuwait's sheikh to the post of *qaimmaqam,* or administrative subordinate, to the provincial governor in Baghdad. Adding further injury, from Mubarak's perch, the agreement allowed the Ottomans to actually assign an agent to Kuwait, a move that Al-Sabah sheikhs had avoided for one hundred and fifty years.

For this concession, however, the Kuwaitis finally received official written confirmation that Sheikh Mubarak's political authority extended a full 80 kilometers from Kuwait City. The map accompanying the convention used a red circle to indicate this zone, which included the major Kuwaiti islands of Bubiyan, Faylakha, and Warbah, as well as several more of the smaller islets. A circle marked by a green line was used to delineate an additional 100-kilometer radius within which Mubarak could collect tariffs and taxes, a considerable financial boon to the Al-Sabah family fortunes. Moreover, Kuwait's position as an "autonomous district" under Ottoman "suzerainty"— both phrases having been carefully selected by the British for their inherent ambiguity—was a tacit sign that the Ottomans would not interfere in Kuwait's affairs domestically or internationally. This was a significant concession on the part of the Ottomans, which should have pleased Mubarak deeply. If it did, however, he kept it largely to himself.

The Ottomans were not happy with the convention, and the Kuwaitis were privately unhappy. Perhaps each side recognized that this convention would eventually foster complications that would have a major effect on Kuwait's subsequent history throughout the twentieth century. The British, for their part, were quite satisfied when they considered the accord solely in relation to the Middle East. Within the context of global strategy, however, the agreement was seen by the British as the half measure that it truly was.

Though the British imperial government was satisfied for the moment with how the Turks had been handled, senior colonial policymakers also noted with concern Sheikh Mubarak's marked displeasure with the bilateral accord between the two superpowers. The very next year, 1914, the British took the needed steps to repair fences with Mubarak and to lock in for the long term their highly favorable foreign policy relationship with Kuwait. Great Britain's resident political agent in the Arabian Gulf wrote a letter to Sheikh Mubarak in which he, as a representative of Her Britannic Majesty's government, recognized Kuwait as "an independent government under British protection."

Mubarak again basked in the glow of security from the Ottoman Empire for which he had long quested. As it turned out, the First World War, and the subsequent collapse of the Ottoman Empire, prevented the Anglo-Ottoman Convention from ever being officially ratified. When the new kingdom of Iraq rose from the Mesopotamian rubble of the fallen Ottoman Empire, the borders of Kuwait would lead to much dispute and, eventually, to bloodshed.

First World War

During the initial years of the First World War, Mubarak was, generally speaking, pro-British, even after the Ottoman Empire took its stance alongside the Central Powers. One contemporary British military observer credited Mubarak with tying down a sizable Ottoman force that could have been fighting the British elsewhere in the Middle East, or perhaps putting down the unrest growing among many Arab tribes in response to harsh Ottoman rule that would lead to the Great Arab Revolt of 1916. This particular assessment of Sheikh Mubarak's contribution to the war effort of the allies, however, is overly kind. Considering the many troubles that some other Arab leaders—particularly Abd al-Aziz Al-Saud, or Ibn Saud as he was commonly known—were causing for Ottoman forces throughout the Middle East region, the half-hearted support for the allies from Mubarak the Great drew scant reaction in Istanbul.

To his credit, Sheikh Mubarak deliberately ignored the call to jihad pronounced by the Muslim authorities under Ottoman sway. Mubarak also kept to a minimum any anti-British propaganda within his domain. In fact, Mubarak contributed thousands of Indian rupees (the coin of the realm) from his personal fortune to the British Red Cross. Perhaps Sheikh Mubarak's most significant contribution to the British war effort was in providing logistical support to British forces operating in Mesopotamia. Moreover, Kuwait City's excellent harbor became homeport to several British hospital ships with drafts too deep to enter the Shatt al Arab. Mubarak's assistance in getting allied wounded personnel to the ships and then evacuated by sea to hospitals in India no doubt saved many lives.

That said, there was much criticism of Sheikh Mubarak's behavior during the war's early years. It is quite possible that, at this early stage of the war, Mubarak was still attempting to calculate which side among the combatants would ultimately win before casting his lot and later living to regret it. As the new sheikh, Jaber had initially taken the same tack, but later he clearly, if not openly, sided with the Ottomans, a development that caused shock waves among British diplomats. Jaber markedly increased the caravan trade from Kuwait to Syria. British concerns that Kuwait was no longer "neutral"—that is, tacitly pro-British—fell on deaf ears in the capital. Eventually the British would conclude that they must do more than just protest. Even though Great Britain's Royal Navy dominated the Mediterranean, the Turkish army in Damascus was able to hold out, thanks to the flow of vital provisions and ammunition that continued to reach the city by camel caravan all the way from Kuwait. Thus, Kuwaiti economic practices, if not policies, effectively broke the British blockade on Ottoman forces stationed in Syria and elsewhere around the eastern Mediterranean Sea.

When Salem became sheikh in 1917, trade with the Ottomans continued. Salem's support of the Turks was tempered by the fear that the British might intervene in Kuwait's growing disagreement with Ibn Saud in Arabia. This time around, the British acted forcefully by slapping a naval blockade on Kuwait until the flow of supplies to the Turks was eliminated. When the British confronted him about the problem in July 1918, Sheikh Salem had argued that the smuggling was outside his knowledge and control. British diplomats countered by pointedly advising the sheikh that the earlier assurances of protection and financial support that the British government had once given to Sheikhs Mubarak and Jaber could just as easily be withdrawn if Salem could not effectively control his own people.

Since the British were actively supporting the Saudis' anti-Ottoman campaign, Salem saw it as a very real possibility that the British would cast their lot against him if Kuwait flaunted its pro-Turkish stance. Practically overnight, the smuggling and gunrunning to the Turks became a mere trickle; soon thereafter it stopped entirely. Thus, Sheikh Salem's efforts to throttle back the caravan trade with the Ottomans had been insufficient to deter a British reaction, but sufficient to keep that British countermove from deposing the ruling Al-Sabah.

Ikhwan Invasion

Following the collapse of the Ottomans, the British formalized the disintegration of that empire by officially repudiating the tenets of the Anglo-Ottoman Convention as they applied to Kuwait. There was no longer any pretense of imperial ties; Great Britain recognized Kuwait as an independent sheikdom in its own right. Great Britain again reiterated its continuing commitment to see to Kuwait's foreign policy and national defense.

The first test of Kuwait's defense, and of British resolve, came from another former Ottoman territory: Saudi Arabia under its de facto ruler, Ibn Saud. Ibn Saud was working hard to cement his control of the entire Arabian Peninsula, and the idea of co-opting the Islamic fundamentalism of the Wahhabis toward that end was an attractive possibility. As early as 1912, Ibn Saud had begun to organize Wahhabi fundamentalists into a militia known as the Ikhwan, or "the Brotherhood." Over the course of the next two decades, he would employ them ruthlessly to cement his control of the Arabian Peninsula and beyond. At the wave of his hand, Ibn Saud could launch an invasion of Kuwait by the Ikhwan. The threat posed by the Ikhwan was dire, and Kuwait's sheikhs and their British protectors took that threat quite seriously.

Several modern scholars now draw distinctions between the traditional Wahhabi movement and the new Ikhwan; some other scholars contend that the Ikhwan movement was wholly spontaneous and that Ibn Saud never had effective control over the movement. Ibn Saud saw it differently. In January 1920, he told a British diplomat that the Ikhwan were the original Wahhabis, though he admitted the Ikhwan contributed a new impetus to that older religious movement. Ibn Saud also bluntly stated to the British resident political agent that he himself controlled every move of the Ikhwan.

Whether he fully orchestrated events or merely took advantage of circumstances on the ground, the ever-present dispute over Kuwait's borders provided the perfect opportunity for Ibn Saud to flex his expansionist military muscle in late 1920. Sheikh Salem claimed control of Kuwaiti territory out to 140 kilometers from the capital city. To the extent that his claim reflected his practical ability to collect taxes and tariffs out to that distance, his claim would be strengthened.

In May 1920, Ibn Saud signaled his ultimate ambitions toward Kuwait when he sent (or permitted) an Ikhwan raiding party into extremely southern Kuwait, where Ikhwan troops quickly destroyed a small detachment of Kuwaiti cavalry operating far from home. From the quick success of this mission, Ibn Saud sensed weakness on the part of the Al-Sabah and, perhaps, hoped that the British lacked the stomach for more battle. Ibn Saud claimed essentially all of Kuwait for his own. In September 1920, he completely rejected Sheikh Salem's official position and asserted that the sheikh's authority did not extend beyond the recently rebuilt and strengthened mud walls of Kuwait City. While the Kuwaitis could point to the Anglo-Ottoman Convention as documentation of their territorial authority, Ibn Saud could counter that the convention had never been officially ratified, as required.

In October 1920, the border war with Najd flared into open warfare when Ibn Saud again sent his Ikhwan warriors into Kuwait—this time in force, and with nothing less than a full conquest of Kuwait their goal. The Ikhwan raided widely and soon approached the walled town of Jahra, 25 miles from Kuwait City. A massive public project had quickly rebuilt a defensive wall around Kuwait City. Later in October, the Ikhwan returned, attacking Jahra, the site of Kuwait's now-famous Red Fort. Sheikh Salem and his troops initially fought on the plain outside the city and were badly mauled by the Ikhwan cavalry.

Rather than surrendering or suing for peace, however, Salem withdrew into the Red Fort and dug in for however long a siege would take. In fact, a resolution was only days away. Not willing to merely sit and watch, the British first dropped leaflets from warplanes advising the Ikhwan to withdraw. When that proved ineffective, a small detachment of Royal Marines was landed to bolster Kuwaiti defenses. With the timely assistance of the guns from patrolling British warships, the siege was soon lifted, and the Ikhwan quickly fell back from Kuwaiti territory. The Wahhabis of Central Arabia had threatened Kuwait since the 1790s. From this point on, however, the threat of the Wahhabi-inspired Ikhwan Brotherhood would recede for Kuwait. This threat would not go away entirely until Ibn Saud was forced to crush the leaders of the Ikhwan, who were no longer responsive to his political will.

When the First World War ended, so too did the Ottoman Empire for all practical purposes. The Ottoman demise would become official with the Treaty of Lausanne, enacted in 1923. The fact that, in the treaty, Turkey also officially renounced any future claims to former Ottoman imperial lands would become of critical importance in subsequent Iraqi attempts to claim sovereignty over tiny Kuwait. Since Great Britain had the postwar mandate over Iraq, it also eventually took the lead in negotiating the boundary status of Kuwait, Iraq, and Saudi Arabia with Ibn Saud.

Uqair Protocol

In the next available period of calm, the British moved quickly to prevent additional economic and political disruption from occurring as a result of growing enmity between Kuwait and Saudi Arabia. Sir Percy Cox, the regional high commissioner of imperial affairs, chaired a convention to resolve the underlying border problems between the Arabian Najd on one hand, and both Kuwait and Iraq on the other. In November 1922, a meeting was convened at Uqair to establish the final boundaries between Kuwait, Saudi Arabia, and

Iraq. The British were represented in the talks by Sir Percy Cox, all the way from Baghdad, who also spoke for the British-controlled kingdom of Iraq. Ibn Saud himself headed the Saudi delegation to the proceedings. Tiny Kuwait was represented by the British resident political agent in Kuwait City, a lowly major. The disparity in rank among these participants was a clear sign, to the Al-Sabah at least, that the deck was stacked against Kuwait, and they were almost certainly correct in that assessment.

Any uncertainty over Kuwait's meager negotiating power was quickly dispelled when Cox expedited the proceedings by drawing proposed new borders on the map. The subsequent treaty among these parties thus established the boundary between Kuwait and Saudi Arabia and also set up the Neutral Zone. Kuwait's border with Iraq remained undefined. In the process, Kuwait lost almost two-thirds of its claimed territory to the Saudi ruler. It was a bitter development, but one that the new sheikh, Ahmad, had no option but to accept. The Kuwaitis were not happy about their southern border, which was now more than a hundred miles closer to the capital city, but at least the boundaries were finally fixed.

The Uqair Protocol, as it came to be known, was successful in the sense that it governed Kuwaiti–Saudi Arabian foreign relations essentially to the present day. Kuwait's borders with Iraq were not so neatly, or so agreeably, defined. As noted, the Ottoman Empire was broken up at the end of the First World War. Turkey was the obvious successor state to the Ottoman Empire, but in the Lausanne Treaty of 1923, Turkey formally relinquished any claim to historical Ottoman holdings. Presumably this left Kuwait's sovereignty in an unassailable position, but Iraq saw the situation differently.

In 1923, Sheikh Ahmad requested in writing that the British formally and finally delineate Kuwait's border with Iraq. It was understood by British authorities that the Kuwaitis expected the border to be set consistent with the earlier "green line" of the Anglo-Ottoman Convention. Within weeks, the British, by way of a memorandum to their resident political agent in Kuwait, recognized that same area as the far limit of Kuwaiti sovereignty. Iraq's King Faisal, whose kingdom was under British mandate following the collapse of the Ottoman Empire, and who had himself obtained the throne with British support, was in no position to quibble. Kuwait and Iraq formally accepted the British finding in August 1923, and again in 1927.

In 1932, the kingdom of Iraq became completely independent from post-Ottoman Turkey and applied for membership in the League of Nations. The Iraqi government once more agreed to the established border with Kuwait since that boundary was included in the documentation that Iraq submitted to the League of Nations as part of its application process. While to the Kuwaitis the issue was now closed, many subsequent Iraqi leaders, including Saddam Hussein, would be unwilling to concede Iraq's claim to the territory of Kuwait.

The exploration and exploitation of oil in the region would up the ante, so to speak, and heighten Iraq's desire to incorporate Kuwait into the fold.

ECONOMIC DEVELOPMENTS

Global economic depression had a powerful negative impact on Kuwait's economy starting in the later 1920s. At its height, Kuwait's pearling industry led the world, regularly sending out between 750 and 800 vessels to meet the world's need for pearls. Unfortunately, in the middle of a depression, luxuries like pearls are the first casualties of belt tightening everywhere. The Kuwaiti pearl industry quickly began to languish. Almost immediately thereafter, the shock waves from the launch of a cultured pearl industry by the Japanese sounded the death knell for Kuwait's once-bustling pearling fleet and its harbor home. A handful of family-owned boats were able to stay afloat, but the vast majority of the sheikhdom's pearl-related workforce was made to look elsewhere for sustenance.

Some Kuwaiti merchant families became rich by smuggling gold into India during these years, but otherwise, there were few new economic opportunities to be exploited. Periodically, Ibn Saud squelched trade between his domain in Najd and Kuwait, which further hindered Kuwaiti economic development. As the economic screws tightened on the people of Kuwait, it was inevitable that a once politically passive people would begin to show interest in effecting change in the politics of the small sheikhdom.

Majlis Movement

During the 1930s, economic problems continued to pile up, adding to social and, soon, political unrest inside Kuwait. The global depression and the collapse of pearling already had many Kuwaitis reeling, and an embargo imposed by the Saudis on trade with Kuwait only worsened the popular discontent with Sheikh Ahmad's economic and taxation policies. The major merchants understood that things would soon be looking up, but only if the expected petroleum revenues were funneled back into the country rather than simply diverted into the coffers of the Al-Sabah family.

When personal pleas to the sheikh failed to bring the desired reforms, most of Kuwait's top merchant families organized into an opposition movement. From among these richest and most influential Kuwaitis, a grassroots legislative assembly, or *majlis,* was elected in mid-1938. While the motive was economic in nature, the shock waves were political and caused quite a scare in the ruling Al-Sabah. Soon the Majlis Movement inside Kuwait began to receive moral and propaganda support from nearby Iraq, which still had its hopes set on acquiring newly rich Kuwait, or at least expanding its access to the Arabian

Gulf by acquiring several of the Kuwaiti islands in the upper gulf, particularly the Warbah and Bubiyan islands.

After allowing the assembly to stay convened for six months, the Al-Sabah, supported by tribal allies, were eventually forced to act, and the sheikh abolished the assembly in December 1938. At the same time, however, the ruling family was forced to make concessions with regard to the spending of oil wealth that in part met the initial demands that had led to the Majlis Movement in the first place. As it was, the sheikh felt compelled to bow to popular pressure and established a "consultative council" to replace the legislative assembly. While *shura,* or consultation, had always marked Al-Sabah rule from the very beginning, this new council codified those shared responsibilities as never before.

Not surprisingly, Sheikh Salem chaired the new council, and four other prominent Al-Sabah family members held key posts. Nine additional members were drawn from Kuwait's elite merchant families. Thus, both sides in the domestic struggle—Kuwait's rulers and Kuwait's people—could claim a moral victory of sorts. Moreover, the abortive assembly and the follow-on consultative council set the necessary precedents for future democratic participation in the governing process. That precedent would become a major contributing factor to subsequent developments in postinvasion Kuwait.

Impact of Oil

As noted elsewhere, Kuwait's economy prior to the exploitation of oil was primarily seminomadic in nature, based on agriculture, fish, pearls, and the caravan trade. By the 1930s, however, these activities collectively were barely allowing a subsistence existence for many Kuwaitis. The pearl trade was crushed by the glut of cultured pearls on the market. The once-lucrative caravan trade had been severely restricted by allied blockades during the First World War, followed by decades of "economic warfare" with the Wahhabis of Central Arabia. When a global depression hit, traditional Kuwaitis were barely getting by financially. Oil soon changed all of that.

It is not that petroleum was newly discovered. Oil had seeped from the ground in spots for centuries. Moreover, European oil companies, and later American oil companies, had begun to actively explore for oil decades earlier, in large part to power the battleship navies preeminent on the oceans of the world. The Anglo-Persian Oil Company (APOC) had begun to develop oil fields in Iran almost a quarter century before. APOC, which would eventually come to be known as the British Petroleum Company in 1954, had requested permission to explore inside Kuwait back in 1911, but the request had been denied by British imperial administrators, as permitted under the memorandum of understanding originally signed by Mubarak and later expanded.

By the 1920s, American companies such as Gulf Oil courted the region's Arab leaders and the British government for permission to explore, though the British generally continued to deny access to non-British firms. APOC and Gulf Oil launched a joint exploratory endeavor in 1932. By 1934, the British government was willing to allow Sheikh Jaber to award the concession. The fact that the Shah of Iran had withdrawn APOC's concession in 1932 perhaps added a sense of urgency to the undertaking that had not existed before.

The new, jointly held firm was called the Kuwait Oil Company (KOC). Active oil exploration inside Kuwait began almost immediately, and survey teams scoured Kuwait throughout 1935. By 1936, KOC was prepared to sink its first well. Drilling equipment and personnel were quickly landed and soon began drilling in the Bahrah field to the north of Kadhima. No oil was found in the first well, but a second well nearby struck oil in 1938. KOC had located one of the largest and most lucrative oil fields in the world.

Like other ruling families around the Arabian Gulf, the Al-Sabah were poised to reap the benefits of oil exploration. More powerful than wealthy going into the petroleum era, the Al-Sabah would soon have almost limitless wealth at their fingertips. The ability of Kuwait's sheikhs to spend most of those funds wisely would shape Kuwait for the rest of the century. Moreover, as the Al-Sabah grew wealthier as a family, and as the extent of the Kuwaiti oil fields became known (approximately 20 percent of known oil reserves worldwide), the country's diplomats were able to negotiate from ever-increasing positions of strength with Western governments and oil companies. Thus, over time, the percentage of oil revenue staying in Kuwait, rather than heading for London or points west, grew ever larger. Additionally, the Al-Sabah were wise enough to insist on ever-greater Kuwaiti participation in the management of joint oil ventures, setting the stage for a time when all Kuwaiti oil production could be nationalized—in 1976.

Full development and exploitation of Kuwaiti oil would have to wait until the Second World War was resolved. Immediately following the war in 1946, KOC and Sheikh Ahmad were jointly ready to open the spigot and quickly pump as much oil as possible. Pipelines and other petroleum-handling facilities were quickly constructed, and commercial exportation was begun in June 1946. Oil production almost tripled from the first year to the second: 5.9 million barrels were produced in 1946, and over 16 million barrels were pumped in 1947. At least seven more oil fields would be located and drilled before oil production would finally peak in 1972. Even then, production was limited only by the decision to do so, not because oil was less readily available than it had been before.

Oil drilling within the joint Kuwaiti-Saudi Neutral Zone was potentially problematic, but the two states equitably resolved the possible difficulties. A consortium of small American oil companies, collectively known as the

American Independent Oil Company (Aminoil), won for a period of six decades, beginning in 1948, the ongoing concession to produce from the Neutral Zone on behalf of Kuwait. The Arabian American Oil Company (Aramco) held the concession to drill in the Neutral Zone on behalf of the Saudis, a concession that was later assumed by Getty Oil. After several years of exploratory drilling, Aminoil began producing and paying royalties to Kuwait, starting in 1954, while Saudi Arabia received royalties from Getty for its production in the zone.

Offshore exploration and production was initially awarded to a number of smaller Western oil companies, which in turn fed royalties back into Kuwait's rapidly filling treasury. In 1957, the Japanese-held Arabian Oil Company (AOC) began to explore for offshore oil in waters claimed by both Kuwait and Saudi Arabia, the arrangement being similar to that of the Neutral Zone. By 1961, the offshore wells were producing revenues that were then split between the two neighbors.

In 1950, Abdullah, known as Abdullah III, replaced Ahmad as sheikh and ruled the emirate until 1965. Having served as trusted advisor and counselor, and having overseen so many of the economic policies and projects of his kinsman, Sheikh Abdullah was ideally prepared to govern the country at this time. Moreover, it would fall to him to prepare Kuwait for the biggest step the tiny sheikhdom could take: full independence. Profits from petroleum production would pave the way for this monumental transition.

By 1953, Kuwait had become the largest producer of oil in the Arabian Gulf. Indeed, the oil industry had grown so large so rapidly, a new city, Ahmadi, named after Sheikh Ahmad, had to be erected to house the petroleum companies' many workers. While these boom times brought money, foreign workers, and hopeful immigrants to Kuwait, the tiny state was ill-prepared to expand in areas other than petroleum. The lack of water, electricity, and natural resources that had plagued Kuwait from the beginning still had to be addressed. Port facilities for massive oil tankers were urgently required. A modern road network had to be built, power plants and distribution grids were needed, and water desalinization was vital. Western oil workers demanded air conditioning during the summer months, and the demand for electrical power skyrocketed. The Kuwaiti government was generally quite proactive in its approach to these complicated issues. For example, by the early 1950s, giant desalinization plants were being designed and planned, and the first was completed in 1953. Even more massive plants would follow, and Kuwait would soon be, and remain, a world leader in potable water production.

By 1951, it had been agreed that oil revenues that on paper had previously belonged to the Al-Sabah family, as owners of the land, would henceforth be split evenly between the rulers and the people. Half of all future profits would be spent on public projects, improvements, and government services.

Unfortunately, once the government began receiving oil revenues, the contribution of other sectors to national income was reduced further still. Economic growth and welfare measures since the Second World War drew workers away from historical pursuits and lessened the role of agriculture.

As petroleum's contribution to the nation's bottom line increased, contributions from other sectors of the economy continued to dwindle. There was little reason for a Kuwaiti to struggle to make ends meet in fishing, herding, or agriculture when a high-paying government-subsidized job, probably somewhere in the oil industry, was readily at hand. Indeed, the Kuwaiti welfare system became so pervasive that many Kuwaiti citizens found it more profitable not to work at all.

Thus, while economic benefits definitely accrued to the populace as a whole, more and more work fell into the hands of immigrant laborers instead of Kuwaitis. The rapidly expanding service industries that surrounded the oil industry were almost entirely performed by non-Kuwaitis, even while management remained in Kuwaiti hands. The critical long-term implications to Kuwait of these nonnative workers would become apparent only later.

As more businesses developed, so too did the need for modern regulations. Kuwait lacked a national banking system and even a coherent monetary system, since the Indian rupee was the most commonly circulated currency in the sheikhdom prior to independence. While the British had built a bank in Kuwait City in 1941 to handle their own transactions, other nations were essentially prevented from building banks since Kuwaiti ownership was mandatory under the law. A national bank was built in 1952, but Kuwait still lacked an entire banking system of its own. Finally, a central bank was established in 1959, and regulation of the banking system became a key function of the new institution.

Kuwait's slowly bloating bureaucracy responded with new Kuwaiti laws borrowed from other countries where they had proven effective. In most cases these regulations were a step forward, but there was no guarantee that every foreign regulation, however effective it had been elsewhere, would readily translate to Kuwait's dynamic business environment. The failure to adequately and effectively regulate speculation in Kuwait's volatile stock market, for example, would eventually prove nearly catastrophic to the Kuwaiti economy.

One of the few native industries to develop was cement. Prior to this time, it had been necessary to import cement, and Kuwait had certainly never experienced a building boom like the one that was about to begin. Soon cement plants were erected locally to meet the building needs of the oil industry and the road building required for the country's infrastructure to keep pace. This also meant that cement did not have to be shipped in from overseas, thereby leaving that much more pier space and cargo-handling capacity available for the steady stream of oil tankers that steamed into and out of Kuwaiti waters.

Kuwaiti technocrats recognized early on that additional revenues could be squeezed from oil if Kuwait refined its own oil rather than shipping raw crude and letting another middleman reap the profits. Thus, refineries were planned and built over time inside Kuwait to ensure the value-added accrued to Kuwait itself. Recognizing the collective power that could be wielded for the benefit of individual nations, a handful of the world's largest petroleum-producing nations formed OPEC (Oil Producing and Exporting Countries) in 1960. Kuwait was one of the organization's original members, along with Saudi Arabia, Iraq, Iran, and Venezuela.

Kuwait's leaders, perhaps much sooner than the rulers of many "oil sheikh-doms," understood that the petroleum that was making them rich would not last forever. Accordingly, by the middle of the 1950s, Kuwait was already investing some of its surplus, perhaps even as much as a quarter of all revenues, in overseas markets. The assistance of British and American financiers helped the Kuwaiti government make wise investment choices for the long term. By the 1960s, Kuwaiti investors would begin to invest in foreign real estate. The other area that saw an influx of Kuwaiti money was foreign aid to friendly nations and entities. Kuwait's leaders also considered this to be a form of foreign "investment."

By no means was all oil revenue pocketed or invested in industry and infrastructure. At least half of that money was spent in turning modern Kuwait into the very model of a welfare state. Whereas in the earliest years of oil development, the sheikhs had used oil money to provide gifts to friends and food for the neediest citizens, Kuwait's rulers from midcentury on began to spend lavishly on health care and education for the Kuwaiti people. A willingness to use personal funds to address social ills had always marked Al-Sabah rule, but the scope of domestic spending now bankrolled by oil wealth exceeded the imagination.

WELFARE STATE

Health care in Kuwait had always been problematic. For two centuries there had been no hospital whatsoever. In 1910, at the urging of Sheikh Mubarak, the Dutch Reformed American Church in America had expanded its small Arabian mission and built a hospital in Kuwait. Sheikh Mubarak had been reluctant to let Christian missionaries into his country, but he understood that health concerns could no longer be ignored. This first hospital was for men only, but a small facility for women and infants was built nearby in 1919. At the time, infant mortality was estimated at as high as 125 deaths per 1,000 live births. By midcentury, the estimated infant mortality rate would fall to as low as 80 deaths for every 1,000 live births, a solid improvement in any country, but of historic proportions in Kuwait.

A host of diseases periodically plagued the population, with tuberculosis perhaps the most persistent of these. Smallpox, however, struck densely packed Kuwait City in 1932 and more than four thousand victims perished in 10 days. Sheikh Ahmad turned to his physicians for advice, and they recommended that the entire population be vaccinated. The sheikh duly ordered that the procedure be carried out for all Kuwaitis. Thousands refused out of ignorance-induced fear. The government responded by forcibly vaccinating young boys enrolled in Kuwait's *madrassahs,* or Islamic schools. When those young lads remained healthy, the people slowly agreed to vaccination for themselves. Both a health care and a political crisis had been circumvented. Another hospital was opened in 1934 and a comprehensive Emiri Hospital, funded entirely by the ruling family, was erected in 1949, paid for by oil revenues. In 50 years, Kuwait saw general mortality fall from around 25 per 1,000 people to a low of about 17 per 1,000.

It was at this point that the country launched a free, comprehensive health care program for every Kuwaiti citizen. With a health care budget that ranked third by proportion of the entire national budget, the new system covered Kuwaitis from cradle to grave. Medical care, dental care, and even veterinary care were now provided to every Kuwaiti. Kuwait's hospital administrators purchased the very latest equipment, though it was not always the equipment that was most needed at the moment. They also brought in hundreds of foreign doctors, especially from Egypt, to provide medical care. It has been charged that the new system focused too much on treatment and too little on prevention, but the overall improvement to the health of the population is undeniable.

Education was the second major area that required serious attention, and spending, once oil revenues began to pour into Kuwait's coffers. Going into the twentieth century, the only schools were the traditional madrassahs, which taught the Qur'an to Kuwaiti boys. Instruction also included reading, writing, and some minimal mathematics. Little formal education was provided for, or available to, young women, other than the basic grounding in Islam. While the wealthiest Kuwaitis, especially the Al-Sabah, had always been able to send their sons to school overseas, for the average Kuwaitis, a proper education was almost impossible.

The Dutch Reformed Church's mission held a small school for future bureaucrats, boys only, to learn basic English and to pick up typing skills. In 1911, a group of wealthy Kuwaiti merchants, with additional personal funding from the Al-Sabah, had established the private Mubarakiyyah School, and in 1921 built the Ahmadiyyah School. An education council was convened in the 1930s, and several private primary schools were built, one of which was reserved for young girls. Most of these measures were private rather than public, though the government had assumed some responsibilities as early as 1939. The private nature of Kuwait's educational system would change dramatically under government control. The Kuwaiti government took over administration of the entire education system. Incorporating the 17 schools in existence already by 1945, the new ministry established a complete system of kindergarten, primary, and secondary schooling for all Kuwaiti boys and girls. Just before independence in 1961, the emirate's schools educated an estimated twenty-seven thousand Kuwaiti boys and eighteen thousand Kuwaiti girls.

As with the new health care system, the new Kuwaiti education system was forced to rely heavily on foreign teachers, many of them Palestinians. One estimate from around 1960 was that 9 out of 10 teachers were non-Kuwaitis. As with all of the other non-Kuwaitis who had flocked to the country beginning in the late 1940s, these people were denied the expanding advantages of Kuwaiti citizenship as a two-tiered social and political system grew inside Kuwait. This issue would continue to plague Kuwait and would flare dramatically following the Iraqi invasion and occupation of the 1990s.

By 1960, a number of unique conditions had developed inside Kuwait, once the most traditional of desert sheikhdoms. The sheikhdom was led by a forward-looking leader in Abdullah III. The treasury was almost full of more oil money than could be counted. New medical and educational systems met the needs of the entire citizen population. An expanding and all-pervasive bureaucracy was in place to oversee future developments. Kuwait was finally ready to take the most dramatic step of its slow march to full independence by formally cutting its ties to the once-protective and also domineering British Empire, now in the form of the United Kingdom.

5

Independence and Nationhood (1961–1990)

On June 19, 1961, Kuwait stepped away from the defensive shield and foreign policy oversight provided since 1899 by Great Britain to become an independent country. Quite a few other countries became independent nations during the 1960s, but few of them had the advantages of Kuwait at the very moment of independence. For that matter, Kuwait also had some unique national disadvantages to overcome, as well. The most critical of both the advantages and the disadvantages were a function of geography. Kuwait was located atop a huge reservoir of oil, which made Kuwait a fabulously wealthy new nation, but which also made it an envied nation and a target of acquisition by powerful and greedy neighbors to the north, south, and east.

The vast wealth from petroleum that was piling up in the Kuwaiti treasury was the most obvious advantage, but by no means the only one. Kuwait's political leaders, the Al-Sabah, unlike the rulers of many other new nations, were well prepared to lead an independent country. This is evidenced by the many steps taken in the intervening decades to get Kuwait to the stage it had attained by 1961. A bureaucracy made up of Kuwaitis was in place to handle domestic issues, so the responsibility to now direct foreign matters was not so large a step. A new national currency, the Kuwaiti dinar, was created, as well as a homegrown banking system to support it. The domestic agenda was well mapped out—to continue to develop as a modern welfare state.

Even when it came to foreign policy, the Kuwaitis were not exactly novices. Long before their partnership with the British, Kuwait's statesmen had been adept at managing both allies and potentially hostile neighbors, large and small, while maintaining Kuwait's de facto independence from the Ottoman Empire. The very nations in the region with which Kuwait would now be negotiating as an equal were countries with which Kuwait had interacted for two hundred complicated years. As long as future emirs could rule with the political savvy of most past monarchs, there was every reason to believe that Kuwait could safely navigate the dangerous international waters ahead.

Kuwait's disadvantages as a new country were also noteworthy. The Majlis Movement of 1938 notwithstanding, Kuwait lacked a strong tradition of popular political involvement in domestic affairs, which left the average Kuwaiti somewhat distanced from the governance of his or her nation. This did not bode well for the future, but events would show this could be overcome with wisdom on the part of the emir and persistence on the part of the citizenry. Kuwait's lack of natural resources (other than oil) would also prove to be a major disadvantage to economic development in the years to come. Kuwait's unskilled labor force would have been a crippling disadvantage to a modern nation had not a horde of foreign workers already flocked to the country to participate in the oil industry. The presence of foreigners, essentially one outsider for every Kuwaiti citizen, was a major problem from the first days of independence, and would become of dire consequences when Kuwait faced Iraqi invasion in 1990.

Kuwait's final disadvantage was its lack of experience in national defense. Had Kuwait been able to defend itself from the Ottomans, the Saudis, or the Persians, it would not have been forced to turn to the British for protection in the first place. Kuwait's position of relative weakness when compared with Saudi Arabia, Iraq, or Iran had not changed substantially since the time of Mubarak the Great. If and when British troops were completely withdrawn from the new nation, Kuwait's ability to deter attack or to effectively defend its sovereign territory was in serious doubt.

Therefore, one way to consider Kuwait's momentous decision to change national status is that to get what it most wanted, independence, the fledgling country had to give up what it most needed, protection. It should be remembered, moreover, that this was indeed a conscious decision on the part of Kuwait. Many new nations in the Third World were "given" independence by the colonial powers that had once ruled them, and that independence was received whether or not those countries were fully prepared for self-rule. Kuwait, on the other hand, chose to become independent, not in a moment of swelling popular opinion but after a decade of tough, open-minded problem solving and decision making. When Sheikh Abdullah as emir formally exchanged memoranda with Great Britain's foreign minister to mark the beginning of

Kuwait's full independence, he did so after sober evaluation of the pros and cons of such a dramatic step. As with every other major decision made by the Al-Sabah rulers in the past two centuries, Kuwait's very survival hung in the balance.

For its part, Great Britain had also made a conscious decision to let Kuwait go. Worn out both militarily and economically by the Second World War, Great Britain had already seen both India and Pakistan become independent in 1947. Once those "jewels in the crown" were gone, it became much less important for Great Britain to secure the sea lines and landlines of communications between the Mediterranean Sea and the Indian Ocean. Moreover, as this was happening, Great Britain was in the process of turning over some of its self-assumed responsibilities as "policeman of the world" to the United States. The United States had become increasingly involved globally at the end of the war, though the Arabian Gulf had never before been a focal point of American foreign policy. That was about to change, as the U.S. economy and the economies of America's major trading partners became ever more dependent on oil shipped from the region. American diplomats and strategists would slowly begin to comprehend the potential importance of Kuwait to regional stability and maintenance of American presence in the Arabian Gulf.

Once Kuwait and Great Britain announced their joint decision, the process of independence moved ahead at a rapid pace. Kuwait was quickly recognized as a sovereign nation by a host of countries. The Arab League, over vehement Iraqi protests, welcomed Kuwait into the organization soon thereafter. The legitimacy that this afforded among Muslim nations was most welcome. Kuwait was designed to be a constitutional monarchy, and so its politicians then began the arduous task of hammering out a constitution for the new nation. It took a year to do so, but on November 11, 1962, the new constitution was finally written and ratified by an ad hoc constituent assembly. Full elections were held, and the first National Assembly of the new Kuwaiti nation convened at the end of January 1963. Kuwait would become a United Nations member later in 1963, by which point all the requisite steps toward nationhood had been completed. The question of national defense had yet to be resolved, however.

Great Britain had taken several steps to foster Kuwait's readiness to defend itself. What had been a Kuwaiti constabulary force of around six hundred men had been slowly converted into a defense force of approximately brigade strength, or 2,500 troops, mostly infantry, but also artillery and light armor in the form of armored cars. Token naval and air forces were also established, but were essentially paper national defense assets. While this defense force was a big step up for Kuwait, it was far from adequate to deter outside aggression.

Almost simultaneously with the announcement of Kuwait's independence, Iraqi diplomats had put forward Iraq's own claim to Kuwait as an Iraqi province. This assertion, hardly far-fetched, was based on the legally ambiguous position of the emirate as an autonomous subprovince of the Basrah region under the old Ottoman Empire during the reign of Mubarak the Great. With claims of national sovereignty over Kuwait as the recognized heir to Ottoman lands in the immediate vicinity, the Iraqi government threatened to invade the new nation. Kuwait quickly requested British defense assistance—help that had been promised at the same time Britain recognized Kuwait's independence.

Beyond the military training mission already on the ground in Kuwait, the British quickly deployed a sizable ground force to deter Iraqi aggression. Soon thereafter, in 1963, the Arab League, which had already ignored Iraq's protest when Kuwait requested admission to the organization, deployed ground forces from other Arab countries to replace British troops. Once the United Nations accepted Kuwait, the Iraqi government backed down on its imminent threat of attack. This defused the situation for the moment, but it clearly did not resolve the matter fully, as Iraq's 1990 invasion of Kuwait would subsequently demonstrate.

While Kuwaitis grew accustomed to the responsibilities of independence, it was helpful that Al-Sabah rule continued without turmoil or disruption. Abdullah ruled as emir until 1965, when he was replaced by his chosen successor, Sabah al-Salem, or Sabah III. Abdullah's choice broke the accepted pattern that had been in place since the succession of Mubarak, in which the reins of authority alternated each time between the descendants of Mubarak's two sons, Jaber and Salem. The country handled the transition smoothly that year, however, and Sabah III's domestic and foreign policies were generally consistent with those of Abdullah III.

For his part, Sabah III, who ruled until 1977, named as his eventual successor Jaber III. This marked a return to the traditional policy of alternating within the family, a relatively new tradition that had been created when Mubarak seized control of the sheikhdom and decided to keep it in his immediate family. In fact, no ruler since Mubarak had independently held total control. The members of the inner family had always been consulted and had often become direct active participants in the selection of the next leader. The new constitution provided for the crown prince to assume the position of emir upon the current emir's death, but it was up to the family to choose the crown prince. Technically, the selection was subject to ratification by the popular assembly. Jaber III's accession in 1977 was also uneventful. With each smooth transition, Kuwait's peaceful political traditions became ever stronger.

NEW CONSTITUTION

Another important difference that set Kuwait apart from many other newly independent nations was its quick adoption of a constitution to establish civil rights and to govern political life. In fact, other than Bahrain, none of the other countries in the region had a constitution. Sheikh Abdullah's willingness to consider this important political step, and its inherent long-term implications for Kuwaiti democracy, was a sure sign of his own maturity, as well as the maturity level of the Kuwaiti people as the nation embarked on self-rule. Of note, however, the constitution contained a clause that allowed the emir to temporarily suspend individual rights and even to disband the National Assembly. The only condition on this authority was that the emir must first determine that national interests dictated the move, leaving the ruler wide latitude.

By law, Islam was the official or state religion of Kuwait. Moreover, the constitution recognized the importance of that religion in civic affairs by stating that a main source of legislation was Shariah, or traditional Islamic law. The article "a," as in "a source of legislation," as opposed to the article "the" was what set progressive Kuwait apart from so many traditional Islamic republics, even today. Though there was a vocal minority inside Kuwait who wished for the country to adopt the Shariah as public law, most Kuwaitis openly rejected any move in that direction.

Notably, Kuwait's constitution was written in an era of Arab nationalism and thus contained obligatory mention that Kuwait is "part of the Arab nation," as well as being a sovereign country in its own right. While there were many Muslims in the world who viewed themselves not as one nationality or another but as part of a larger Islamic entity, Kuwaitis had learned over the intervening years that they were Kuwaitis first, Muslims second, and Arabs third. The horrific experience of invasion and occupation by Iraq, addressed fully in the next chapter, would further etch these uncommon priorities deep into the national consciousness of Kuwait, the nation's constitution notwithstanding.

The constitution also confirmed Kuwait's status as a hereditary emirate and defined in explicit detail the lawful succession to the throne among the descendants of Mubarak the Great. At the same time, however, the constitution spelled out that Kuwait would have a democratic system of government. The constitution even noted that Kuwait's national sovereignty resided in the people, who were also described as the source of all ruling authority. Few monarchies, especially in the Arab world, have ever had such liberal democratic ideals enshrined in their basic political documents, as was the case in Kuwait.

The legal rights of Kuwaiti citizens were carefully delineated in the new constitution. These included equality before the law, freedom of belief, freedom of expression, and the presumption of innocence. Private property was protected under the constitution, and inheritance was established in accordance with Shariah law. Deportation and torture were specifically forbidden. Collective liberties that the constitution delineated include freedom of the press, freedom of association, and freedom to establish trade unions. Social rights were also mandated by the constitution, which required the government to provide the extensive services in effect under the current welfare system. These social rights included guaranteed employment, health care, public health services, and public education.

While freedom of expression and freedom of the press were guaranteed under the constitution, a 1961 law governing the press and publishing industries put practical limits on these important freedoms. Inside Kuwait, certain written material could be banned at the discretion of the government, and this commonly occurred, especially with content considered offensive or pornographic to Muslim sensibilities. News reports critical of the government in general, and of the Al-Sabah family in particular, could be and often have been prohibited. The mechanism for full press censorship was in place in the Ministry of Information, and Kuwait's emirs sometimes determined to utilize that repressive tool at several points in Kuwait's subsequent history. That said, relative to other countries in the region, and Arab countries in general, Kuwait was a model of freedom of the press.

Not only did the constitution place restrictions on the government, but Kuwaiti citizens had certain obligations imposed on them under the new constitution as well. These included prompt payment of taxes, maintenance of public order and public morals, and contribution to national defense (i.e., conscription for males). As with the rights just mentioned, the responsibilities here applied only to Kuwaiti citizens. The half of the population that was non-Kuwaiti was not affected by these constitutional provisions. As will be addressed in the final chapter, international concern has long existed for the civil and human rights of the many non-Kuwaitis living inside Kuwait simply because their legal status has never been fully resolved.

While the voting public played an active role in Kuwaiti politics from the start, the right to vote as established under the new constitution was far from universal. In order to vote, a Kuwaiti male had to be able to prove that his family was in Kuwait in 1920. Subsequent immigrants were denied suffrage. With voting thus restricted to Kuwaiti men who met these tight conditions, Kuwaiti women and later immigrants were essentially disenfranchised. While the issue of women's rights in general, voting in particular, would be decades in coming, Kuwait is today embroiled in a healthy public debate about how to best balance modernization with traditional Islamic values. This question will be covered more fully in the last chapter.

The drafters of Kuwait's constitution understood that, while the Islamic Shariah provided traditional legal guidance for many aspects of the law, secular considerations were equally important in establishing a fully functional legal system for a modern country. If nothing else, the domestic legal implications of Kuwait's petroleum-based economy absolutely required an up-to-date judicial system. Toward that end, the new constitution established an independent judicial branch of government. In fact, for practical purposes, a Kuwaiti judiciary had been in place since 1961, which was when the United Kingdom ended its oversight of legal matters for all foreigners inside Kuwait. Initial Kuwaiti courts enforced laws borrowed from other Arab countries, especially Egypt. These laws were then tailored to Kuwait by an Egyptian judge brought in specifically to oversee this important task.

Lastly, but of key importance, the constitution spelled out the role of the government in managing Kuwait's economy. While built along free-market principles, Kuwait's economy had always been subject to the whims and manipulations of others. Kuwait's constitution recognized this linkage, and also that Kuwait's success as a welfare state was dependent upon a thriving national economy. Thus, the constitution obligated the government to intervene in the national economy to ensure social justice, a balance between the common good as measured privately with that measured publicly in the areas of living standard and overall prosperity.

NATIONAL ASSEMBLY

The new National Assembly (Majlis al-Umma) was limited by the constitution in its authority and, ultimately, subject to arbitrary dissolution by the emir as he deemed appropriate. Nevertheless, the assembly also allowed for much greater participation by the Kuwaiti people in their governance. As the people became more a part of their own government, they would also become more committed to the survival of the new nation. This connection to the country, with Kuwaitis seeing themselves as Kuwaitis and not as Arabs, would become crucial during the time of the Iraqi invasion, occupation, and subsequent liberation and reconstruction. Whether or not the emir understood what he was doing when he permitted the assembly to be established, this was arguably the most critical element in Kuwait's ultimate survival as a nation three decades later.

The role of the National Assembly was originally envisioned as a place where legislation could be initiated, pending official approval by the ruler. The assembly had the right to hold hearings and to question government ministers about national policies. Most members of the first National Assembly did not come from the merchant class, which had always had a say in Kuwait's affairs since the election of the first Al-Sabah leader in the mid-1700s. Instead, most assemblymen came from the middle class, dependent on Kuwait's welfare system for their well-being, but also eager to ensure that the system ran smoothly and efficiently. These young, well-educated, politically astute assemblymen served as middlemen between the average Kuwaiti citizen and the emir. Thus, the common people had a way to express their concerns locally and to know their voice was being heard at the seat of government. Moreover, the assemblymen and the Al-Sabah had an effective mechanism in place for communicating about issues and building popular support for policies and positions.

Strategically positioned between the National Assembly and the emir was the cabinet. Almost invariably, the crown prince or heir apparent was named prime minister and oversaw the daily operations of the cabinet. Membership to the cabinet was through appointment by the emir and, not surprisingly, was often heavily weighted in favor of the Al-Sabah family. The 15-person cabinet seated following independence contained a dozen Al-Sabah family members in key ministerial positions. Over time, the proportion has dropped as more and more cabinet ministers have been drawn from the ranks of the National Assembly, though tribal allies of the Al-Sabah and top Kuwaiti families were also represented in the executive body. All ministers served at the discretion of the emir, however, as did district governors and commanders of military services. Since religion would soon become a complication for Kuwaiti domestic politics, it is worth noting that, along with the royal family itself, the vast majority of cabinet officials were Sunni Muslims, not Shiites.

One distinctive feature of Kuwait was the huge—some would even say bloated—bureaucracy that oversaw virtually every aspect of the welfare state. Since Kuwaitis were guaranteed employment, and because so much of the work of the petroleum industry and the service economy was performed by foreigners, the only place left for Kuwaitis to work was in their own government. By a wide margin, the government of Kuwait was the largest employer in the entire country. While underemployment was rife and waste was easy to find, the advantage of the welfare system was that it further cemented the bonds between the Kuwaiti citizen and his or her government. Kuwaitis were invested in their nation to a degree rarely seen, especially among the countries of the Middle East region. Moreover, this marked a major change from the time when British bureaucrats and Western oil men made so many of the key decisions affecting the daily lives of Kuwait's citizenry.

Elections for the initial National Assembly were held in 1963, and subsequent elections were held every four years thereafter through 1975. The emir dissolved the assembly from 1976 to 1981. Some civil rights, such as freedom of speech and freedom of assembly, were also temporarily rolled back at this time by the emir. After elections in 1981 and again in 1985, the assembly was temporarily dissolved yet again. This political turmoil was a direct reflection of the ability of political opposition to get elected and thereby influence Kuwait's internal affairs. Despite periodic charges of heavy-handedness by the emir, seen in hindsight, it is clear that a healthy political climate and process were developing internally. The political difficulties inside Kuwait were also symptoms of the social turmoil experienced by Kuwait and the entire region as oil, religion, and terrorism intersected. As all of these events unfolded, Kuwait's rulers found themselves under increasing scrutiny and criticism from neighboring monarchies, especially Saudi Arabia, which feared that democratic reform in Kuwait would spur demands for increased political participation among Saudi citizens.

The Iranian Revolution of 1979, inspired and led by the radical Shiite cleric Ayatollah Ruhollah Khomeini, changed the political landscape of not only the region as a whole but also the area inside Kuwait. By 1980, with the growth in the Iranian threat, which will shortly be discussed more fully, the new emir, Sheikh Jaber, felt compelled to hold new elections and to reinstate previously suspended civil rights. Though the next several national assemblies were confrontational, these measures had the intended overall effect of legitimizing Al-Sabah rule at a time when that legitimacy was under attack from without and within. As had previously been the case, increased political participation fostered stronger national sentiment among Kuwaitis. The political roller coaster continued its ups and downs. Following the crash of the Kuwaiti stock market (discussed later), the National Assembly was highly critical of the Al-Sabah, who responded by again dissolving the body and further restricting civil liberties. The emir was nevertheless compelled to fire the minister of justice, another Al-Sabah family member, amid charges of corruption related to the crash. This action by the emir reflected the slow shifting of power from the ruler to his people.

By 1989, the Constitutional Movement had formed inside Kuwait. Its goal was to first restore and then strengthen key provisions of the constitution, limiting the arbitrary authorities of the emir and boosting those of the people's elected representatives. This certainly was not the first attempt to revise or fine-tune the original constitution. Indeed, though they were ultimately withdrawn a year later, the government put forward a long list of recommended constitutional changes in 1982. These proposals ranged from adjustments in the size of the legislature and term limits for assembly service to provisions for the declaration of martial law, if deemed appropriate by the emir.

This latest constitutional reform and general antigovernment opposition movement was the broadest to date, since it included liberal reformers, merchants, and even Islamic fundamentalists. Members of the dissolved National Assembly took their complaints directly to the people, and vice versa, and a groundswell of political discontent began to grow. Soon antigovernment demonstrations spilled onto the streets of Kuwait City. While clearly afraid that giving into the many demands would forever cripple his power, the emir could ill afford to stonewall the growing and increasingly loud calls for political progress. The emir's compromise was to replace the National Assembly with a new national council. The national council would have 25 members appointed by the emir and 50 members elected by the voters. The authority of this national council was also trimmed substantially by the emir. Many pro-democracy advocates protested this change in representative government and boycotted the elections; however, those elections were held in June 1990. The new national council was in place when the Iraqis invaded later that summer.

WELFARE STATE

The process of turning Kuwait into a modern welfare state continued un-abated after independence. A host of health-related statistics clearly docu-ments the progress made over this period. From 1960 to 1990, life expectancy increased by 10 years for both males and females. As determined just prior to Iraq's invasion in 1990, an average Kuwaiti male could expect to live 72 years and an average female 76 years. Life expectancy for both males and females in Kuwait was thus comparable to the expected averages in virtually every major industrialized nation.

These results were not accidental. Over the same period, the number of phy-sicians in Kuwait grew from 362 to over 2,600. Even as Kuwait's population was spiking, the doctor-patient ratio was cut in half. Infant mortality dropped to 15 per 1,000 live births. By any measure, Kuwaitis were the healthiest and best cared for that they had ever been. Just prior to the Iraqi invasion, the United Nations ranked Kuwait first in the world on its index of human devel-opment, which included life expectancy and per capita GDP.

Significant strides were also made in education. By 1965, education was made compulsory for Kuwaiti children through age 14, a step that would have been taken sooner had it not been for resistance from many tradition-minded Bedouin families. A preschool program followed, as did a national university system, in 1966. At independence, there were 140 schools inside Kuwait. By 1990, five hundred additional schools had been built. Moreover, the tiny coun-try that had only about three thousand teachers at independence now boasted around twenty-eight thousand educators.

State financial support covered not only the cost of tuition, but also the cost of books, meals, uniforms, and transportation. Even though public educa-tion was not fully funded for the children of non-Kuwaitis, it was still heavily subsidized for noncitizens. In fact, by 1990, most students in Kuwait's public schools were noncitizens. By the late 1960s, a network of private schools was in place to handle the scions of Kuwait's political and economic elites, though many chose to take advantage of the best schooling that the United States and Western Europe had to offer. Another surprising statistic was that Kuwaiti women made up more than half of the student body at Kuwait University, largely because Kuwaiti families were more likely to let their sons, as opposed to their daughters, study abroad. Immediately prior to 1990's invasion, overall literacy in Kuwait was at an all-time high of over 73 percent.

ECONOMIC DEVELOPMENT

The rulers and financiers of Kuwait had long understood that the key to the country's long-term economic success would be astute management of its oil resources. When the oil companies operating in and around Kuwait were foreign owned, even the Al-Sabah were frustrated by a lack of control over the country's finances. Thus, a concerted effort was launched early on to convert the oil and related industries into wholly Kuwaiti-owned organizations. Toward that end, the Kuwait National Petroleum Company (KNPC) was launched in 1960 and chartered to facilitate involvement in all aspects of the oil industry inside and outside the country. Initially, the company's stock was 40 percent privately held and 60 percent government owned. In 1975, the government took over complete control of the company. Beginning with control of local distribution of oil inside the country, KNPC expanded into in-country and overseas refineries before adding oil marketing to its portfolio. A branch of the company was formed to oversee additional exploration, in collaboration with foreign oil companies.

KNPC invested heavily in a new, state-of-the-art oil refinery at Ash Shuaybah, which went fully operational in 1968. In-house development of production facilities for petroleum by-products further expanded the company and boosted profits that accrued directly to Kuwait. Additionally, since the Kuwaitis owned and ran KNPC, individual Kuwaiti managers gained invaluable industry experience, making overreliance on foreigners less problematic. A similar approach was taken when Kuwaiti executives looked upstream and downstream of oil production to identify promising investment opportunities. The Petrochemicals Industries Company (PIC) was established in 1963 with split funding from the government and private investors. PIC's major chemical products included ammonia and urea. By 1976, the government was ready to assume total ownership and management of the firm. By investing in local facilities and by developing an innovative gas-gathering system, Kuwait's new petrochemical facilities cornered the local market and replaced foreign control of these vital income-producing industries. Other than oil itself, this became Kuwait's largest industry.

Also in 1976, the government of Kuwait took total control of KOC, Aminoil, and AOC, essentially nationalizing the entire oil industry in the country. KOC took control of Aminoil's oil-production operations, and KNPC took over refinery and port operations that had once belonged to Aminoil. KOC continued to focus on domestic exploration and production. KNPC continued to oversee refining operations. The Kuwait Oil Tanker Company was formed to handle shipment to new trading partners that included Japan and Pakistan. By the 1980s, Kuwait began to move into the European market via a new Kuwaiti-owned firm, Q8.

Kuwait's oil production peaked in the early 1970s and then leveled off. In conjunction with OPEC, Kuwait cut oil production to 3 million barrels per day (bpd) in 1973. The OPEC oil embargo of 1973 caused prices to skyrocket, and Kuwait benefited from the increased revenues. While higher levels of production were possible, it was by limiting production that OPEC nations maintained the artificially high prices on which those countries were counting. In 1976, Kuwait reduced production further to 2 million bpd. By around 1980, refined oil products replaced crude oil as Kuwait's major export.

The global drop in oil prices of the mid-1980s had a negative effect on Kuwait's economy, but Kuwait reluctantly continued to abide by OPEC's lower limits. Production was further reduced to 1.5 million bpd. Only in 1989 did Kuwait openly violate an OPEC-directed cut in production to just over 1 million bpd, a move that the government felt was needed to maintain the oil revenues necessary to continue Kuwait's vast welfare system. Little did the Kuwaitis know that Kuwait's refusal to abide by the final OPEC cut would become one excuse used by Iraq for invading the country a year later.

To manage the country's growing family of oil industry–related corporations, Kuwait launched the Kuwait Petroleum Corporation (KPC) in 1980. KPC, one of the largest corporations in the world, was more than a reorganization of existing business entities. It entailed massive investment overseas through the Kuwait Foreign Petroleum Exploration Company. Soon Kuwait's oil companies were drawing profits from the pumping of oil in the United States and the North Sea.

Having introduced the Kuwaiti dinar at independence, Kuwait's currency board handled the minting of money and maintained the required reserves. In 1971, the financial concessions held by British banks expired, and the Kuwaiti government purchased majority ownership in the National Bank of Kuwait. Other new banking companies soon formed. The Credit and Savings Bank and the Real Estate Bank were geared toward private investors. The Industrial Bank of Kuwait and the Investment Bank of Kuwait were built to help finance major industrial developments. From the 1970s on, the country's industrial development was strategically coordinated by the Kuwaiti government's Industrial Development Committee.

Mina al Ahmadi was developed as Kuwait's largest ocean terminal for oil and related products. With numerous offshore berths to speed the process, the port could eventually load as many as 2 million gallons of oil each day into the largest tankers afloat. Ash Shuwaykh, Kuwait's main ocean terminal for everything other than petroleum, was built in 1960. Ash Shuwaykh quickly became one of the busiest deep-water ports in the region, loading and unloading around eleven hundred cargo vessels annually in 1988.

In 1964, the industrial zone of Ash Shuaybah was built, with some construction lasting until 1967. The zone included distilling plants and electrical power production facilities to support any kind of manufacturing, as well as the necessary road and sewage networks to tie these endeavors together. Factories to produce cement, asphalt, and various industrial chemicals such as chlorine were built. Port facilities were built or expanded to facilitate import of raw materials and export of finished products, though many of the products were intended for domestic consumption. Housing to shelter the zone's many workers was also provided. The other required infrastructure to turn the industrial zone into a population center of sorts would eventually be added to the surrounding area. Just prior to the Iraqi invasion, Ash Shuaybah was almost as large as Ash Shuwaykh. For calendar year 1988, the port transported between 3 million and 4 million tons of cargo.

To back up these considerable physical and financial resources, the Kuwaitis made legal changes to further foster industrial development. By law, every company formed in Kuwait required 51 percent Kuwaiti ownership. The intention was not simply to ensure that Kuwaitis profited by these new endeavors, but to facilitate the day-to-day operations of outside businesses inside Kuwait. Despite the many efforts of the government, Kuwaiti state support for industrial development never reached the levels of some other nations in the region, nor did development build up the needed momentum to transform the country.

Kuwait's relatively open economy meant that foreign competition always impacted on internal developments. A small and largely unskilled labor force was another obstacle, while the promise of a government dole dampened the ambitions of many potential workers. Even tradition had a negative effect. Kuwaitis were historically traders, not manufacturers. As long as Kuwaiti investors saw themselves as middlemen rather than the actual creators of wealth, Kuwait's economy could never fully diversify.

As more Kuwaitis worked for the government or in the petroleum industry, the numbers involved in agriculture and fishing declined dramatically. Just prior to invasion, fewer than ten thousand Kuwaitis were estimated to be involved in agriculture. Despite considerable government investment in hydroponics, Kuwait's farmers produced only modest quantities of tomatoes, onions, dates, cucumbers, and eggplant. Of those, tomatoes were Kuwait's largest crop, and the only one to be even partially exported. In part due to overfishing in the Arabian Gulf during the 1970s, Kuwait's dwindling fleet of vessels regularly plied the Red Sea and the Indian Ocean, and sometimes wandered as far as the Atlantic Ocean, in search of fish—especially shrimp and prawns. During the Iran-Iraq War, Kuwaiti fishing vessels were severely hampered by the threat of Iranian attack. Thus, over time, increasing quantities of food had to be imported to feed the growing population, thereby making Kuwait all the more dependent on the sea lines of communications through the Arabian Gulf.

The Kuwaiti government determined to heavily invest much of its oil wealth overseas. The Reserve Fund for Future Generations was created in 1976, and about $7 billion was initially invested. Moreover, the government planned to add 10 percent of its oil revenues each year to the fund. Initially, investments were made in blue-chip companies in the United States and Western Europe. By the 1980s, large investments were added in Asia, especially Japan. By the late 1980s, the annual income from the fund's investments actually outpaced the annual income from oil production. Just prior to the Iraqi invasion, Kuwait's overseas holdings were estimated at more than $100 billion. These available funds would become absolutely critical to Kuwait's ultimate survival following the invasion of Iraqi forces in 1990.

Stock Market Crash

While their government was heavily investing, so too were thousands of private Kuwaiti citizens. Unfortunately, the weakest area of Kuwait's entire economy was the one least regulated by Kuwait's ministerial bureaucracy— the local stock market, or Souk al Manakh, which had started in Kuwait City largely on its own. With oil wealth aplenty, private Kuwaiti investors had millions to invest, and the official stock market could not keep up with the business. Thus, an alternative, wholly unregulated stock market that relied on the trust and familiarity that Kuwaitis held for other Kuwaitis came into being. Among neighbors and friends, a personal promise or a handshake had been more than enough for business purposes when the commodities to be exchanged were measured in camel loads or even pearls. With the billions of dollars in oil profits in play by the 1980s, however, the highly volatile, illicit trade in stocks, often based on personal credit, was only one bounced check away from total collapse.

The end came in 1982, when, in fact, a bad check created a cascading failure. Before the financial collapse was complete, all but one of Kuwait's banks were technically insolvent. Virtually every Kuwaiti family was directly affected by the disaster. The official investigation that followed estimated that $94 million in investments was irrevocably lost by about six thousand Kuwaiti investors. The few Kuwaitis who weren't directly affected by the crash were indirectly impacted as the entire economy shuddered into recession. Tougher regulations were quickly legislated, but the effect was only to prevent new crashes, not to mitigate the effects of the current disaster. Given the scale of the problem, the government had no choice but to bail out private investors by enacting the Difficult Credit Facilities Resettlement Program. Some of the ministers and bureaucrats whose negligence allowed the situation to develop were held accountable and fired. The domestic political repercussions were apparent in the contentious popular elections and the loud antigovernment rhetoric that ensued.

FOREIGN AFFAIRS

Following independence, Kuwait's foreign policy took the country in several directions. Friendly relations in the region and across the Arab world were expanded. In 1966, the Kuwaitis agreed in principle with the Saudis to divide the Neutral Zone, which had been established by the Treaty of Uqair following the siege of Jahra. In 1969, the agreement went into effect over the area to be known henceforth as the Divided Zone. Revenues from the sale of oil from inside and offshore of the Divided Zone continued to be equally shared, to the substantial benefit of both countries.

In the face of the Iraqi threats of invasion, which arose immediately after independence, pragmatism had required that Kuwait continue to rely on Great Britain for defense. During the 1960s and 1970s, Iraq continued to instigate minor border incidents, while diplomatically keeping the pressure on Kuwait to cede the islands of Bubiyan and Warbah. In 1973, Iraq went as far as massing troops along the border before finally standing down under pressure from other Arab countries.

Once the British essentially pulled out of the Arabian Gulf militarily in 1971, Kuwait sought out another protector. A bilateral agreement was established with the Soviet Union, which brought some Soviet military advisors and defense equipment, but neither nation ever really warmed to the relationship. For their part, wise Kuwaiti diplomats always took pains to appear neutral in relations during the Cold War between the Soviet Union and the United States.

In 1979, the Iranian Revolution dramatically changed the political landscape of the entire region. Suddenly, the major threat to Kuwait was from Iran, then ruled by the Ayatollah Khomeini and other radical Shiite clerics who aggressively spoke of spreading their revolution to the Shiites around the Arabian Gulf. Kuwait's leaders concluded that the threat posed by Iranian troublemaking was very real indeed. Domestic security problems increased noticeably, and Kuwaitis were convinced that Iran was behind the rash of increasingly violent internal incidents.

Beyond the raucous political demonstrations that were stirred up, Kuwait's internal difficulties included the fires set at oil facilities, bombings of the U.S. and French embassies, numerous car bombings and airplane piracy, and even an abortive assassination attempt on the emir in 1985. Eventually, an underground Shiite terror cell linked to Iran was uncovered. Its members were prosecuted and punished severely, with several receiving the death penalty. The domestic tensions that this exacerbated among the Kuwaiti population were reflected in the contentious political environment highlighted by the worsening relationship between the Al-Sabah and the National Assembly, which culminated in the Constitution Movement of 1989–1990.

Iran-Iraq War

When all-out war erupted between Iran and Iraq in September 1981, the Kuwaitis soon backed the Iraqis as the lesser of two evils. During the nearly decade-long war that followed, Kuwait provided billions of dollars in loans to Iraq and also allowed Iraqi goods to be transshipped through the country. The Kuwaitis also sought collective protection among the remaining friendly neighbors. In May 1981, Kuwait joined with Saudi Arabia, Bahrain, Oman, Qatar, and the UAE in the newly formed GCC.

Since Iran had already backed violence in Saudi Arabia and even a coup attempt in Bahrain, it was fear of the Iranian threat that tied together these neighbors at this time. The initial GCC meeting set up only the mechanisms for trade and other economic cooperation. It did not specifically initiate military cooperation among the pact's members, but additional meetings were soon held among the defense chiefs from the six countries. Political differences among the members, which reflected differing conditions inside those countries, held up implementation of any major cooperative defense measures.

In 1984, however, the Peninsula Shield, a joint air-ground task force under Saudi Arabian command but including forces from other GCC members, was formed. The force was based at Hafar al Batin, in Saudi Arabia south of the border with Kuwait. In theory, this force might have been able to deter or defend Saudi oil fields from Iranian or Iraqi attacks, but it was ill-conceived and ill-located to serve Kuwait's needs. Cooperative measures implemented among GCC members to identify and eliminate Iranian-sponsored terrorists, however, were largely effective.

In 1986, the Iranians widened the war to the nonbelligerent shipping of Kuwait and Saudi Arabia. The tanker and merchant fleets of these technically neutral countries had, in fact, been used to the advantage of Iraq. Around the Arabian Gulf, the Iranian move was seen as retaliation against unfriendly neighbors. Around the world, however, in the capitals of the major economic powers, the Iranian attacks on shipping were clearly seen as a threat to entirely shut down the flow of oil coming from the Arabian Gulf—oil on which the economies of Japan and Western Europe already depended, and on which the United States was becoming increasingly dependent.

When viewed in this international economic context, the Iranian threat begged for a forceful response. The Kuwaitis formally requested American help, though help was also requested of Great Britain and the Soviet Union. Moving quickly, the United States reflagged half of Kuwait's fleet of modern tankers so they sailed under the American flag instead of the Kuwaiti flag. In May 1987, the United States Navy began to provide military escorts for Kuwaiti and Saudi tankers into and out of the Arabian Gulf to prevent or severely punish any Iranian attacks by warplanes or small missile boats. While there were several small clashes, and one tanker was badly damaged by an Iranian sea mine, the active patrols of the United States Navy generally put a stop to the Iranian aggression.

The Iran-Iraq War ended with a ceasefire in August 1988. Though the United States had posted a consul general in Kuwait as early as 1951 and had opened a complete embassy at independence 10 years later, the two countries had never been especially close. Prior to the Iran-Iraq War, the United States and Kuwait could be described at best as merely friendly, not friends. However, the shifting regional environment caused by the Iran-Iraq War changed their relationship dramatically. This improved international relationship with the United States would quickly become another key element in Kuwait's ability to survive Iraqi invasion.

Foreign Aid

As part of its overall diplomatic strategy of ensuring survival during the 1980s, Kuwait spent lavishly when it came to foreign aid, with most of those funds going to economic development in fellow Arab countries. The instrument for this financial support was the Kuwait Fund for Arab Economic Development (KFAED). When oil revenues were abundant, foreign aid could amount to as much as 4 percent of Kuwait's GDP. When oil profits were down, Kuwait generally cut back on the loans and grants, but Kuwaiti generosity far exceeded the norm of other countries in the region. During these years, outright grants and low-interest loans from the Kuwaiti government underwrote major industrial projects across the region, as far away as North Africa. Syria, Jordan, Egypt, and the Palestine Liberation Organization (PLO) were all recipients of extensive Kuwaiti funding during the 1970s and 1980s.

For their part, the Kuwaitis hoped their largesse would buy them friendship. While that was certainly the case for most recipients of Kuwaiti aid, a few, Iraq especially, grew less friendly rather than more friendly over time. Though Kuwait had provided perhaps as much as $13 billion in invaluable support to Iraq during the Iran-Iraq War, Iraq seemed increasingly less likely to repay those loans over time. Iraqi requests that Kuwait forgive the loans fell on deaf ears. A strong financial motive soon existed for Iraq to want to absorb tiny Kuwait, and the time was fast approaching when diplomacy alone would not appease the Iraqi dictator, Saddam Hussein.

NATIONAL DEFENSE

As previously noted, the Kuwaiti military at the time of independence was of extremely limited size and scope. Conceived of initially as a mere constabulary force to patrol Kuwait's desert area, the Kuwaiti army was ill-prepared to defend the entire country from outside invasion. With oil wealth, however, Kuwait was able and willing to invest in national defense assets. A 1989 U.S. government report ranked Kuwait as sixth in the world in per capita military spending, with most of that equipment coming from Great Britain. Kuwait's high level of spending notwithstanding, it is now clear that the defensive steps taken after independence were far from adequate.

Approximately 1 in 10 Kuwaitis was tied in some way to national defense, though the ratio itself is deceiving. Unlike most nations in the region, Kuwait had a system of military conscription. The accepted standard was two years of military service, from age 18 to 20, for all of Kuwait's young male citizens; college graduates, however, served only a one-year tour. During the prewar period, a very small number of Kuwaiti women served in support positions such as public relations and administration.

Despite liberal opportunities to receive deferment from the draft, such as for education or being the head of a family, many Kuwaiti men served a short stint in the army and received a minimal amount of military training before returning to civilian life. Recalling those men to active duty in the army or national guard, however, was problematic, since they also served as functionaries in Kuwait's massive civil bureaucracy. Moreover, the low level of training received at the start of their careers was clearly inadequate for operating or employing some of the high-tech equipment Kuwait was purchasing to defend itself.

Making matters worse, from the perspective of Kuwait's strategic planners, on the eve of invasion in 1990 only about a quarter of Kuwait's military personnel strength consisted of Kuwaiti citizens. Many Kuwaiti Shiites had already been removed from the military during the Iran-Iraq War due to suspicions about their trustworthiness. The other three-quarters of Kuwait's uniformed frontline troops were foreign nationals, largely from Palestine, Pakistan, India, Egypt, and the Philippines. There was serious doubt among senior Kuwaiti officers that these *bidun,* or stateless people, would vigorously fight to defend a country other than their own homeland. Subsequent experience during both invasion and liberation would be mixed when these non-Kuwaitis were placed in active ground combat roles.

While the lowest ranks in all the services were primarily bidun, all of Kuwait's officers were citizens, and all were well educated and well trained. Any Kuwaiti officers considered unreliable had already been removed during the 1980s, so expectations were high for the prewar officer corps. Whether from the army, air force, or navy, Kuwaiti officers received some of the best military training available worldwide, most commonly from Great Britain, the United States, France, Germany, and even the Soviet Union.

Kuwaiti army equipment was also of diverse backgrounds. Kuwaiti battle tanks came from Yugoslavia. France provided most of Kuwait's artillery, and the United States, France, and Great Britain provided antitank munitions. Air-defense missiles came from the Soviet Union. In 1984, Kuwait requested American-made Stinger shoulder-fired antiaircraft missiles, but the United States rejected the request out of fear the deadly weapons could fall into the hands of Islamic terrorists. Kuwait turned to the Soviet Union, which quickly supplied its own shoulder-fired missiles, albeit of inferior quality to the American system. Even though many of these foreign weapon systems were of first-rate quality, the fact that they came from all over the planet made maintenance an absolute nightmare for Kuwaiti military logisticians.

The situation was similar for the Kuwaiti naval force and air force. In 1990, the air force was manned by just over two thousand men and the navy by around eighteen hundred men. In both services, as had been true in the army, the lowest ranks were filled by bidun. The air force maintained almost 80 aircraft, from the French F-1 Mirage to the American A-4 Skyhawk, as well as about 40 combat helicopters that were also of French origin. The air force also operated American-provided Hawk antiaircraft missile systems designed to defend Kuwaiti air bases. Moreover, the air force was partially connected by radar and computer into the U.S. Airborne Warning and Control System (AWACS), which, flying out of Saudi Arabia, had patrolled the Arabian Gulf since the Iran-Iraq War. Since 1984, the Kuwaiti naval force had operated eight corvette-sized boats built in Germany. These Exocet missile-firing craft were high-speed, high-tech vessels that, when employed aggressively, provided a credible deterrence to seaborne assault. Fully armed and deployed early, these missile crafts could potentially defend successfully in the event of invasion through the restricted waters of the Arabian Gulf's upper reaches. As events transpired, however, these Kuwaiti warships would never get a fighting chance to defend their nation from Iraq's assault.

6

Invasion and Occupation (1990–1991)

On August 2, 1990, Iraqi infantry and armored forces invaded Kuwait. Initial Iraqi pronouncements claimed the invasion was intended to support a popular uprising by Kuwaitis dissatisfied with Al-Sabah rule. The initial Iraqi propaganda theme was that the Al-Sabah had been deposed to popular Kuwait acclaim. There was no true spontaneity to the invasion, however, since the Iraqi blitz had clearly taken at least several months to plan and stage. Nor was there any popular revolt by the Kuwaitis. In fact, practically no Kuwaiti citizens were willing to collaborate in the Iraqi farce. Within days of the invasion, an Iraqi governor was named to fill the seat of power in Kuwait City. A series of proactive Iraqi diplomatic announcements then boldly put forward a host of rationales for having subdued Kuwait.

Only a week after the invasion, Iraqi officials announced that Kuwait would henceforth be permanently merged into Iraq. The occupying Iraqi forces quickly subdivided Kuwait into two parts. The northern half of Kuwait, including the controversial Ratqa oil field and the islands of Bubiyan and Warbah, officially became part of the Iraqi province of Basrah. The islands, in particular, were especially crucial to unhindered Iraqi maritime access to the Arabian Gulf. No longer would Iraq be bottled up in the Shatt al Arab. The southern section of Kuwait was renamed Kadhima, the 19th and newest province of Iraq. The most searing and costly period in Kuwait's history as a people and a nation had begun. Moreover, if the international community wanted to help Kuwait, and it was by no means certain to do so, it would be long months, possibly years, before anything could be done to roll back the Iraqi occupation garrison.

IRAQI ARGUMENT FOR INVASION

Going into August 1990, Iraq's claim on the land and people of Kuwait was a major theme of both Iraqi diplomacy and Iraqi propaganda. Iraq's position under international law combined two contradictory precepts. Foremost, Kuwait had never been independent and had always been part of Iraq. The embedded Iraqi fallback position was that Kuwait had been independent, but that the borders between the two countries had never been definitively established.

The primary basis for the Iraqi claim is that Kuwait was once part of the Ottoman Empire. As such, the Iraqi argument went, Kuwait was governed by the Ottoman chain of authority through nearby Basrah and Baghdad, which was only a little farther away, relative to the seat of Ottoman power in Istanbul. Iraq maintained that, when the Ottoman Empire collapsed following the First World War, the territory of Kuwait thenceforth belonged to Iraq as the Ottoman successor state in the region. From the Iraqi point of view, Sheikh Mubarak the Great, a serving Ottoman official, lacked the authority to enter into agreement with Great Britain in 1899.

The Iraqis also pointed to when the British and Ottomans penned the Anglo-Ottoman Convention of 1913, which mentioned Kuwait as a *qaza* as evidence of Kuwait's subordinate status. The fact that the rest of the convention definitively established the border between Iraq and Kuwait was disregarded by the Iraqis because the Anglo-Ottoman Convention of 1913 had never been officially ratified, another logical inconsistency in the Iraqi position. Iraqi lawyers held that subsequent international treaties, such as the 1920 Sevres Treaty and the 1923 Lausanne Treaty, were inapplicable. The Iraqis also argued that when Iraq's prime minister, in 1932, had officially acknowledged Kuwait's independence to the British, he had been serving as a puppet of Great Britain's mandate government of Iraq. Unfortunately for Iraq, all of these selective facts pale when compared with the official minutes of a diplomatic meeting held in 1963 in Baghdad, in which Iraq officially abandoned these earlier claims to Kuwait and subsequently voted to allow Kuwait to join the Arab League and the United Nations. For Iraq to suggest afterward that Kuwait was not historically an independent country is self-serving.

Historical claims aside, Iraq offered additional reasons for its invasion of Kuwait. Just inside Iraq's southern border with Kuwait was the large, valuable Rumaylah oil field. Iraqi diplomats accused Kuwait of "slant drilling"—that is, building oil wells just inside Kuwaiti territory that angled down, across the border—to steal oil from beneath Iraq. The Kuwaitis did have an oil well at Ratqa, immediately across from Rumaylah, but it had been there since the mid-1960s and actively pumping since the mid-1970s. If Kuwaiti oil wells just across the border were also tapping Rumaylah oil, it was because the oil deposits were actually connected. This was not uncommon, and international law did not consider it sufficient justification for resorting to war.

Iraq subsequently accused Kuwait of violating OPEC's internal policy by exceeding oil production, thereby flooding the world market and hurting the Iraqi economy in the process. Although Kuwait was, in fact, exceeding its OPEC quota, other members of OPEC were, at times, also highly selective in adhering to production guidelines. Moreover, it was noted that OPEC itself, under U.S. law, was inherently an illegal organization established solely to fix prices and manipulate the market. Did Kuwait deserve punishment for not gouging its international customers? In any case, at a July 1990 OPEC meeting, Kuwait committed itself not to exceed established OPEC quotas in the future.

Finally, the matter of money also played prominently in Iraqi calculations. Kuwait had extensively bankrolled the Iraqi war machine during the Iran-Iraq War. Iraq owed Kuwait approximately $13 billion and wanted that debt forgiven permanently. At an Arab League summit in May 1990, Iraq declared that the Kuwaiti loans were only partial payment for the protection from Iran that Iraq provided to Kuwait and other small Arabian Gulf states. At a subsequent Arab League meeting in July, Iraq claimed that Kuwait's oil production had cost Iraq alone $89 billion. In a speech on July 17, Saddam Hussein accused Kuwait of not only robbing oil revenues and territory but actually conspiring with the United States and Israel against Iraq. That same day, the first of Iraq's armored divisions began to redeploy just north of the border with Kuwait.

For the next two weeks, a series of bilateral and multilateral discussions and negotiations ensued across the region. Kuwait was willing to address some of the Iraqi demands but was unwilling to consider losing territory. Saudi Arabian officials were willing to contribute billions in Saudi money to avoid war, but Iraq continued to push for more while its troops continued to carry out so-called military exercises in plain sight along the Kuwaiti border. Egypt's president, Hosni Mubarak, attempted to mediate, as did Jordan's King Hussein. Saddam Hussein promised both leaders that he would not invade Kuwait.

On July 25, 1990, U.S. ambassador to Iraq April Glaspie forwarded a diplomatic note to the Iraqis that urged Iraq to avoid both coercion and intimidation. Later that same day, Ambassador Glaspie was summoned for a meeting with Saddam Hussein. In that meeting, according to Ambassador Glaspie's later testimony before a congressional committee, she informed Saddam Hussein that the United States had "no opinion on the Arab-Arab conflicts like your border disagreement with Kuwait." For his part, Saddam Hussein asked the ambassador to inform President Bush that there would be no invasion of Kuwait. During the weeks preceding the war, the Kuwaitis received repeated assurances from the United States, the Saudis, and other well-meaning third parties that there would be no invasion, as long as Kuwait itself did not precipitate a crisis. Accordingly, Kuwaiti ground, air, and naval forces were deliberately denied ammunition and approval to take up defensive positions on the eve of war.

On July 31, 1990, the Kuwaitis and the Iraqis met face-to-face in Jeddah, Saudi Arabia, to resolve their differences. By this point, there were about one hundred thousand Iraqi troops deployed along the Kuwaiti border. The Kuwaiti delegation was led by Crown Prince and Prime Minister Sheikh Sabah al-Ahmad. The Kuwaitis had already resolved the issue of oil quotas, were willing to forgive Iraq's debt, and were willing to offer an additional $9 billion loan to Iraq. With regard to territorial concessions, however, the Kuwaiti delegation was unbending. Talks finally broke down on August 1, 1990, with the Kuwaitis and the Saudis anticipating another round of negotiations in a few days. By midnight that very day, Iraqi commandos and infantry were already crossing the border to open the roads for follow-on tank regiments. Iraq's invasion of Kuwait was under way.

IRAQI INVASION

An Iraqi invasion force, estimated at around 120,000 troops supported by about 2,000 tanks and armored vehicles, was assigned the job of conquering Kuwait. This gave Iraq an attacker-to-defender ratio of about six or seven to one and overwhelming superiority in tanks and artillery. The Iraqi air force also vastly outnumbered its Kuwaiti opponent. The Iraqi navy was of only marginal capability, except for a handful of top-notch Soviet-built Osa missile boats with Styx antiship missiles. Iraqi commandos were assigned the task of capturing the bases of the Kuwaiti naval force. Once these commandos had completed their tasks, the battle at sea would essentially be over.

Iraqi commandos began infiltrating the Kuwaiti border prior to midnight, in preparation for capturing the border crossing sites to facilitate the movement of Iraqi armor. Major units began the attack at the stroke of midnight, with most crossing the border around 1:00 A.M. The Iraqi attack had two prongs, with the primary attack force driving south straight for Kuwait City down the main highway, and a supporting attack entering Kuwait farther west, but then turning and driving due east, cutting off the capital city from Kuwaiti defensive positions in the southern half of the country.

In addition to the geographic objective of Kuwait City itself, Iraq's military objectives were destruction of Kuwait's armed forces and capture of the emir, the crown prince, and other key ministers. In support of this operation, several hundred Iraqi commandos had already infiltrated Kuwait and were poised to strike the Dasman Palace, home to the emir, and Kuwait's key naval bases. This group also served as "pathfinders," capturing the international airport and establishing additional landing zones for Iraqi infantry deployed by helicopter to fly directly into Kuwait City.

Kuwaiti defenders, unable to stem the onslaught, fell back rapidly. By 3:30 A.M., Iraqi tanks were in Jahra. By 4:00 A.M., Iraqi commandos, in civilian clothes, were attacking around Kuwait City. Their assault on the Dasman Palace was especially aggressive and continued into midafternoon. Despite a spirited defense by the Emiri Guard, the Iraqis eventually took the site. In the process, the Iraqis killed Sheikh Fahd al-Ahmad, a well-liked member of the ruling family. Sheikh Fahd, the emir's youngest brother, was the only Al-Sabah to die in the invasion. The emir and many of his advisors had moved to General Headquarters much earlier that morning to follow the battle. From there, the emir and key ministers headed south along the highway for refuge in Saudi Arabia.

By about noon on August 2, Iraqi forces essentially controlled all of Kuwait City. Scattered Kuwaiti units, ships, and aircraft were still in the fight, but the Iraqis had only to mop up the rest of the small country before their victory was complete. After destroying Kuwait's military forces and gaining control of the entire country, Iraqi ground forces redeployed along the border of Saudi Arabia. This indicated to many intelligence analysts that Kuwait was only a stepping-stone to the overall Iraqi goal of Saudi oil fields and oil terminals along the Arabian Gulf.

KUWAITI DEFENSE

As the new day began at midnight on August 2, 1990, the Kuwaiti defense force was ill-prepared to defend the country from an Iraqi assault. The muster rolls of the military carried about eighteen thousand names, but the length of the list was not indicative of the actual defense situation. Nor was the list of Kuwaiti army units, which included a mechanized infantry brigade, three armored brigades, and an artillery brigade, an accurate measure of combat capabilities. Had all those units been at full strength—but in fact, all were severely understrength—Kuwaiti military commanders still would have been hard-pressed to defend their nation. For one thing, overmatched militaries prefer to trade space for time. The tiny country of Kuwait had no strategic depth, meaning that Kuwaiti defenders could not engage in a fighting withdrawal, stalling for time while waiting for help from abroad. Kuwait's defenders had to meet and defeat the Iraqi tanks right at the border if they wanted the chance to conduct a successful defense.

When war came to Kuwait in 1990, approximately one-fourth of Kuwait's military personnel were on leave, many out of the country. Included in that group were several commanders and key staff officers. The situation below these officers was equally problematic. After independence, Kuwait had put in place a system of mandatory conscription. On paper, every Kuwaiti male was subject to military service. In practice, however, deferments were routine. In a country where every Kuwaiti was already assured of a government job and pension, there was little incentive to serve in the military.

Senior posts in the Kuwaiti defense establishment were filled by Kuwaitis, but, over time, many non-Kuwaitis, including bidun, were enlisted to fill critical needs in the enlisted ranks. Approximately one-quarter of Kuwait's army consisted of non-Kuwaitis. For example, Palestinians filled many technical roles in the Kuwaiti military; when the war commenced and the PLO officially backed Iraq, the loyalties of some of those Palestinian soldiers became open to question. At a time when Kuwaiti forces suddenly found themselves fighting for their national existence, many of those non-Kuwaitis would think twice before dying in the attempt to stop Iraqi troops. Thus, some Kuwaiti units that were at fighting strength on paper were, in fact, not always able to put up a solid defense of their assigned positions.

The Kuwaiti government's fateful decision to avoid arming and deploying its forces so as to avoid aggravating the situation meant that Kuwaiti tanks, warplanes, and guided-missile naval craft were without ammunition when the Iraqi forces crossed the border, invaded Kuwaiti airspace, and steamed into Kuwaiti waters, intent on overrunning the small country. As one example, the Kuwaiti naval force's only two operational modern guided-missile craft had been fully armed and placed on alert a week before the invasion. As the policy to avoid appearances of belligerency filtered down from the government, Kuwaiti General Headquarters ordered the French-made Exocet antiship missiles removed from those two ships and returned to the ammunition depot. On the morning of the invasion, the two guided-missile craft could engage Iraqi warships only with guns; later in the day, after destroying as many Iraqi vessels and helicopters as possible under the circumstances, the two Kuwaiti missile boats had no choice but to withdraw from the battle as ordered into Saudi Arabian territorial waters.

The commander of a Kuwaiti armored battalion, on his own authority, had provisioned his vehicles and deployed them in readiness for the Iraqi attack several hours before other Kuwaiti units had begun to prepare. With little more than training ammunition, this battalion was able to conduct a robust defense near Mutla'a Ridge, perhaps the only defensible geographical line in the entire country. Those Kuwaiti troops, at heavy cost, managed to slow the

Iraqi assault in their sector. The rest of Kuwait's battle units were not officially put on alert until after the invasion was already under way.

This is not to suggest that no Kuwaiti units held their ground. Midgrade and senior Kuwaiti officers from all services were well trained and highly motivated. Under their leadership, despite overwhelming odds, some Kuwaiti units remained in place and held their ground, at least until the situation became untenable. Postwar analysis would indicate that 90 percent of Kuwait's military installations had sustained combat damage during the initial Iraqi invasion. The Kuwaiti army's 3rd Brigade, which included the aforementioned armored battalion, later became known as the Martyrs' Brigade, in recognition of its spirited defense over the course of the first few days of the Iraqi invasion.

From two bases in southern Kuwait, Ali-al-Salem and al-Jaber, Kuwaiti air force fighters and helicopters were still flying sorties on the morning of August 3. The main runway at al-Jaber air base had been bombed and mined by Iraqi aircraft, so Kuwaiti pilots were using a perimeter road as their landing strip in order to continue the fight. In their defense, Kuwaiti pilots shot down a number of Iraqi helicopters. Kuwaiti defenders also used shoulder-launched surface-to-air missiles (Soviet-made SAM-7) to shoot down several Iraqi warplanes and hold off the surrender of the two bases. When it was clear their position was untenable, the local commanders sent their remaining aircraft to Dhahran, Saudi Arabia. The Iraqis captured the two bases shortly thereafter. Soon even the remaining Kuwaiti military units were surrounded and out of ammunition. Though isolated skirmishes occurred throughout Kuwait for the next few days, it was clear that sporadic resistance was insufficient. Iraq had conquered Kuwait.

Beyond the numbers of killed and wounded, most of Kuwait's troops were captured. Approximately seven thousand troops escaped into Saudi Arabia, along with about 40 tanks and other fighting vehicles. Along with the warships and aircraft already mentioned, these forces would make up the Kuwaiti contingent of the coalition that would soon attempt to overturn the results of the Iraqi invasion.

INTERNATIONAL RESPONSE

The Kuwaiti government urgently petitioned the United Nations to condemn the Iraqi invasion of Kuwait, and the Security Council was quick to act. On the very day of the invasion, it passed Resolution 660, which called for Iraq's immediate and unconditional withdrawal from Kuwait. Of note, a veto by the Russians had been a distinct possibility. That Russia endorsed the resolution should have been a clear sign to Saddam Hussein that Cold War–era geostrategic calculations would no longer be in his favor.

On August 6, in a 13–0 vote (with Yemen and Cuba abstaining), the United Nations Security Council enacted Resolution 661, which imposed economic sanctions on Iraq in the form of restrictions on financial dealings and trade. Resolutions 665 and 666 added more definition to the economic sanctions. The target of these sanctions was specifically oil; if Iraq could be denied the profits from sale of its petroleum, now including Kuwaiti oil, Saddam Hussein might be persuaded to withdraw his forces from Kuwait. Subsequently, Resolution 669 further stiffened the sanctions on Iraq while attempting to lessen the impact on third-party nations. Resolution 670 added airborne commerce to the list of banned commercial activities.

The number of nations that both privately and publicly condemned the attack is indicative of the widespread perception of Iraq as a regional threat. Eventually, 34 countries would contribute military forces to the coalition. One notable exception was the PLO, which strongly supported Iraq. What the PLO hoped to gain by this support is unclear. The PLO position would have minimal effect on the war itself, but once Kuwait was liberated, it would have a huge negative impact on the thousands of Palestinians who lived and worked in Kuwait, and also on the liberal financial support that Kuwait had formerly provided to the Palestinian Authority over the years.

Over this same short period of time, the initial positions of the United States, Great Britain, and Saudi Arabia were able to coalesce into a united position. President G.H.W. Bush condemned the invasion on the morning of August 2, but afterward, the United States could do little but evaluate the strategic alternatives. Without a standing military pact with Kuwait, unilateral American action was never contemplated. At the same time, Saudi Arabia was especially concerned that Iraqi forces would continue to advance southward, and recognized that it could not defend itself from an Iraqi invasion without outside military assistance. The United States and Great Britain, with time to assess the economic impact of Iraqi aggression, realized that no further Iraqi gains could be tolerated under any circumstances. Secretary of Defense Dick Cheney hastily visited Saudi Arabia on August 7. During the meeting, Saudi King Fahd requested the deployment of U.S. forces to his country. These American troops, it was conceived, would immediately take up defensive positions to prevent any Iraqi advances into Saudi territory. On August 8, President Bush announced his decision to the American people.

American ground, air, and naval elements were already moving into position to defend Saudi Arabia. Navy aircraft carrier battle groups and lead elements of the 82nd Airborne and the 1st Tactical Fighter Wing were quickly dispatched to Saudi Arabia, but it would be weeks before substantial U.S. forces arrived. By October, however, coalition forces in Saudi Arabia would be strong enough that defense of Saudi Arabia could be taken as a given. American, British, Saudi Arabian, and even Kuwaiti strategic planners could begin to consider how to retake Kuwait from Iraq, without destroying the country in the process.

Going into the war, Kuwait and the other members of the GCC had hoped that their combined military capabilities would be sufficient to deter aggressive neighbors like Iraq and Iran. Iraq's invasion of Kuwait pointed out the hopelessness of "self" defense in the near term. It was obvious that if Saddam Hussein's Iraq wanted to attack Saudi Arabia and the other countries along the Arabian Gulf, the token Peninsula Shield defenders from the GCC would be unable to prevent it.

Almost all the Arab nations of the Arabian Gulf supported the attempts to roll back the Iraqi aggression, though some of those countries kept their support more private than those that played a public role in countering Iraq. The availability of ports and air bases in these nearby countries would prove invaluable during Operation Desert Storm. Moreover, military forces from several GCC nations would eventually fight against Iraq as part of an Arab task force in that operation. In the long term, this realization of weakness would encourage Kuwait to establish an especially close defensive relationship with the United States after liberation.

After escaping from Kuwait City, the emir proceeded to Saudi Arabia. Soon a Kuwaiti government in exile was established at Taif in that country. Kuwaiti diplomats also worked feverishly in Washington, DC, New York, London, and Paris, as well as in most Arab capitals. The Kuwaitis no longer had revenue from petroleum to bankroll their national defense. Fortunately, lucrative foreign investments made in previous decades (some estimates were $100 billion) meant that the Kuwaiti government had access to at least a small portion of its financial resources to stay in the fight over the long term. Kuwait could contribute only modest military forces to the collation. Monetary contributions were substantial, however. Around $16 billion was eventually pledged by the Kuwaiti government to the United States, and another $6 billion to Egypt to cover expenses for Operations Desert Shield and Desert Storm.

Coalition naval forces, especially from the United States, were quick to implement the Arabian Gulf blockade necessary to give Security Council–endorsed economic sanctions the teeth needed to hurt Iraq financially. On August 17, just 15 days after the invasion, vessels of the United States Navy intercepted three Iraqi-flagged oil tankers. As soon as it was clear that the Iraqi air force had no interest in attacking coalition warships, the blockading vessels were able to aggressively enforce the sanctions throughout the Arabian Gulf.

The naval blockade begun during Operation Desert Shield continued through Operation Desert Storm and was carried over into the postwar period. By war's end, 13 nations had supplied more than two hundred warships to the coalition's flotilla in and around the Arabian Gulf. Those warships conducted more than ten thousand intercepts in support of the two operations.

It has been estimated that, as a result of the blockade, Iraq's GNP was halved, its imports cut by nine-tenths, and its exports virtually shut down. With no way to sell the oil of Kuwait, Iraq found it increasingly difficult to provide logistical support to its military, especially the Iraqi occupation forces in Kuwait. As the situation worsened for Iraqi troops in Kuwait, the circumstances of the Kuwaiti populace under occupation—as well as for foreigners, especially westerners, trapped in the tiny country—grew even worse, as food and other scarce commodities were diverted to Iraqi use.

IRAQI OCCUPATION

From August 4 to August 8, Alaa Hussein (no relation to Saddam Hussein) served as the first civilian governor of Iraqi-occupied Kuwait. Hussein was a member of Iraq's Baath Party (Socialist Arab Rebirth Party), which became the first and only legal political party in Kuwait during occupation. Hussein was soon replaced by General Ali Hassan al-Majid, a first cousin and close confidante of Iraq's president, Saddam Hussein. Known to many inside Iraq as "Chemical Ali" and the "Butcher of Kurdistan," the new military governor had already made a name for himself by employing chemical weapons to murder thousands of Iraqi Kurdish civilians in 1988. The new military governor's marching orders from Saddam Hussein were straightforward: impose ironclad Iraqi rule in Kuwait by any means necessary. (After the U.S. invasion of Iraq in 2003, al-Majid was apprehended. Convicted by an Iraqi court for crimes against humanity, he awaits a death sentence and may be executed before ever being tried for war crimes in Kuwait.) In November, with Iraq in firm control of the Kuwaiti populace, a new governor arrived. Aziz Salih Numan, another Iraqi Baath Party stalwart, held the job until February 27, 1991, when coalition troops rolled into downtown Kuwait City.

Throughout the actual occupation, numerous reports of Iraqi atrocities were circulated. Some of those accounts were exaggerated, and others were probably demonstrably false and the product of either ignorance or wartime propaganda. Extensive postwar research by the United Nations' Special Rapporteur, as well as by other nongovernmental organizations such as Human Rights Watch and Amnesty International, has been conducted, however. These studies were quite thorough and have resulted in solid documentation of conditions inside Kuwait during and after Iraqi occupation. From such nonpartisan sources it is known that Iraq's repressive measures to subjugate Kuwait's populace began immediately after the invasion and lasted for the entire period of occupation. For better understanding, however, it is helpful to consider Iraqi occupation as occurring in three distinct phases.

The initial phase of repression began with invasion and was largely focused on capture of Kuwaiti military personnel and senior Kuwaiti officials.

Obviously, the Iraqis were especially interested in detaining members of the Al-Sabah family. At a minimum, every captured Al-Sabah was one fewer to work against the Iraqis and overthrow of the occupation. If the Iraqis managed to co-opt a senior Al-Sabah family member, the possibility of using him as a puppet governor would have been an attractive option. Estimates are that six thousand to seven thousand Kuwaitis, mostly military personnel, were captured and detained during this phase.

Perhaps Iraqi troops believed their own propaganda that the Kuwaiti population would greet them as brothers, even as liberators. In any case, the Iraqis were stunned when popular resistance to the occupation began to spring up. The second phase of Iraqi repression started in mid-August, a few weeks after the invasion. Many of the people detained during this phase included more Kuwaitis in key government posts and anyone even suspected of supporting the resistance. Perhaps not coincidentally, this is also the time that Saddam Hussein adopted the policy of using "human shields" to protect Iraqi forces and facilities in Kuwait and Iraq.

The Iraqi "human shield" policy was intended to preclude allied attack. Since foreigners, especially Americans and Europeans, were considered especially valuable as human shields, Saddam Hussein issued an order on August 24, 1990, that any Kuwaiti civilian detected trying to conceal a foreigner would be treated as a spy and shown no mercy; public hanging by the neck until dead was the preferred method for these mandatory executions. A month later, Saddam Hussein issued another order, directing Iraqi troops in Kuwait to be extra vigilant in locating Pakistani professionals, such as scientists and engineers. Presumably, these were people who could help with Iraq's missile and nuclear weapons development programs. The number of people detained during this second phase is unknown.

Roughly coinciding with these first two stages of Iraqi occupation, the United Nations attempted to address the worsening situation inside Kuwait. Resolution 664, on August 19, demanded the release of foreign nationals. Resolution 666, on September 13, authorized the shipment of food and medicine to alleviate humanitarian concerns inside Kuwait. Resolution 667, on 16 September, demanded the protection of diplomats and other foreign national civilians under occupation. Resolution 674, on October 29, specifically demanded protection of the rights of civilian nationals. Finally, Resolution 677, approved in November, specifically targeted Iraqi attempts to alter Kuwaiti demographics and Iraqi destruction of Kuwaiti public records.

The final phase of Iraqi repression inside Kuwait began on February 19, 1991, more than a month since the allied air campaign had begun, and just prior to Iraqi withdrawal. People detained during this phase were mostly Kuwaiti males, estimated to be at least two thousand in number. In all, probably around eight thousand people were deported to Iraq. Most were Kuwaitis, but the total also included Jordanians, whose home country opposed the Iraqi invasion, and Palestinians, whose homeland supported Iraq. Several hundred biduns were also included in the total.

Throughout the occupation of Kuwait, Iraq argued that because Kuwait was part of Iraq, the matter was purely domestic in nature and, therefore, Iraq was not obligated to abide by the prisoner administration requirements of the International Committee of the Red Cross. Only at the very end of the First Gulf War did the Iraqi government begin to allow the International Committee of the Red Cross to visit a small number of prisoners in a few of the Iraqi detention facilities. Iraq's "show prisoners" were usually Kuwaiti military personnel. Rarely were deported Kuwaiti citizens displayed.

When Kuwaitis were arrested by Iraqi troops, a similar pattern was generally followed. Initial interrogation of the so-called suspect took place at the local police station. This interrogation usually included verbal and physical abuse, and often included actual torture. If not released, the Kuwaiti detainee would then be transferred to a larger interrogation center in Kuwait City. There, additional sessions of beatings and torture were periodically conducted. This phase generally lasted several weeks, during which the suspect's family was not informed of his or her status or condition.

At this point, Kuwaiti detainees could be handled in three different ways: some suspects were released from custody; others were escorted to their homes, where they were summarily executed in front of family and neighbors; and Kuwaitis in the final category of detainees were deported to prison in Iraq for more torture and questioning. Again, thanks to nongovernmental organizations like Human Rights Watch and Amnesty International, the forms of Iraqi torture are generally known and well documented. Fairly typical torture included *falaqa,* or beatings on the soles of the feet, burning with cigarettes and lighters, and electrical shock from cattle prods and other devices. Rape was widespread, though the social stigma associated with it prevented many Kuwaiti women from reporting their sexual assaults. Fingernails were routinely ripped off. Isolated reports exist of Iraqi interrogators forcing Kuwaiti prisoners to play Russian roulette until a fatality occurred.

Several homemade Iraqi torture devices were discovered after liberation. These included headphones through which an ever-increasing volume of sound could be transmitted, culminating in the rupture of eardrums, and a helmet that gave electrical shock. Mock executions were not uncommon. Many detainees reported seeing Iraqi interrogators pluck out the eyeball of a victim. Evidence of the practice does exist, but not of the widespread use of the tactic. It is possible that some of the several thousand Kuwaiti detainees who disappeared in Iraqi custody were victims of these practices who were later murdered. The truth may never be known.

Detention aside, "extrajudicial execution" or summary execution could occur on the spot when suspects, especially those suspected of resistance membership, were captured. More often, these suspects were escorted directly to their homes or neighborhoods, displayed to family and friends, and then shot. Iraqi occupation policy was that the body of the person executed would be left undisturbed as a warning to others. The family of the deceased was not allowed to move the body, sometimes for six hours, and possibly for as long as several days.

In mid-December 1990, the General Assembly of the United Nations expressed its "grave concern at the grave violations of human rights and fundamental freedoms during the occupation of Kuwait." Also in December 1990, Saddam Hussein issued an order to the Iraqi occupation force to maintain control of the Kuwaiti civilian population "with a hand on the trigger." Since the date of the order was not included, it is unclear if Saddam's directive preceded or followed the United Nations' resolution, but clearly the resolution itself was insufficient to alter Iraq's draconian policies in occupied Kuwait.

Throughout the period of occupation, the systematic appropriation of Kuwaiti property by the Iraqi army proceeded apace, especially of Kuwaiti-owned vehicles. For months, some of the nicest private homes in wealthy Kuwait City neighborhoods had been arbitrarily confiscated for use by Iraqi authorities. The Iraqi army promulgated official directions to document confiscation of Kuwaiti property and to govern its transportation to Iraq. Buildings that weren't confiscated outright were sometimes destroyed, purportedly because of a failure to cooperate with occupation troops on the part of their Kuwaiti owners.

By January 1991, six months into occupation, Iraq had almost total control of Kuwait. Roughly 50 percent of Kuwait's preinvasion population, Kuwaiti and non-Kuwaiti alike, had fled the country. As Human Rights Watch and other nongovernmental organizations have reported, virtually all of Kuwait's institutions, from the media to medical facilities to higher education, were officially run by an Iraqi, often a military officer. Freedom of assembly and freedom of expression, two things that had always set the modern Kuwaitis apart from other Arab nations, no longer existed.

The Iraqi occupation forces were very successful in their attempts to cut off virtually all outside communications. For Kuwaitis under the occupation, any attempt to communicate with the outside world was almost out of the question. Most international telephone lines had been cut on the day of the invasion. Even owning a satellite telephone was dangerous, and using that satellite telephone might be suicidal for practical purposes. Kuwaiti television had been taken off the air right after the actual invasion. Kuwaiti radio stations were told to retransmit Baghdad stations or cease transmission altogether.

A single Kuwaiti newspaper remained in print following the invasion, but it was used by the occupation government and served no other public purpose per se. Even that newspaper, *al-Nida*, or "The Call," was shut down in January 1991, after which the only newspapers available inside Kuwait were published in Iraq. The coalition forces of Operation Desert Shield put up temporary transmission facilities in northern Saudi Arabia that provided a modicum of both news and much-needed moral support to the Kuwait people.

The Iraqi army's deliberate destruction of Kuwaiti oil facilities that occurred during Iraq's withdrawal will be discussed in the next chapter. Of note here, however, is that the massive vandalism was not a spontaneous act, as it was once portrayed. Translation of Iraqi documents found inside Kuwait after liberation tells a different story. A December 1990 Iraqi army directive delineates the official chain of military command for the operation and lays out specific responsibilities for destruction of Kuwait's oil infrastructure. The document lists January 12, 1991, as the anticipated date of execution. This clearly indicates that Saddam Hussein was at least contemplating withdrawal from Kuwait long before the passing of the United Nations' deadline of mid-January. On January 10, 1991, a second military directive reiterated the earlier instructions for demolition of the oil fields. Thus, at that late date, complete withdrawal from Kuwait was still considered a possibility by Iraqi authorities.

KUWAITI RESISTANCE

A resistance movement against Iraqi occupation, which began on its own inside Kuwait, was already apparent by mid-August 1990, only a few weeks after the invasion. Later the Kuwaiti resistance would receive guidance and support, such as money and small arms, from the United States and Saudi Arabia, but it was never a tool of foreign powers. The resistance was homegrown and focused solely on driving out the Iraqis and restoring the legitimate government of Kuwait. Many members of the resistance had been in the Kuwaiti military when Iraq invaded, and they managed to avoid capture since that time. Others in the resistance were civilians. Most, but certainly not all, were actually Kuwaiti citizens.

Initial resistance measures included maintaining contact with the Kuwaiti government in exile and hiding foreigners from Iraqi troops. Several safe houses were established, between which the hidden foreigners could be moved to avoid Iraqi searches. When it could, the resistance movement also clandestinely printed and distributed antioccupation publications such as "Steadfastness of the People" (*Sumoud al-Sha'ab*). As the military capabilities of the resistance grew, so did its tactics. In the mass confusion during the first few days of the invasion, some former military officers had been able to sneak away with small arms, explosives, and even some shoulder-fired surface-to-air missiles. With these ordnance items, sniping at Iraqi troops was a favorite resistance tactic. Car bombings, especially during December 1990, were a serious problem for the Iraqi occupiers. In one of these bombings by the resistance, 4 Iraqi troops were killed and 12 were wounded. Records are sketchy, but 18 other people, presumably Kuwaiti or bidun, were also injured in this bombing.

Occasionally, the Kuwaiti resistance would engage in isolated hit-and-run skirmishes with occupying Iraqi troops. Whether it was a bombing by or a gun battle with the resistance, the Iraqi response was invariably swift and brutally effective: roundup of likely suspects, torture possibly leading to "confession," followed by summary execution. Afterward, Iraqi forces often destroyed the homes of suspects and their families as a means of deterrence. In one case, when a handful of resistance fighters had sniped at Iraqi troops from a nearby house, the Iraqis retaliated against the entire city block to make their point.

These and similar Iraqi tactics definitely had a localized effect as a deterrent. Iraqi measures were insufficient, however, to prevent the Kuwaiti resistance movement from establishing a liaison with coalition forces in Saudi Arabia during Operation Desert Shield. During Operation Desert Storm to liberate Kuwait, the resistance would conduct a number of military and intelligence operations in support of coalition forces; these operations, though small in scope, were crucial to coalition success and minimization of allied casualties.

Under virtually every single Al-Sabah sheikh, Kuwait's foreign policy historically hinged on two complementary objectives: to appease serious outside threats and to foster protection from powerful friends. In that sense, then, the Iraqi invasion of Kuwait represented a failure of Kuwaiti foreign policy: Kuwait was not able to avoid direct confrontation with one of its most powerful neighbors. On the other hand, Operation Desert Storm, the coalition military campaign to liberate Kuwait and restore its legitimate government, represented the complete success of the second prong of Kuwait's historic diplomatic efforts. Several powerful friends, in particular the United States and Great Britain, came to Kuwait's defense when needed most.

7

Liberation (1991)

As early as August 8, 1990, less than a week after the Iraqi invasion but many long months before any realistic hope of pursuing these key strategic objectives, President Bush spelled out the overarching political goals of the United States with regard to Kuwait and the Arabian Gulf. These policies were four in number: immediate and unconditional withdrawal of Iraqi forces from Kuwait, the legitimate Al-Sabah government reseated, establishment of political stability and economic security throughout the region, and protection of American citizens currently inside Kuwait and Iraq.

The president's political objectives were quickly translated into the military objectives that Operation Desert Storm was later designed to accomplish. That task fell to coalition military strategists in Washington, DC; London; and Tampa, Florida, headquarters to the U.S. Central Command, which would actually carry out the mission. Those allied military staffs quickly began to lay out a campaign plan that would remove Iraqi forces from Kuwait; if the Iraqi units refused or failed to withdraw, then the coalition forces would cut off those Iraqi forces and destroy them, while minimizing civilian casualties and destruction of Kuwait's infrastructure. Next, the coalition military was tasked with restoring the emir to power in Kuwait City. Beyond these first two military objectives, which were directly tied to Kuwait, coalition military forces had two additional, broader objectives related instead to Iraq: destruction of Iraq's Republican Guard as a fighting force, and sufficient destruction of the other repressive instruments of Saddam Hussein's power, such as the Baath Party and the Iraqi Intelligence Service. Finally, coalition forces intended to destroy Iraq's weapons of mass destruction (WMDs) and demolish the means to develop, build, and deliver WMDs in the foreseeable future.

While military strategy was being mapped out, the diplomatic front focused on coalition building. British and American statesmen were especially eager to avoid the appearance that the campaign was a Western one waged against a Muslim nation. Military contributions from more than a mere token number of moderate Arab nations were considered vital. Saudi Arabian leadership, along with Kuwaiti promises of significant financial support, soon won the participation of Arab-world heavyweights such as Egypt and Syria. Keeping these key Arab countries in the coalition also meant, however, that Israel, militarily the most powerful nation in the region and a key ally of the United States, would have to remain on the sidelines throughout any military campaign. Saddam Hussein worked hard to portray the war as about Zionist Israel, not about tiny Kuwait. If the war was mistakenly perceived across the Muslim world as Iraq against the Israelis, then popular support, already doubtful at best in several Arab nations, might plummet precipitously. For the allies to keep Israel out of the fight, however, meant that the coalition had to do all in its power to prevent Iraq's military harassment from eliciting a defensive Israeli response.

On August 17, 1990, President Bush activated the Civil Reserve Air Fleet (CRAF), which essentially impounded American-owned commercial aircraft to carry U.S. troops and equipment to the Arabian Gulf. Considering the economic impact on the airline industry, this was a major move. On August 22, President Bush followed with an even bolder move, when considered within the context of American domestic politics. By executive order, the president called up forty thousand reservists to active duty, primarily in the Army Reserve and the Air Force Reserve. Another executive order would come on January 18, 1991—this time to direct the reserves to remain on extended active duty, as long as 24 months if deemed necessary. Collectively, the call-up and deployment of reservists would be the largest for America since the Korean War. This major commitment clearly signaled the severity with which President Bush viewed the Iraqi occupation of Kuwait. Significantly, during the coming Operation Desert Storm, more than 40 percent of the American forces would be members of the Organized Reserve and the National Guard. In the interim, United Nations Security Council Resolution 678, enacted on November 29, 1990, made equally clear the degree to which the international community had coalesced against Iraqi aggression. The resolution authorized the use of necessary force to compel Iraqi withdrawal from Kuwait.

MILITARY PLAN

Operation Desert Storm was designed to be conducted in four phases that were intended to be completed sequentially, but the military planners allowed for overlap of the phases, as well. Often referred to collectively as the "air campaign," phases one, two, and three of the operation all involved coalition airpower, which was of sufficient strength to allow the coalition aircraft to fly approximately twenty-five hundred "sorties," or individual missions, and, theoretically, to attack up to that many Iraqi targets on a daily basis. In practical terms, however, it was possible to strike only a few hundred targets daily. Cruise missiles, such as the long-range Tomahawk land-attack missile with pinpoint accuracy, were also factored into the allocation of Iraqi targets, at least for the first two weeks of the air campaign. Coalition targets in phase one were Iraqi military communications, air defense forces, airfields, and warplanes, wherever they could be located, even if deep in Iraq.

When those initial targets were neutralized, phase two would commence, with coalition aircraft switching the focus to Iraqi supply and ammunition bases, as well as highways, railroads, and bridges between Iraq and Kuwait. Once those targets were destroyed or at least severely degraded, phase three air strikes were designed to pulverize entrenched Iraqi army divisions, especially the Republican Guard divisions, both in Kuwait and inside southern Iraq itself. Phase four of the campaign, if necessary, would involve a ground offensive to dislodge Iraqi defenders and recapture Kuwait City and the rest of the small country. As part of these campaign plans, the surviving Kuwaiti forces were expected to play an active role. Those Kuwaiti air force fighters that remained operational would fly defensive missions over Saudi Arabia. The missile craft of the Kuwaiti naval force would be actively engaged in maritime interception operations in the Arabian Gulf in support of the naval blockade of Kuwait and Iraq. Kuwait's ground forces, which had been quickly reorganized, rearmed, and retrained, were already preparing to contribute to the liberation of their capital when the time came.

In total, around seven thousand Kuwaiti troops were anticipated to participate in Operation Desert Storm, a small but vital portion of the six hundred thousand troops making up the coalition. From the west, the United States provided the largest numbers of troops, followed by Britain and France. From the Muslim world, Saudi Arabia contributed more than twenty thousand troops. Other nations of the GCC, specifically Bahrain, Oman, Qatar, and the UAE, provided another three thousand troops. The contingents from Syria and Egypt were surprisingly strong on paper, but in actual combat power, they were less imposing. In all, 34 nations joined the coalition, and almost 30 of those countries provided significant military forces of some kind.

Leading the multinational coalition was American General H. Norman Schwarzkopf, commander in chief of the U.S. Central Command. His head-quarters and staff had deployed to Riyadh, Saudi Arabia, by mid-August and remained there for both Operations Desert Shield and Desert Storm. Lieuten-ant General Khalid ibn Sultan ibn Abd al Aziz Al Saud was General Schwarz-kopf's Saudi Arabian counterpart. General Sultan, a prominent member of the Saudi royal family, was in command of the Arab and non-Western troops and worked closely with General Schwarzkopf on the key details of the coalition's battle plan for the upcoming campaign to liberate Kuwait.

General Sultan had forces from the member states of the GCC as well as other Arab nations, most notably Egypt and Syria, under his command. From these Arabic-speaking units, two joint task forces were organized. Within this strate-gic military context, "joint" means that ground, air, and naval forces were inte-grated into the larger force; these were not simply ground combat units. "Task" means that the Arabic-speaking force was organized to accomplish a specific mission or task as part of the larger allied campaign plan to liberate Kuwait.

Units from Joint Forces Command East (JFCE) took up positions due south of Kuwait just inside the Saudi Arabian border. JFCE's components were con-tributed by Kuwait, Saudi Arabia, Qatar, and Bahrain. On paper, there were five brigades in JFCE, though the actual strength of these units was signifi-cantly less than a brigade of the U.S. Army. The same was true of the Arab brigades that made up Joint Forces Command North (JFCN), which consisted of troops from Egypt, Saudi Arabia, Syria, and Kuwait. JFCN's troops were positioned to the west of Kuwait, also inside the Saudi Arabian border. Some of these forces fought as national units; others were incorporated into larger divisions along with troops from other nations. For example, Kuwaiti, Saudi Arabian, and Egyptian troops were integrated into the Khalid Division, which formed the heart of JFCN.

The campaign plan to liberate Kuwait was sequential in nature. In the first phase, coalition air power, including cruise missiles, would cut Iraqi com-mand and control, and destroy Iraqi air and air defense forces. Once total air supremacy was obtained, coalition air forces would begin to isolate the battlefield by interdicting Iraqi supply lines all the way from Baghdad to Ku-wait City. The final phase of air operations would focus on whittling down Iraqi ground units that were actually dug in inside Kuwait or just inside the original Iraqi border. Throughout the air campaign, simultaneous diplomatic efforts hoped to persuade Saddam Hussein to withdraw his forces uncondi-tionally from Kuwait. Should Iraq do so, the coalition campaign could cease on short notice.

In case air strikes alone turned out to be insufficient to compel Iraqi compliance with United Nations' demands, however, detailed plans were laid for a three-pronged ground offensive to physically retake Kuwait. In that event, JFCE and U.S. Marines would proceed from Saudi Arabia directly up the coast road toward Kuwait City. JFCN would move eastward, also in the rough direction of the capital, essentially cutting Kuwait in half. Meanwhile, American, British, and French armored units hidden in the desert farther to the west would launch a broad, sweeping maneuver to cut off all Iraqi forces in Kuwait; once isolated, those Iraqi forces would either surrender or be destroyed.

ACTUAL MILITARY OPERATIONS

The coalition allies began massive offensive air strikes in the early-morning hours of January 17, 1991. The overwhelming air campaign was waged almost as precisely as it was designed. Each day, allied strategic planners picked new Iraqi targets, in Kuwait and in Iraq, and reassigned available air and cruise missile assets almost like clockwork as the campaign moved toward its almost inevitable conclusion. Barring a catastrophe, there was little doubt how these operations would end. That said, wars breed catastrophe, and allied military commanders fretted constantly as they explored contingencies and worst-case scenarios.

The coalition's campaign plans as written were based on the critical assumption that Iraq would not employ nuclear, chemical, or biological weapons in the defense of Kuwait. Allied diplomats pulled out all stops to communicate to Saddam Hussein that the coalition was interested only in liberating Kuwait, not in invading Iraq and removing Saddam Hussein from power. If, out of fear of removal from power, Saddam Hussein had decided to employ any of his WMDs, most likely his chemical air-dropped bombs and artillery shells, American and British statesmen assured him that his demise as dictator of Iraq would have been certain and swift. Allied strategists understood that if it came to that, the casualties on both sides, and especially among innocent Kuwaiti and Iraqi civilians, would undoubtedly skyrocket. As it was, the military campaign remained conventional in nature, and allied warplanes and tanks were well positioned to dominate the battlefield.

Throughout the air campaign, Saddam Hussein had numerous opportunities to withdraw his forces from occupied Kuwait. Whatever his geopolitical calculations, he elected not to do so. Instead, concerted efforts were made to draw Israel into the war through a barrage of Scud missiles that rained down on Israeli population centers. While the Scud missiles were so inaccurate as to be militarily useless, these attacks held the potential to elicit an Israeli military response should the allies prove incapable of destroying Iraq's Scud missiles on the ground or in the air.

American Patriot missiles, designed to shoot down both aircraft and surface-launched missiles like the Scud, were quickly deployed in and around Tel Aviv, Israel's capital city, to provide a protective shield for the Israeli population. With this reliable but not impervious air defense umbrella in place, allied air forces went Scud hunting with a vengeance; often as much as 40 percent of allied air power was relegated to the role of locating and destroying Scud missiles prior to their launch. In that respect, the Iraqi Scud missiles turned out to have a major, though temporary, impact on the ensuing campaign.

Following weeks of devastating air bombardment, primarily by U.S. and British warplanes, the ground offensive to capture or destroy Iraq's occupation troops and to retake Kuwait was launched on February 24, 1991. Allied combat engineers had worked hard in the preceding days to plot out, remove, or circumvent Iraqi obstacles on the battlefield. The minefields, sand berms, and "fire trenches" that Iraqi troops had so meticulously created to slow or stop the allied ground assault proved of little consequence. The Khalid Division, around which JFCN was built, quickly breached Iraqi defenses and moved north at a rapid pace. Ahead of their advance, Iraqi forces abandoned strong defensive positions to either flee toward the north or surrender en masse.

At the same time, JFCE, with Kuwaiti units in a prominent role, assaulted due north straight up the coast road. On this front, as well, Iraqi forces, though initially well dug in, were quickly sent reeling back toward Kuwait City or were captured by the thousands. The allied forces, especially the Martyrs' Brigade of battle-hardened Kuwaiti veterans, were eager to fight, but it was clear that the typical Iraqi foot soldier had no stomach for battle under the circumstances. The combined Kuwaiti, Saudi, Bahraini, and Qatari forces were barely slowed by the opposition they faced. By the third day of the operation, allied troops were converging on Kuwait City.

The Kuwaiti Martyrs' Brigade was given the honor of officially liberating the capital. By the afternoon of February 26, 1991, Iraqi occupation of the tiny nation of Kuwait was at an end. Armed members of the Kuwaiti resistance movement essentially controlled the city and its suburbs. On the morning of February 27, 1991, the Kuwaiti flag was officially run up a flagpole in downtown Kuwait City. Following 42 days of allied military operations, the Kuwaiti people had survived the nightmare of invasion and occupation. Their spirited and joyous victory celebration went on almost unabated for days. Though President Bush unilaterally declared a cease-fire, the Gulf War did not officially end until a cease-fire agreement was formally signed by General Schwarzkopf and a deputation of Iraqi generals, though not actually Saddam Hussein, at Safwan in southern Iraq.

In all, an estimated seven thousand Kuwaiti troops participated in the liberation of their country under Operation Desert Storm. The largest Kuwaiti units to fight in the campaign included the renamed Martyrs' Brigade, the 15th Infantry Brigade, and the Liberation Brigade, which was formed from the remnants of Kuwaiti units destroyed during the Iraqi invasion. The Kuwaiti naval force's two missile craft played a prominent role in operations at sea to retake Kuwait's offshore islands. The Kuwaiti air force contributed two dozen combat aircraft, only one of which was shot down by the Iraqi army.

Many other military men and women fought alongside those heroic Kuwaiti warriors. The combined coalition force included practically 700,000 troops, almost 200 warships, and more than 1,000 warplanes from 18 nations. Leading up to the war, and throughout the campaign, the United Nations as a body functioned in an exemplary manner, setting a standard for international unity at a time when the potential for such united action routinely drew scoffs from critics.

WARTIME DAMAGE

Even as Kuwaiti flags were dramatically raised on available flagpoles to replace Iraqi pennants, and while portraits of His Highness, the emir, were being plastered atop the ubiquitous pictures of a gloating Saddam Hussein, it was apparent to the Kuwaiti people and their rulers that liberation had come at a terrible price. Allied offensive efforts, while intentionally avoiding civilian casualties and peacetime infrastructure, had nonetheless demolished a large proportion of the telecommunications and transportation facilities upon which the government of liberated Kuwait had hoped to capitalize. Making matters infinitely worse, however, was the deliberate and malicious damage done by Iraqi troops on their hasty withdrawal from Kuwait. According to plan, demolitions were exploded and fires were set at the majority of Kuwait's valuable oil pumping and storage facilities. In all, almost 750 oil installations were damaged or destroyed by the Iraqis even as they pulled out from the tiny country.

Since oil is the economic lifeblood of modern Kuwait, the fiscal ramifications of this state-sponsored vandalism would have to be measured in the billions of dollars. Twenty-five of 26 storage facilities were damaged; the oil pipeline that tied together all of Kuwait's petroleum facilities was cut at too many points to begin listing them all. The transfer and pumping controls at the massive oil refinery at Mina Abdullah were totally unsalvageable. Upon liberation, and before repairing or replacing the damaged petroleum infrastructure, Kuwait's GNP was estimated at around 30 percent of its prewar value.

The damage did not stop with the destroyed facilities, however. At undamaged petroleum facilities across Kuwait, retreating Iraqi troops opened wide the massive valves; millions of gallons of oil gushed onto the sands of Kuwait or into the dark waters of the Arabian Gulf. These lakes of oil soon seeped into the already-limited underground water table, and in a country where every drop of potable water was precious, the impact would be felt for decades. The effects on plants and animals, as well as the long-term prospects for farming in Kuwait, were equally dire. The oil, once evaporated, added dangerous and toxic chemicals to the atmosphere, which were then returned to earth via precipitation.

As the fires burned, the situation grew worse. As much as 3 million gallons of petroleum burned each day. Every day that it continued, thousands of pounds of pollutants blackened the skies, first over Kuwait, then over regions downwind. The black clouds themselves weren't the problem, but the "black rain" that followed was. Indeed, many Kuwaitis who lived through the occupation maintained that the sight of black rain was their most vivid memory of the entire experience.

What the survivors would not realize for months was the damage caused to their lungs from breathing this polluted air. Reports of severe respiratory ailments would soon explode, especially in the very young and the very old, and debilitating illnesses such as lung cancer would begin to strike more frequently than ever recorded in Kuwait. Subsequent reports of medical problems by troops from the United States and Great Britain, popularly summed up in the catchphrase Gulf War syndrome, multiplied dramatically the number of severe health problems that could be at least indirectly tied to the environmental conditions in Kuwait caused by the war. Debate among scientists continues today regarding the degree to which chemical weapons, ambient radiation, and environmental pollution contribute to the spike in reported medical cases.

While the black rain helped clear the atmosphere, it dropped those polluting chemicals back on Kuwait and the Arabian Gulf, to be absorbed back into the soil, the water table, and the coastal marine environment. Kuwait's soil grew more acidic, which would have an ongoing negative effect on the prospects for farming. Because of the spilled oil and the other pollutants, Arabian Gulf waters were severely damaged. The temperature of the Arabian Gulf was markedly raised, and bacteria levels rose accordingly, which in turn made the production of drinking water through desalinization more problematic. As plankton absorbed the oil and chemicals, the toxic components were then distributed throughout the marine food chain; Kuwaitis hoping to feed themselves and their families by fishing were placed in a difficult position.

In all, it took nine long months to extinguish the flames from the oil wells and stop the continuous polluting of the atmosphere. Between eight thousand and nine thousand oil firefighters, generally private contractors drawn from as many as three dozen countries, had to converge on Kuwait to bring the necessary experience and specialized equipment to bear on the environmental and economic crisis. By the time that the many oil fires of Kuwait were finally extinguished, a new term had been coined by scientists and diplomats to capture the essence of what Saddam Hussein's Iraqi troops had done to Kuwait: environmental terrorism. Timed deliberately to coincide with the day the last oil fire was put out, the United Nations on November 6, 1991, announced that date as the International Day for Preventing the Use of the Environment in Military Conflicts. Whether this symbolic statement will prevent similar environmental terrorism in the future remains to be seen.

Putting out the hundreds of oil fires had been delayed and hampered by the presence of Iraqi landmines in the vicinities of major facilities. Mine-clearing operations were necessary before some of the oil fires could even be approached, let alone extinguished. Most of these Iraqi mines had been laid defensively to protect the facilities, initially from the Kuwaiti resistance movement and later from allied military forces. Thousands more Iraqi landmines had been strewn almost haphazardly around the Kuwaiti landscape. One official estimate placed the total number of Iraqi antivehicle and antipersonnel landmines laid in tiny Kuwait at 2 million, approximately one mine for every Kuwaiti man, woman, and child. To this day, Iraqi mines continue to threaten the lives of Kuwaiti civilians, and Kuwaiti papers have run hundreds of articles on civilians who have lost hands, feet, and lives to these Iraqi weapons nearly every month since liberation in 1991.

On official orders from their chain of command, perhaps directly from Saddam Hussein, Iraqi naval forces, contrary to international law, also deployed thousands of drifting naval mines in the Arabian Gulf during the war. For months afterward, these unguided, dangerous munitions threatened local fisherman (those lucky enough to have saved their boats), as well as oil tankers and other merchant ships. When these floating naval mines washed up on the shores of the Arabian Gulf, they were usually handled by demolitions experts, but occasionally these mines took the lives of incautious civilians, primarily but not exclusively Kuwaitis.

The physical damage inside Kuwait was far more extensive than just that related to the oil fires. The first-rate telecommunications system enjoyed by Kuwait prior to the war was almost nonexistent afterward, as a result of allied bombing intended to deny the use of these facilities to the occupying Iraqi forces, as well as due to the malicious damage caused by the retreating Iraqis. The four fixed ground stations that made up the Kuwaiti element of the Intelsat (International Telecommunications Satellite Organization) and Arabsat (Arab Satellite Communications Organization) systems were obliterated. The television studios, the modern recording and transmission equipment, and the transmitting towers and buildings that originally housed the Kuwaiti Ministry of Information were all but destroyed by bombing and Iraqi vandalism.

The buildings of Kuwait University were fire damaged, and the Kuwaiti Institute for Scientific Research (KISR) was utterly devastated.

Kuwait's modern network of highways and bridges was pulverized by coalition bombs and by harsh use of Iraqi and allied military vehicles. Kuwait International Airport was severely damaged and would take months to be restored to prewar operational levels. Out of Kuwait Airway's fleet of 23 airliners, 15 were stolen by Iraq—a single loss estimated at more than a billion dollars. Many of Kuwait's banking facilities were looted or razed. The monetary funds they had secured on the day of invasion were transferred to Iraq and are thus irrecoverable despite ongoing efforts.

Other economic damage included the looting and burning of downtown hotels and resorts that were once the envy of the Arabian Gulf. Museums, the capital city's zoo, recreation facilities, and restaurants were vandalized or destroyed. Not only had the soil and water table been damaged, but the fixed irrigation systems were badly broken. Water purification and desalinization plants were degraded, as was the fertilizer factory. Kuwaiti-owned fishing boats had been burned. The departing Iraqi troops even targeted neighborhood mosques before pulling out of their prepared defensive positions.

Perhaps most devastating of all was the destruction of Kuwait's state-of-the-art medical facilities. Prior to the war, the people of Kuwait had grown accustomed to the best medical care in the Arab world and, per capita, as good as any on the planet. The Iraqi occupation had changed all of that. The hospitals left behind by the Iraqis were merely shells. The critical equipment these facilities had once held was stripped and carted off to Baghdad in an organized fashion. The negative effect on the Kuwaiti public, under occupation and since, cannot be overstressed. A series of statistical studies has documented the skyrocketing instances of miscarriage, infant mortality, underweight babies, birth defects, heart disease, and a host of other debilitating, previously uncommon ailments.

Psychological scars caused by the invasion and occupation will be erased only when future generations have replaced those who survived the hardships of the war. Because so many of Kuwait's public spaces had been used by the Iraqis as detention centers, torture chambers, and execution grounds, the people of Kuwait are reminded daily of the atrocities committed by Iraqi forces—everywhere they look, they see the scenes of those crimes. Emotional and psychological problems—for example, severe depression and post-traumatic stress disorder (PTSD)—have been widespread since liberation.

Loss of life should not go unmentioned. The latest estimates of known dead inside Kuwait as a direct result of the war are 113 Kuwaiti civilians, 118 Kuwaiti soldiers, and 439 non-Kuwaiti nationals. In the aggregate, these Kuwaiti deaths are proportionately the equivalent of four hundred thousand Americans or one hundred thousand British citizens. These figures reflect on the documented deaths related to the war. Soon after liberation, the Kuwaiti government released a list of more than six hundred Kuwaitis, both military personnel and civilians, who were missing and remained unaccounted for. Eyewitness accounts, testimony from family members and friends, and, in some cases, official Iraqi military or judicial documents corroborated that these people were last seen alive in Iraqi custody. Kuwait's National Committee for the Missing and PoW Affairs (NCMPA) was formed solely to pursue the matter as long as it takes to be resolved. The NCMPA continues to work with the United Nations, the Red Cross, the Arab League, and, as of 2007, the new Iraqi government to ascertain the status of these missing Kuwaiti citizens.

RETURN OF THE EMIR

Even though the country was now in the hands of the Kuwaiti people and their liberators, the emir elected to remain in Saudi Arabia for another three weeks before returning on March 14 to reassume his throne. While at the time his belated return seemed to indicate a return to the status quo, domestic troubles were brewing for the Al-Sabah. By this point, the Kuwaiti people had finished their victory celebrations and had begun the soul-searching and problem-finding to be expected under the circumstances. Prewar policies of the Al-Sabah—policies that might not have caused the Iraqi invasion but in their failure certainly contributed to the attack—drew scathing attention from a Kuwaiti people who had once been more passive in their censure of the government. The Al-Sabah spent the rest of 1991 disarming their now-vocal critics, appeasing the people, and creating the conditions outside the country necessary to ensure Kuwait's survival in the future.

In the back of their minds, Kuwait's rulers were clearly aware of growing unrest among some elements of the Kuwaiti population, which was made all the more dangerous by the presence of so many small arms in the hands of Kuwaiti citizens. Kuwait's resurgent media establishment fed some of those governmental fears. Kuwaitis were accustomed to freedom of opinion, but opinion is quite different from free speech. Upon liberation, groups dissatisfied with the autocratic rule of the Al-Sabah were outspoken on the need for freedom of the press. The Al-Sabah recognized they were in a position of weakness, since the opposition had ridden out the invasion and occupation inside Kuwait, while the rulers themselves had lived in relative luxury in exile in Saudi Arabia. If the Al-Sabah failed to astutely defuse the developing situation, they potentially faced the greatest threat to their authority since the assaults by the Ikhwan early in the century.

The actions of the United Nations immediately following the war came as some relief to Kuwait's government. On March 2, 1991, barely a week after

Kuwait was liberated, the United Nations Security Council enacted Resolution 686, which demanded that Iraq immediately and irrevocably renounce its claims on Kuwait. Soon thereafter, the Security Council formed a five-member commission determined to examine the historical border issue between Kuwait and Iraq as documented in the 1963 agreement, signed between the two nations upon Kuwait's independence from Britain, as well as the earlier 1932 border agreement between the same countries. Under Resolution 687, the commission delineated the border between Kuwait and Iraq in April 1992. In general, the border between the two countries was moved only about one-third of a mile to the north. This new border gave Kuwait effective control of six additional wells in the Rumaylah oil field, as well as a significant portion of the former Iraqi naval base at Umm Qasr. The United Nations boundary commission's official findings pronounced the newly demarcated border "inviolable" under the United Nations charter. Though at the time Iraq refused to recognize the new border, it formally agreed to do so in November 1994.

MARTIAL LAW

While international support of its borders came as a comfort, the situation inside Kuwait was turbulent. The first measure enacted by the returning emir and his legitimate government of Kuwait was the imposition of martial law. Clearly the entire country was a war zone, but the biggest concerns involved mob violence against non-Kuwaitis, a segment of the prewar population that was almost universally believed to have collaborated with the occupying Iraqis.

This is not to suggest that the Kuwaiti government was not otherwise interested in dealing with collaborators. Perhaps because the entire government had spent the war in exile, it took this opportunity to reestablish its standing as a defender of all things Kuwaiti. Military tribunals, which in prewar times had only had jurisdiction over military personnel, were quickly set up and trials were conducted apace for those suspected of collaboration. Before martial law was ended in midsummer 1991, almost six thousand were arrested on charges of collaboration, many of whom were held for lengthy periods before being released without ever facing trial.

The Martial Law Court existed only in 1991. It was replaced by the Special State Security Court, which was abolished only in 1995. During the period of martial law, around three hundred people were tried for collaboration, a felony under Kuwaiti law, in one of these courts, but many more alleged collaborators were still in custody 18 months later awaiting trial. Besides Kuwaitis, most of the alleged collaborators were Palestinian and Syrian nationals.

Of those actually tried, 115 were convicted, about a quarter of whom were sentenced to death for their wartime actions. At the time, several nongovernmental organizations, most notably Amnesty International, determined that these trials were not judicially fair. The primary criticism involved the lack of appeal afforded to those convicted by the courts. Following criticism from around the world of what was perceived to be a case of serious violation of human rights, the Kuwaiti government later commuted those sentences to life imprisonment. That adequate protection of basic civil rights was lacking is now generally conceded, but questions also remain about how many confessions had been obtained through torture or other coercive measures. Some reports suggest that as many as four dozen non-Kuwaitis died while in the physical custody of Kuwaiti military or government authorities.

These postwar conditions had an immediate impact on the workforce available to rebuild Kuwait. For example, prior to the war, around four hundred thousand Palestinians lived and worked in Kuwait. When the Palestinian Authority elected to support Iraq's invasion of Kuwait, the stage was set for retaliation against those Palestinians regardless of their personal feelings about the matter. In the immediate aftermath of the war, facing suspicion of collaboration, as well as overt discrimination in the workplace, the Palestinians left in Kuwait were estimated at about thirty thousand. The number of other non-Kuwaiti nationals also dipped markedly.

NATIONAL SECURITY

In the area of national defense, almost immediately after liberation the restored Kuwaiti government began to take the necessary measures to ensure the country's security. These measures were hastened by the scheduled rapid departure of American and British troops. Toward the end of 1991, the GCC, at the formal behest of Oman, considered the feasibility of establishing a standing joint military command, one hundred thousand strong, to defend against Iraqi or Iranian aggression. Though the recommendation, sometimes referred to as the Damascus Agreement since that was the location of the session, was serious, the GCC member states quickly ruled out the maintenance of such a force as being well beyond the capabilities of their limited military personnel strength, and also expressed concern at having Syrian or Egyptian troops stationed in the Arabian Gulf region for an undefined length of time. Both Egypt and Syria subsequently offered to formalize a defensive arrangement directly with Kuwait to arrange for the country's protection, but Kuwaiti statesmen deemed these promises inadequate under the circumstances. In the absence of a unified Arab defensive posture in the Arabian Gulf, Kuwait realized it would have to look elsewhere for help.

The United States and Great Britain independently worked bilaterally with Kuwaiti military officials to assess the continued threat posed by Saddam Hussein's Iraq, and also to hammer out both short- and long-term defense strategies to deter or defeat that threat. Defense agreements were quickly signed with the United States, Great Britain, and France. Kuwaiti strategists were adamant that only a massive level of Western military equipment and training could prevent or preclude another Iraqi invasion in the near future. A survey of the overall condition of the Kuwaiti military pointed up the wisdom of this approach. While the Kuwaiti army, naval force, air force, and coast guard had all fought well in the liberation of their country, they were far from ready to maintain Kuwait's security without significant outside assistance.

The popular discontent of the country was also reflected inside Kuwait's military establishment. Military policies that had failed to make the country defensible in the face of Iraqi aggression were roundly criticized, and the senior officers who had championed the failed approach were seen as a detriment to the effective rebuilding of a strong Kuwaiti defense. There were also serious morale issues among military personnel that again paralleled the schism within the overall population. Those who had fought and those who had sat out the war in Iraqi prisoner of war camps were not likely to easily reconcile their differences at a time when unity of purpose was a prerequisite for progress. A group of reform-minded midgrade officers, known collectively as the Second of August Movement, petitioned Jaber III to overhaul the military's hierarchy. The situation quickly came to a head, the emir faced the issue head on, and by the end of summer 1991, a large number of senior military officers were forced into retirement to clear the decks of discontent and obstacles. The postwar Kuwaiti military was now ready to move forward.

In September 1991, Kuwait inked a 10-year defense pact with the United States. Though the agreement did not call for the permanent stationing of American troops in Kuwait, it did call for the transfer of massive amounts of defense equipment and materials. Indeed, Kuwait needed so much military help that it went on to sign 10-year defense agreements, albeit more limited in scale, with Great Britain and France, as well. Moreover, Kuwaiti naval forces continued to be equipped and trained by Germany. Through the deal, the United States received the facilities needed to pre-position its own defense materiel in case of further action in and around the Arabian Gulf. Training of Kuwaiti military forces by teams of American and British officers began almost immediately under these new defense agreements.

Because of the top priority placed on military affairs, by early 1992, the Kuwaiti army would once again occupy its refitted barracks, the main naval base was back in action, and the Kuwaiti air force would soon move from its temporary home at a civilian airfield back to its own combat-hardened facilities around the capital. The Kuwaiti army at this time carried around eight thousand troops on its muster rolls, organized into four understrength mechanized or armored brigades, an artillery brigade, and a reserve brigade. In trade for oil, Kuwait's armored units received two hundred aged M-84 tanks from Yugoslavia while awaiting new equipment from the United States and Great Britain. The Kuwaiti air force had 34 combat aircraft and 12 helicopters. The Kuwaiti naval force was down to around five hundred men and the two missile craft that had survived the war.

In an address to the American people televised nationwide on February 27, 1991, President Bush announced, "Kuwait is liberated." At that point in time, and throughout the remainder of 1991, it was certain that the coalition's first two military objectives had been met, and it was widely believed that the third and fourth objectives—destruction of the Republican Guard and elimination of Iraqi WMD capabilities—had also been accomplished. Months later, when it became clear that the initial declaration of complete victory had been overly optimistic, it was too late to do anything about it. More than 10 years of "cold war" would ensue with Iraq, and Kuwait would be in no position to remain out of the crossfire. The continuing presence of American troops within Kuwait, even in relatively small numbers, while offering much-wanted security from further Iraqi aggression, would soon begin to play a role in Kuwait domestic politics in the postwar era.

8

Reconstruction (1992–1999)

As 1991 drew to a close, the dust from the war had largely settled, and the more than seven hundred oil fires set by the Iraqis were finally extinguished. Kuwaitis were finally able to look at their country and begin to make decisions regarding the nation's future. Kuwait faced a number of huge national problems. The country's ability to defend its sovereignty had to be overhauled and rebuilt almost from the ground up. That a belligerent Saddam Hussein was still in power in Iraq made the timing of the undertaking all the more critical. Kuwait needed to forge new international alliances that accomplished three goals: ensure national survival, reward friends, and punish enemies. The massive issue of domestic demographics, the presence of and overreliance on foreigners inside Kuwait, had to be resolved. The Kuwaiti social fabric had long required mending. Finally, Kuwaitis needed to effectively confront long-standing social and political inequities that now threatened to tear the nation's social fabric in the postwar period. Only when these collective goals were accomplished could reconstruction be considered complete.

In facing this daunting list of national goals, Kuwait had numerous disadvantages that hindered success: the country was strapped for cash, the vital oil sector was nonfunctional, and the workforce was depleted. And, as noted, Saddam Hussein was still in power. Lastly, the Kuwaiti people would not tolerate the prewar status quo. Fortunately, Kuwait had several advantages working in its favor. The vast majority of Kuwait's prewar petroleum reserves, which had been estimated at 100 million bpd, were still on hand, ready to be refined and sold. The country held extensive overseas investments and other reserves. Kuwait's ties to the United States were stronger than ever. In the postwar period, the sense of Kuwaiti national identity grew more powerful by the day, at the same time that the Kuwaiti sense of Arab brotherhood was diminishing. Moreover, the Kuwaiti people and their government now held a "never again" mentality, a refusal to ever make mistakes similar to those that had resulted in invasion and occupation.

INFRASTRUCTURE

A survey of Kuwait's oil infrastructure highlighted a grim reality for those planning Kuwait's postwar recovery. As a result of coalition bombing and, especially, Iraqi vandalism, oil pipelines had been cut, pumping stations had been demolished, refineries had been stripped of machinery, and almost every petroleum-related physical asset had been damaged or diminished in a measurable fashion. Once the seven hundred oil fires were extinguished, which had taken months and cost more than $1 billion, the costs of additional repair of war damage to Kuwait's oil facilities was estimated at slightly more than $5 billion. That figure is a little deceiving, however, because, rather than merely restoring the oil infrastructure, the Kuwaitis took the opportunity to modernize many of the existing facilities. Thus, while most of the money went to repairs, some paid for improvements. New oil wells had to be drilled to replace 19 older wells that either had been totally destroyed or, after the engineering survey, were deemed to be beyond economical repair.

Specific numbers are hard to find. Kuwait's oil minister offered a budget showing $1.5 billion spent in putting out the fires and projecting $8 billion–$10 billion to repair the rest of the damage. Kuwait's National Bank estimated repairs to the oil infrastructure at $6.5 billion through 1995. The same is true when discussing overall costs of Kuwait's reconstruction. Some estimates for all reconstruction including oil were as high as $100 billion, but a few were as low as $20 billion–$25 billion. Regardless of the eventual cost, it was the job of the government to determine whence those funds would come. Kuwait had already tapped into its cash reserves to help pay to run the government while in exile during Iraqi occupation and, especially, to cover the war-related expenses of Kuwait's coalition partners. While more could come from overseas investments, Kuwaitis understood the long-term negative implications of doing so. The alternative was to restore the petroleum facilities and turn on the gas pump to pay for as much of reconstruction as possible.

By making this the top recovery-related priority, Kuwait was able to commence production of crude oil in 1992, though at reduced levels compared with before the invasion. To make up for some of the difference, Kuwait dipped into its strategic oil reserves, which held perhaps as much as 90 billion barrels of oil at liberation. While this had long-term ramifications that would eventually need to be addressed, over the short term it immediately put oil money to work funding Kuwait's reconstruction. Just prior to the invasion, Kuwait had been refining about seven hundred thousand bpd. At liberation, refinery output was essentially zero. By dipping into crude oil reserves, Kuwait was able to restore its refining capacity and was producing more than three hundred thousand bpd in its three prewar refineries. Going into 1993, Kuwait had already met prewar production levels and went on to exceed the prewar levels that next year. The production level went up so steadily that the Kuwaiti government optimistically planned to boost overall production to 2 million bpd, possibly higher. Thereafter, the only constraints on Kuwaiti production were the production limits set by OPEC. In 1994, the OPEC quota for Kuwait was set at 2 million bpd.

By 1993, oil once again accounted for nine-tenths of Kuwait's exports. The primary markets for Kuwaiti oil were, in descending order, Japan, the Netherlands, the United States, and Pakistan. The country's economy showed a growth rate of 35 percent for 1993. This is a phenomenal accomplishment that reflects the priority that the Kuwaitis placed on rebuilding and also an indication of the difference that readily available capital can make.

While exports exceeded $11 billion, imports for the tiny nation were also very high in 1993. Kuwait spent more than $6.5 billion on food, construction materials and equipment, personal automobiles, and clothing. The majority of that business went to the United States. Some Kuwait watchers had opined that the invasion and occupation had all but destroyed Kuwait as a country and, moreover, that the Kuwaiti people would show no interest in rebuilding. The relatively high level of imports clearly indicates that the Kuwaiti people were eager to return their lives to normal. The Kuwaiti government definitely did all in its power to restore public confidence in the nation and its future prospects.

Rebuilding of transportation and telecommunications infrastructures, both badly damaged by the war, was almost as high as oil facilities on the national priority list. Transportation came first because it was a prerequisite for bringing in the equipment necessary to make all the needed repairs to every other area of the economy. Major repairs had to be made to Kuwait International Airport before it was ready to resume international flights. The airport, which had last been upgraded and expanded in 1979, was back in full operation by 1992. Kuwait's roadways were not so quickly or easily repaired.

Kuwait's prewar highway system had been first rate. The system itself consisted of almost four thousand kilometers of road, with three-quarters being fully paved. Postwar, however, bombed bridges needed to be replaced and in some cases relocated. Many major roadways were crumbling, not having been built to handle the amount of traffic they received from heavy armored vehicles over the past year. Some sections were so badly deteriorated that they could not handle additional traffic of heavy construction equipment. Once the local production of cement was restored, however, Kuwait could begin to meet the road-building needs around the country.

Focus was on rebuilding roads in and to the south of Kuwait City. This hastened restoration of the connection with industrial and marine facilities. It also delayed repairing the roadways the Iraqis had used to blitz the country in 1990. Knowing the Iraqis were still a threat, Kuwaiti planners saw no reason to facilitate another Iraqi invasion before Kuwait's military was ready to defend the country. As roads were repaired and Kuwaitis returned to their private driving habits, the Kuwaiti government publicly discussed in May 1992 the possibility of privatizing Kuwait's gas stations, in part to encourage entrepreneurship and also to speed recovery. Not said, but clearly a factor in the decision to privatize, was the additional money this move was expected to bring into public coffers.

Kuwait's telecommunications system, also top-notch prior to the war, was in dire straits as reconstruction began. Several of the coaxial cables that had connected Kuwait to its neighbors had been cut. Repairs were completed to most cables by the end of 1992, but the cable to Iraq took longer to repair. Before the war, Kuwait had four ground satellite stations that had been tied into Arabsat and Intelsat. All four were inoperative following coalition attacks. It took more than a year to make these systems fully operational, which meant that regional television signals and international phone calls were disrupted in the meantime. As it had done with gas stations, and likely for similar reasons, the government announced its intention to privatize parts of the telecommunications network, a move that some experts estimated would bring in as much as $1 billion in new revenues.

Kuwait's entire system of banking was also high on the priority list for repair or overhaul. In late 1991, additional steps were taken to alleviate the lingering negative effects of the prewar Souk al-Manakh stock market failure. The government purchased the entire debt load directly associated with the crash, as well as the entire domestic debt load. The total cost of this debt relief was estimated at $20 billion. This included more than $1 billion in consumer loans and more than $3 billion in loans for housing.

With those measures already taken and the physical damage from the war to banking facilities considered to be minimal, the government now believed it had a strong foundation on which to base the nation's financial recovery. Kuwait's National Bank, headed by an Al-Sabah family member, had felt almost no effect from the war, largely since it had handled the finances of the government in exile from Saudi Arabia. The rest of Kuwait's banks had been less lucky but still looked to be solid. Toward the end of 1992, however, additional internal accounting discrepancies were identified. If not addressed immediately and in a forthright manner, these irregularities threatened a financial scandal on the scale of the Souk al-Manakh disaster. At a time when the government was doing all it could to restore the people's confidence, swift action was called for. The government again dipped into its investment portfolio to cover losses, while visible changes in high-ranking personnel indicated that accountability had been fixed. At that point, Kuwait's bankers were ready to look at consolidation, and serious consideration was given to orchestrating bank mergers to solidify Kuwait's finances.

Additional government actions to alleviate the impact of the war on its citizens included a cash payment to every Kuwaiti family that had remained in the country during the Iraqi occupation. The government, which employed more Kuwaitis than any other company in the nation, then paid back salaries to all public employees for the duration of the occupation. Government salaries were raised for all employees. Finally, in mid-1992, the costs for all government-provided utilities, such as electricity, water, and phone service, that had been provided during occupation were also waived. While this new debt was a huge burden for the government, the debt relief afforded to the population went a long way toward dispelling any possible qualms about rebuilding the country.

The one sector of Kuwait's economy that needed no help to recover was trade. Especially with the debt relief provided by the government, Kuwaitis spent lavishly on themselves and their homes. Moreover, all personal property that had been destroyed or stolen by the Iraqis had to be replaced. Virtually all of these goods came from overseas, and Kuwait's merchant families reaped the benefits of this frenzy of buying. Though of short duration, this buying spree provided a much-needed boost of money and enthusiasm to propel the local economy through the rest of the reconstruction era. A related benefit to Kuwait's local economy came from a law enacted in July 1992 that required foreign companies that won major Kuwaiti government contracts to invest 30 percent of the contract's value inside Kuwait.

The single biggest expense in the reconstruction period was not in payments for repair or for new construction. It was payment on the debts that the Kuwaiti government incurred to coalition partners that helped liberate the country, as well as international borrowing that continued after the war. For example, in late 1991, Kuwait took out a $5 billion loan on the international market, the single biggest loan in the nation's history. Above and beyond all of the new expenses, the cost of this debt was estimated to be at least $20 billion, and possibly as much as $37 billion. Payments on this debt were expected to account for approximately 30 percent of all government spending in 1993. With all other revenues at half their prewar levels, this new expense forced the government to cut into its overseas investment portfolio yet again, specifically the Fund for Future Generations and the General Reserve Fund. A reliable Western financial institution estimated that Kuwait had spent about $30 billion of its investment portfolio, roughly 30 percent of its preinvasion value, during 1992 alone.

POLITICAL DEVELOPMENTS

After the euphoria of liberation wore off, the political environment of Kuwait during reconstruction can only be described as stormy. The emir's late return to the country still did not sit well with those Kuwaitis who had remained in the country under Iraqi occupation. The temporary period of lawlessness followed by the brief experience of martial law might have dampened open dissent with the government, but probably just pushed popular discontent off the streets and into the homes of everyday Kuwaitis. Kuwait's security apparatus collected the many guns left behind by the invasion, though many Kuwaitis were less than willing to give up their weapons, and the streets were again peaceful. Once martial law was rescinded, it was clear that Kuwaitis would once again grow more vocal in their complaints about and demands of their government. The seeds of these circumstances had been planted a year earlier.

While Kuwait was under Iraqi occupation, the emir and his government had been in exile in Saudi Arabia along with thousands of other Kuwaiti citizens. In October 1990, Jaber III had met with more than a thousand members of the prewar opposition who had originally been behind the Constitution Movement. He sought their support for the restoration of his throne. They sought promises of widespread constitutional reforms once the country was liberated. These opposition leaders also made clear that they expected to see popular participation in the governing process dramatically enhanced. For his part, Jaber III swore that his restoration would bring with it political liberalization.

When those members of the Constitution Movement returned to Kuwait after liberation, however, they quickly discovered that their popular support had dwindled. A new faction, consisting of the leaders of the Kuwaiti resistance movement who had remained in Kuwait, now had popular sentiment on its side. Those who had resisted had little use for those who had spent the war in luxurious exile. Almost immediately a squabble ensued between these groups, which soon subdivided into distinct political units. The Democratic Forum included many of those who had supported the original Constitution Movement before the war and who saw the struggle in secular terms. The rest of the opposition divided along religious lines. Sunni opposition splintered into the Islamic Constitutional Movement and the Islamic Parliamentarian

Alliance. The Shiite opposition formed in the National Islamic Coalition. Though political parties were forbidden by law in Kuwait, these were all essentially political parties, and the Democratic Forum openly declared itself a party contrary to standing law.

It has been suggested by some observers that had the emir returned to Kuwait immediately after liberation, while the thrill of liberation still filled the average Kuwaiti, he might have been able to unify the country in short order. The emir did not return immediately, however, and during the short delay before his return, the political situation hardened and the emir's moral authority waned. The only thing on which the opposition could agree was that any return to Al-Sabah authoritarian rule, however benevolent it had been in the past, had to be tempered by democratic reforms. Jaber III was forced to accede by calling for elections the following October (1992) for the National Assembly.

In the interim, the handpicked cabinet or national council would convene and continue to govern Kuwait's reconstruction. Once a new National Assembly was elected, this group would be disbanded. Of note, while Al-Sabah family members filled all of the key posts in this interim body, representatives from the Salem branch of the family were more prominent than members of the ruling Jaber branch. Key shifts in personnel included new ministers of foreign affairs, finance, and defense, though the new ministers generally were already cabinet members who moved up to these more powerful slots.

Also in early 1991, looking ahead to the run-up to the first crucial national election, the various opposition parties united briefly in calling for a free and uncensored press. The Kuwaiti constitution, while recognizing every citizen's freedom of opinion, specifically placed legal limits on that freedom. The opposition wanted those legal limits eased or removed entirely. In January 1992, the government removed the censorship that had existed since liberation, but that only restored the prewar norms of government oversight of the press. For practical purposes, the Kuwait News Agency (KUNA) was directly overseen by the Ministry of Information. Three radio stations and one television station were also government run. There were seven daily newspapers and a handful of weekly papers in Kuwait. All were privately owned, but subject to the same restrictions placed on all journalists, with possible sanctions for strong political criticism of the government or any criticism of the royal family.

ELECTION OF THE NATIONAL ASSEMBLY

As the emir had directed and the constitution had provided, elections for a new National Assembly were held on October 5, 1992. In all, seven major political factions (parties still being technically banned) ran candidates for the available seats, though by far the largest of the new organizations were the

Islamic Constitutional Movement (Sunni), the Democratic Forum, the Islamic Parliamentarian Alliance (Sunni), and the National Islamic Coalition (Shiite). Overall, the elections were peaceful. Opposition candidates won two-thirds of the assembly's 50 seats. Pro-government politicians took the remaining third of available seats. Nineteen of the 50 total seats were now held by Islamic candidates, a showing roughly double of the posts held in the prewar National Assembly. Of note, only one-third of the newly elected assembly members had served in the National Assembly previously.

Thus, while the people were represented in the new deliberative body to a degree never before seen and, beyond the widely held view that democracy needed to be expanded, the disparity of positions on key political and social issues was bound to cause waves. The schism between opposition and government was the widest it had been. Moreover, some assemblymen were elected to enact a return to Shariah law, while others had openly advocated suffrage for women. Some in the assembly were focused solely on fixing blame for the invasion; others sought to provide oversight of future expenditures to ensure reconstruction dollars were being spent wisely. Given these many deep political differences and disparate goals, this was bound to be a contentious National Assembly.

Shortly after the October elections, the emir's new cabinet was formed. The new cabinet held fewer Al-Sabah family members than any previous cabinet. Moreover, opposition politicians held 6 of the 16 cabinet positions, clearly mirroring the new reality of postwar Kuwaiti politics. That said, the key ministerial posts—for example, that of foreign affairs—were still firmly held by the Al-Sabah or their allies. The balance of power in the cabinet between the family's two branches, Jaber and Salem, was also restored for the moment.

After the National Assembly convened, things settled down somewhat for Kuwait as popular attention was diverted to reconstruction of the country as a whole. The efforts made by the government to relieve individual debt went a long way in appeasing the opposition's popular base. The National Assembly proceeded to review those decrees that the emir had instituted in its absence, as was the assembly's constitutional right. Other than that, only minor squabbles periodically popped up in the political realm over the short term. Massive social changes were sweeping Kuwait, however.

SOCIAL DEVELOPMENTS

The government was determined to reduce Kuwait's dependence on foreigners, especially Palestinians and others who could not be relied on to remain loyal to their adopted home in the event of another crisis like the Iraqi invasion. In May 1991, the government openly encouraged all refugees to return, as long as they were Kuwaiti citizens, that is. Nonnationals had a much more difficult time getting back into the country, regardless of how long they had lived there in the past. Palestinians had the hardest time of all nationalities, due largely to the support thrown to Saddam Hussein by the Palestinian Authority. This had an immediate negative impact on the restoration of some services since foreigners had held so many important positions throughout Kuwait's economy, medical system, and educational system. Moreover, non-nationals who had stayed behind during the Iraqi occupation were often suspected of collaboration, regardless of evidence to the contrary. Again, it was the Palestinians who experienced the most difficulty.

Once brought into the judicial system as suspects, these non-Kuwaitis had a very difficult time indeed. A large number of human rights abuses, such as unlawful arrest, imprisonment, torture, and even murder by vigilante groups, were documented by international observers such as Amnesty International. Quite a few non-Kuwaitis were convicted of collaboration in high-profile trials and then sentenced to death. Following an international uproar, many of those sentences were commuted by higher courts or by the emir. By late 1992, however, most observers agreed that Kuwait's judicial system once again met international standards of justice, though the Special State Security Court would not be officially abolished until 1995.

In March 1992, Kuwait's National Bank estimated the country's total population at just over 1.1 million people. This was roughly one-half of Kuwait's total prewar population, which had been about 2.3 million. In 1992, however, slightly more than one-half of the population consisted of Kuwaiti citizens, while before the war, Kuwaiti nationals made up only about a quarter of the total. The government intended to maintain this new ratio and enacted legislation to keep the presence of non-Kuwaiti workers to less than 50 percent of the total population in the future.

At the same time, the government announced plans to manage the nonnative population so that no one nationality represented more than 10 percent of Kuwait's overall population. Generally this meant fewer Arabs and more Asians. Again, this had the largest impact on Palestinians in Kuwait. When the purge of foreigners was completed, about 30,000 Palestinians were left in Kuwait, though the prewar Palestinian population had been estimated at more than 400,000. Again, while popular politically, and perhaps necessary socially, this move had an immediate negative effect on Kuwait's economy, education, and health care fields. Kuwait's banks, schools, and hospitals had a very difficult time filling the many low-skill, low-pay positions that day-to-day operations demanded. Kuwait's domestic recovery was slowed at a commensurate rate, though Kuwait's comprehensive school system was back in operation by September 1991, albeit at reduced student capacity.

New regulations were put in place in early 1992 to restrict the hiring of foreigners as domestic workers. Visa regulations were enacted that limited the ability of the dependents of many lower-paid nonnationals to get into the country. To instill a degree of fairness to the new immigration policy, the government set aside more than $8 million to cover termination payments to non-Kuwaitis who lost their jobs as a result of this new policy. This huge outlay was more than offset by the immediate savings to be garnered from not having to provide government services to hundreds of thousands of non-Kuwaitis, as had been the case before the invasion.

The Kuwaiti government recognized, however, that the same factors that had driven the need for workers before the war were still operative in the postwar era. If nonnationals were not to fill those positions, then Kuwaitis would have to do so. Moreover, it would take several years, at a minimum, to train Kuwaitis to fill these jobs, and it might even take multiple generations. The government quickly enacted legislation to pay a $14,000 lump sum to Kuwaiti men on their wedding day. This was intended to encourage both marriage and large families.

Kuwaitis also understood that there was a huge, essentially untapped pool of workers readily available to fill the void: Kuwait's female population. Throughout the reconstruction period the subject was debated but never resolved. In mid-1999, Jaber III arbitrarily decreed that Kuwaiti women would have the right to vote in the next election for the National Assembly, scheduled to take place in 2003. The emir also made it legal for women to serve in the cabinet. Later that same year, however, the National Assembly overruled the emir and withdrew these new women's rights. The opposition to these progressive moves was based partly on traditional Islamic values and partly on the fact that the emir had made his decree while the National Assembly was convened, thereby depriving the assembly of its constitutional right to oversee legislative actions. As will be seen in the next chapter, Kuwaitis to this very day continue to grapple politically, socially, and religiously not only with the roles of women in Kuwait, but also with their basic civil rights in the future.

NATIONAL DEFENSE

In 1992, Kuwait began to reestablish its national defense. Defense agreements were signed in 1991 with the United States and Great Britain, and in 1992 with France. These agreements provided much-needed assurance, as well as equipment and training. For the United States, the agreements offered vital port access and pre-positioning of equipment and spare parts, all of which would be needed should the United States have to intervene again in the Arabian Gulf region. The United States established the Office of Military Cooperation in Kuwait City to both manage foreign military sales of American hardware and track defense-related sales from commercial U.S. sources.

Prior to the war, Kuwait had ordered more than three dozen F/A-18 Hornet fighter-bombers from the United States. Delivery of those combat aircraft was expedited, and Kuwaiti pilots began to train on the new warplanes in 1992. Other major purchases from the United States included several batteries of state-of-the-art Patriot antiaircraft missiles, several batteries of Hawk antiaircraft missiles, and the M-1A2 main battle tank. Kuwait's naval force looked to Germany to replace its small flotilla of missile corvettes. The Kuwaiti military paid for much of the initial equipment in hard currency, estimated at about $9 billion for fiscal year 1992 alone.

By 1993, as final repairs were made to Kuwait's air and naval bases, the Kuwaiti defense forces possessed a credible defense capability if based solely on military equipment. Having the trained personnel to operate that equipment and aggressively defend the country, however, would take longer. On paper, the Kuwaiti military was planned to reach a postwar strength of 30,000 personnel. Early in the reconstruction period, however, this did not look achievable. Once thousands of bidun were removed from the ranks, there was serious doubt that the military could grow to the necessary size. For example, with the bidun removed, Kuwait's naval force was down to only 500 personnel in 1992. By 1993, the combined naval force and coast guard still only numbered about twelve hundred personnel. The air force stood at about 2500. The army contained between nine thousand and ten thousand personnel of all ranks.

Kuwaiti officials realized that even an improved system of conscription, with far fewer possible exemptions, could not make up the difference, especially when eligible Kuwaiti men had so many more financially rewarding options available to them across the economy. The defense forces were left with two options: readmit nonnationals to the military or begin to tap the large pool of Kuwaiti females. A protocol was put in place to screen bidun for loyalty, following which limited numbers were allowed to serve in the army. Some bidun were even promised Kuwaiti citizenship in return for an extended period of loyal service. At the same time, a small number of Kuwaiti women were brought in for training and limited assignment to short-term support positions within the army and air force. Greater employment of women would require a national consensus, which did not exist in the middle of the 1990s.

The Kuwaiti military stepped up its international training exercises, especially with the U.S. military forces in the Arabian Gulf. This was done not only to enhance the readiness of Kuwaiti forces, but also to send an unmistakable message to Iraq, which continued to act provocatively just across Kuwait's largely indefensible border to the north. Kuwait plans to build an electronic fence and defensive minefield along the border were laid, but the overall long-term efficacy of these measures was hotly debated. At best, these measures would reduce infiltration, but probably never preclude Iraqi assault.

Thousands of American troops came to Kuwait for joint military training in August 1992 and were back again in late 1994. This second "training" deployment had been sparked by a huge Iraqi "exercise" in which armored forces had massed along the border with Kuwait in October. In November, the Iraqi government formally recognized the international boundaries set by the United Nations in Security Council Resolutions 773 and 883, which helped defuse the tense situation. Despite this de-escalation, however, the long-term threat of a rearmed Saddam Hussein certainly kept Kuwaiti strategists awake at night throughout the decade.

To complement the aggressive steps taken to strengthen its military, Kuwait also pulled out all the stops in its diplomatic efforts. Kuwait actively courted permanent members of the United Nations Security Council, even Russia and China. Kuwait also used large reconstruction contracts, both military and commercial, to increase the odds of future support by politically powerful nations. While talks went on apace with GCC countries about unifying air defense, an unwillingness to turn over strategic responsibilities for national airspace, even to friendly Arab neighbors, kept real progress from being made. The GCC held discussions about developing a joint weapons production industry to reduce dependence on Western governments, but these talks also garnered little support among the Gulf countries and made minimal progress. The Damascus Agreement, which had provided for Egyptian and Syrian forces to defend Kuwait, had never gotten off the ground. On paper, both Syria and Egypt were still obligated to do so, but no one expected it to ever happen, and, moreover, the Kuwaitis had no intention of requesting such intervention by any nations other than the United States and, possibly, Great Britain.

As a general rule, then, during the era of reconstruction, Kuwait rewarded those nations that had supported it through liberation. For example, in 1993 Kuwait stopped complying with several aspects of the long-standing Arab boycott of the state of Israel, which further increased Kuwaiti business with U.S. firms that had previously worked with Israel. Conversely, by direction of the national council in June 1992, Kuwait did what it could to punish those countries that had supported Iraq, including Cuba, Jordan, Sudan, Yemen, and the Palestinian Authority, by withholding economic aid that, in the past, had been given freely and without strings attached.

From the focused steps taken to reestablish national defense, and from analysis of Kuwaiti foreign policy, two things become apparent. First, the Kuwaitis viewed national security as their top priority bar none. Saddam Hussein's Iraq was seen as the most immediate threat, but a radical Iran was also threatening to Kuwait, even if only in the domestic sphere. Second, it is clear that Kuwait believed, correctly, that it would be incapable of defending itself. Only an incredibly close relationship with the United States could provide the tiny country with the peace of mind its people craved as the century drew to a close.

9

Kuwait Today (2000–)

Several key developments occurred during the first years of the twenty-first century that have had, and will continue to have, a powerful, long-term impact on Kuwait and the Kuwaiti people. One event was external and one was internal. First was the forceful removal of Saddam Hussein from power ordered by President George W. Bush in 2003. Overall, the long-standing Iraqi threat to reinvade Kuwait was removed. Continuing instability inside Iraq, including sectarian violence, has substituted an uncertain future for a Kuwait that would be profoundly affected by either civil war in or partitioning of Iraq. Internally, the continuing move toward democratization in general, and in particular the major political and civil rights strides made by women in Kuwait, hold momentous potential to reshape the desert emirate. This final chapter provides a snapshot of the country in the first decade of the twenty-first century and identifies some of the likely developments expected in the future.

ECONOMY

Kuwait's dynamic economy continues to grow at an admirable rate, with estimates between 5 and 7 percent for recent years. Inflation hovers around 2 percent annually. The government annually invests a fixed amount of 8 percent of the GDP. Annual purchasing power is more than $22,000 per capita, among the highest in the world. The total labor pool is around 1.5 million people, but about 80 percent of those workers are not Kuwaiti citizens. The service industry, which employs almost 40 percent of the workforce, supports the tourist industry and provides domestic labor in most Kuwaiti homes. Over 60 percent of Kuwait's workforce is employed in oil-related labor. Kuwait's economy is based almost entirely on petroleum, which provides just under half of Kuwait's annual income, the rest coming from strategic overseas investments. The Kuwaiti dinar, closely pegged to the fluctuating values of the U.S. dollar and several other international currencies, remains one of the highest-rated currencies in the entire world.

Kuwait's laborers have a constitutional right to join a union, but there are practical limits imposed on this right. Kuwait recognizes only one union for every trade, and places restrictions on how unions may be organized and operated. About 1 in 20, or 5 percent, of Kuwait's laborers are members of unions. Under the direct supervision of the Ministry of Social Affairs and Labor, Kuwait's labor law also puts limits on the rights of unionized workers to strike. Arbitration is mandatory by law, so strikes are exceedingly rare in Kuwait, and of short duration when they do occur. Kuwait's oil industry, of vital interest to the government, is not covered under the same labor laws that cover the rest of Kuwait's economy.

Kuwait's petroleum industry is government owned and generally abides by OPEC production limits. Daily petroleum production fluctuates around 2–2.5 million bpd, and exports around 2 million bpd. Kuwait's proven oil reserves are more than 95 billion barrels, with 77 billion barrels deemed fully recoverable. Annual natural gas production and domestic consumption are around 9 million cubic meters, with proven reserves at more than 1.5 trillion cubic meters. Almost 800 kilometers of pipeline move crude and refined oil and natural gas.

Kuwait's national oil industry is managed through its parent corporation, KPC, which directly oversees international marketing. KPC is further subdivided into tailored units, such as the KOC, which handles exploration; the KNPC, which directs refinery operations; and the PIC, which covers petrochemical production. Kuwait's leading export partners, in descending order, are Japan, South Korea, the United States, Singapore, and Taiwan. Kuwait's imports of food, clothing, and automobiles are purchased primarily from the United States, Germany, and Japan, though the United Kingdom, Saudi Arabia, France, and China have sent a growing amount of goods to Kuwait in recent years.

Local agriculture barely exists in modern Kuwait at the moment, though expensive research and long-range investment in hydroponics may result in an increase in importance for this sector of the economy. Currently only about 1 percent of Kuwait's territory is arable. This is why most of Kuwait's food must be imported. Another reason is the lack of fresh water. While Kuwait has the largest and most modern desalinization facilities in the world, they meet only the needs of the population and the oil industry. There is little potable water left over for agriculture. Kuwait continues to grapple with a number of environmental issues, with acute desertification and pollution of air and water at the top of the list.

Kuwait's fishing industry provides some locally produced food, but the contribution is tiny when compared with what it was early in the twentieth century, when seafaring was the country's largest employer. Other than oil drilling and refining, Kuwait's other industries include petrochemicals, cement, and fertilizers. The tourist industry, devastated by the Iraqi invasion, has come back slowly. Today Kuwait boasts 15 five-star hotel resorts that continue to attract visitors from around the world.

Kuwait's highways are top notch, and its paved road system is already 50 percent longer than when reconstruction began in the early 1990s. While there are engineering concerns with the state of many bridges, these roadways are capable of supporting population and industrial growth in the foreseeable future. The country has seven airports and dozens of heliports. Kuwait International Airport is one of the most modern facilities in the world. Three huge seaports handle the steady stream of massive oil tankers and containerships, the lifelines that connect Kuwait to the world's most powerful economies. Kuwait's merchant marine fleet is currently 39 vessels and growing. Nineteen additional Kuwaiti-owned oceangoing vessels are registered overseas.

Kuwait's telecommunications system was completely rebuilt following liberation and now ranks as the most modern communications system in the entire region. Kuwaitis are closely connected by telephone to their neighbors and the world. Coaxial cables and microwave relays tie Kuwait to Saudi Arabia. A fiber-optic cable connects the country to Bahrain, Qatar, and the UAE. A broad spectrum of satellite downlink stations connects Kuwait to the economic and political capitals of the world. The satellite system includes three Intelsat stations, one International Marine Satellite System (Inmarsat), and one Arabsat station. Eighteen local radio stations and 13 local television stations, 4 of which are controlled by the government, backed by numerous satellite television channels, keep today's Kuwaitis abreast of world developments. Moreover, the rate of Internet usage among Kuwaitis is probably the highest in the Arab world.

Estimates of literacy for the whole population exceed 83 percent, with Kuwaiti men scoring slightly higher and Kuwaiti women scoring slightly lower than that figure. Kuwait's public education system, free to all Kuwaiti citizens, is still very dependent on foreigners to fill the ranks of teachers, but the system provides the typical Kuwaiti boy or girl with a solid education. At the university level, technical or scientific preparation for demanding jobs generally requires additional schooling overseas. This long-standing shortcoming contributes to Kuwait's continuing reliance on more non-Kuwaitis to fill top engineering and managerial positions throughout the high-tech economy.

Kuwait's comprehensive cradle-to-grave health care system provides Kuwaiti citizens with some of the finest medical treatment in the world. Any care or expertise that Kuwait's state-of-the-art hospitals cannot provide is accomplished instead by sending Kuwaitis to where that treatment can be had. From prenatal care to hospice care for the elderly, today's Kuwaitis enjoy medical care that would have been unimaginable only a few generations ago, before oil wealth forever changed the emirate. Health care for non-Kuwaitis, however, lags behind what citizens receive. Kuwait's level of care, indeed all social services provided to nonnationals, requires serious attention. Until the disparity in the welfare system is effectively resolved, half of Kuwait's population will continue to harbor some degree of resentment toward the country and its ruling family.

SOCIETY

In 2005, the latest year for which official figures are available, Kuwait's population stood at just over 2.3 million people, though almost 1.3 million do not hold Kuwaiti citizenship. The estimates for 2006 are almost 2.9 million people. The country's population growth rate of 3.4 percent does not adequately reflect the nation's birthrate. This is because the figure also includes the many non-Kuwaitis who continue to flock to the country seeking employment. Overall, males outnumber females by a ratio of around 3:2. Infant mortality is low at just under 1 percent. Life expectancy is high at 77 years overall, with males at 76 years and females averaging 78 years. The median age is 26. Kuwaitis make up 45 percent of the total population, other Arabs 35 percent, Asians 9 percent, and Iranians 4 percent. The remainder comes from a broad range of ethnic groups. Arabic is the official language, but English is widely spoken in Kuwait's economy, if not routinely in Kuwaiti homes.

As is common throughout the Arab world, Kuwaitis take great pride in their hospitality. Though gender segregation remains the norm, Kuwaitis are eager to bring visitors into their homes. In that, today's Kuwaitis are identical to their forebears. Where today's Kuwaitis differ from the people of Kuwait only a century ago is in sophistication and technology. In 1900, Kuwait was an insular people, isolated by sand dune and sea wave from distant trading partners. Kuwait's citizens lived in a small, cozy world of their own making. Though the emirate was always affected by the actions of distant empires such as Great Britain and the Ottomans, on the day-to-day level, the average Kuwaiti was oblivious of the fact.

Nowadays, it is rare indeed to come across a Kuwaiti who has ever even sat on a camel, let alone owned a herd of the animals. Modern Kuwaitis, as status conscious as ever, are instead addicted to their automobiles. Kuwaitis drive everywhere and, at high speed, cover the country's breadth and depth in ways their nomadic ancestors would find incredible. Moreover, today's Kuwaitis are connected with the outside world to an incredible extent. Kuwait has as many cell phones as it does people, and there are almost as many computers with Internet access. Thus, contemporary Kuwaitis are a cosmopolitan people who fully realize the interdependent relationship between their own tiny but oil-rich country and the rest of the wide world.

Despite the excellent health care facilities available inside Kuwait, serious and widespread health-related problems linger from the Iraqi invasion and its aftermath that affect the mortality and morbidity rates within the Kuwaiti population. A United Nations Compensation Committee (UNCC) set up just for this purpose continues to adjudicate Kuwaiti claims against Iraq for many health-related problems. With funding by the United Nations, a team of scientists at Harvard University's School of Public Health is in the process of a long-term comprehensive research study of those effects. A sampling of five thousand Kuwaiti citizens was closely followed for 14 years as part of the intensive research. It is clear that Kuwaitis who remained in Kuwait during the occupation show markedly higher rates of mortality.

One likely cause of the increased mortality rates appears to be exposure to the smoke from the more than seven hundred oil fires set by the retreating Iraqi army. Additional contamination might also have come from the hydrocarbons and toxic heavy metals that leached into the soil from the oil lakes, as well as depleted uranium from coalition antitank munitions that were widely used during liberation. In addition to the higher mortality rates, the incidence of PTSD is also dramatically higher for those Kuwaitis who remained in the country under Iraqi occupation. Kuwait continues to document premature deaths and increased medical costs caused by the Iraqi landmines that turn up regularly today, often with tragic human consequences.

Some international critics argue that a rich country like Kuwait should not receive compensation from a poor country like present-day Iraq, especially if that compensation comes at the expense of the already financially strapped Iraqi people. Seen in isolation, this may be true, but in a global context the question takes on added long-term importance. The precedent that this sets will be important for years to come under international law. Holding Iraq accountable for having committed environmental terrorism will serve as a deterrent to other aggressor nations in the future. Until fully resolved by the United Nations, it remains uncertain how much monetary compensation, if any, will be awarded to the state of Kuwait or to individual Kuwaiti citizens.

Islam is the official state religion of Kuwait. Almost all Kuwaiti citizens are Muslims. A large majority of Kuwaitis are Sunni Muslims, though Shiites form an important minority in Kuwait. Within Kuwait, there is a sectarian division between Sunni Muslims and Shiite Muslims, because Sunnis believe that a religious leader or caliph can be elected, while Shiites hold that only true descendants of the prophet Mohamed, Islam's founder, can serve as caliphs. Kuwait's 1962 constitution openly acknowledges the role of Shariah law as a major source of legislation. Under the law, harsh sentences are provided, and have at times been applied, for journalists who criticize or ridicule Islam. In aspects of national life other than domestic politics, the country seems to be becoming more, rather than less, conservative, largely driven by traditional Islamic values. This will affect, and possibly even effect, the trend toward increasing civil and political rights for Kuwait's female population.

While Islam clearly predominates inside Kuwait, members of some recognized religions can register and practice their faiths in Kuwait. At least seven Christian churches are represented in Kuwait, though all are subject to government oversight. Kuwaiti authorities are especially vigilant to prevent proselytizing by Christian evangelicals, thereby wooing Kuwaiti citizens away from Islam. Practitioners of religions that are not recognized by the Qur'an, specifically Buddhists, Hindus, and Sikhs, can practice their faiths in the privacy of their homes, but are not allowed to erect houses of worship. Though Mormons, for example, are hindered by this restriction, the law has a disproportionate negative effect on many of the foreigners, lately drawn from East Asia rather than Arab countries.

Foreigners still make up more than half of Kuwait's population, which, from the Kuwaiti perspective, remains a serious problem. The nation attempted to rectify the situation during reconstruction, when laws were passed to prevent an overreliance on foreign labor from occurring again, but the measures were largely ineffective. The same compelling reasons for attracting and utilizing foreign labor prior to the war are still in existence today. Kuwait's oil economy requires technical training and engineering expertise that Kuwait's educational system is unable to provide. At the same time, Kuwait's service sector offers low-paying jobs that are very unattractive to Kuwaitis, who receive government benefits whether or not they work. A new wrinkle comes from the recent popularity of betting on camel racing in Kuwait. This activity draws hundreds of young men and even boys, especially from Sudan and Eritrea, to serve as jockeys. Though there are fewer Arabs and more Asian nationals than before the war, Kuwaiti citizens are once again a minority in their own country.

Bidun of primarily Palestinian origin and the many Saudis and Syrians make up about one-eighth of the foreign nationals inside Kuwait. All non-Kuwaitis struggle under the same inequitable conditions relative to Kuwaiti citizens. Kuwaiti citizenship is almost impossible to attain, and, except for the highest-paid foreigners, it is equally tough to bring dependents into the country. Though the 1993 law that barred bidun from military service was dropped in 2001, bidun in particular and foreigners in general have a hard time getting ahead in Kuwait's armed forces. Regardless of where they work, foreigners do not receive complete access to the various segments of Kuwait's welfare system, particularly education and medicine, and must pay at least a token fee for the services they do receive. While in limited instances the nationals of GCC countries may own stock in Kuwaiti companies, as a rule other non-Kuwaiti nationals are denied that economic opportunity.

Kuwait's fairly progressive labor laws unfortunately do not apply to domestic workers, which hurts tens of thousands of non-Kuwaitis. There is no minimum wage in Kuwait's private sector, which further adversely affects non-Kuwaitis who fill the vast majority of the low-pay, low-skill positions in Kuwait's economy. Physical and emotional abuse of female domestic servants has been repeatedly documented. The problem is only slowly being brought under control by the government, which has been reluctant to intrude into the private homes of Kuwait's wealthiest and most influential citizens.

POLITICS

Kuwait remains a constitutional monarchy ruled by an emir. Since the mid-1700s, Kuwait's rulers have come solely from the Al-Sabah family, which, since that time, has ruled in consultation with other powerful merchant families. Sheikh Sabah Al Ahmad Al Jaber Al-Sabah has been Kuwait's emir since January 2006. His elevation, brought on by the extreme ill health of the crown prince and heir apparent, was the result of both infighting among members of the ruling family and direct intervention by the National Assembly, as provided for under the 1962 Kuwaiti constitution. The constitution, which spells out the rights of Kuwaiti citizens and the obligations of government, also makes provisions for the emir to suspend the constitution, in whole or in part, and to dissolve the National Assembly under certain circumstances.

The emir appoints the prime minister, who under normal circumstances would also be the crown prince and heir apparent. The emir also appoints a cabinet of ministers that oversees Kuwait's extensive bureaucracy that runs the nation's oil industry, as well as Kuwait's comprehensive welfare system. The emir also appoints (and removes) military officers at his discretion. For political purposes, Kuwait is separated into six regional districts or governorates. Popular elections for a National Assembly (Majlis al-Umma) to represent those governorates are held every four years.

The unicameral or single-chambered National Assembly consists of 50 popularly elected members, though up to 15 cabinet ministers appointed by the emir are automatically made members of the National Assembly. Elected members can always vote. Appointed members are restricted from voting in specific instances, such as no-confidence votes directed at cabinet officials. Unless the National Assembly is dissolved early by the emir, members hold their seats for a term of four years. The cabinet cannot exceed one-third the size of the elected members of the National Assembly. For its part, the National Assembly has the power to hold a no-confidence vote and, practically speaking, to remove any of the cabinet ministers, to include the prime minister. The National Assembly also has significant power in the selection of each new emir, which allows it to reject the emir's first choice, and then to actually pick the next emir from a list of three candidates provided to them by the emir.

The procedures as spelled out in the constitution were followed in spirit, if not to the letter of the law, in the selection of the current emir. Jaber III, who had been severely ill for an extended period, died in January 2006. The crown prince and heir apparent, Sheikh Saad Al Abdullah Al Salem Al-Sabah, automatically became the nation's new emir. As Saad was quite elderly himself, his health was also failing badly. In fact, in 2003 his poor health had resulted in his replacement as prime minister by Sheikh Sabah Al Ahmad Al-Sabah. Suddenly elevated to emir, Saad's diminished mental capacities raised serious doubts about his fitness for the position of ruler. Facing simultaneous action by the National Assembly calling for him to be deposed under the constitution, Saad abdicated after only nine full days as emir. Sheikh Sabah Al Ahmad Al-Sabah, who had also served previously as foreign minister before becoming prime minister, was immediately nominated by the cabinet to be the new emir. On January 29, 2006, the National Assembly unanimously confirmed the appointment of Sabah IV as the new emir.

Though political parties are technically forbidden under Kuwaiti law, groups with shared political interests have formed, generally in opposition to the government. Islamic traditionalists, separated by their Sunni and Shiite sects, secular reformers, and progovernment nationalists make up the three largest political factions in the country. Only Kuwaiti citizens, who make up only half the total population, are allowed to vote. In practical terms, non-Kuwaitis have no say in the things that affect them, other than leaving Kuwait and seeking employment elsewhere.

CIVIL RIGHTS

In May 2005, the National Assembly for the first time legally awarded Kuwaiti women the right to vote beginning with municipal elections and leading to the expected National Assembly elections slated at the time to be held in 2007. Though Islamic and tribal politicians, who filled 21 of 50 total seats in the 2003 National Assembly, had initially attempted to withhold suffrage from Kuwaiti women, the municipal elections of 2006, in which women not only voted but actually ran as candidates for some offices, had these same traditionalist parties courting the women's vote. Turnout of women voters was not as high as had been hoped, and in the end no women candidates were elected, but the election was nevertheless historic and clearly demonstrates the momentous political and social changes that could engulf Kuwait in the near future. When a Kuwaiti woman was nominated in 2005 to join the emir's cabinet and to serve as minister of Kuwait's administrative development, there was no public uproar, just a few murmurs of dissent.

Despite the recent attainment of suffrage, Kuwaiti women still face institutionalized discrimination that will probably take years to eliminate from Kuwait's social fabric. For example, though Kuwait's criminal courts do not follow the discriminatory practice, in family courts where divorce proceedings are adjudicated, the Kuwaiti woman's testimony carries half the legal weight of the man's testimony. Shariah law, which heavily favors males, is used to establish inheritance. A husband's permission is required before a Kuwaiti woman can apply for and receive a passport for international travel. Kuwaiti women are forbidden to marry non-Kuwaiti men, and when it does happen, the couple's children do not automatically become Kuwaiti citizens, which is the opposite of what happens when a Kuwaiti man marries a non-Kuwaiti woman. Among Kuwaitis, men are legally permitted to have multiple wives, but the practice is generally rare except among the remaining Bedouin.

Even though about one-third of Kuwait's women are employed, most in administrative positions for the state, the typical Kuwaiti woman is expected to stay at home and raise her children. By law, women are not allowed to hold most positions in the military or in dangerous industrial occupations. Only recently have Kuwaiti women been employed by the police department in airport security, where they frisk female suspects, and in selected criminal investigations. Women who wish to pursue political careers are especially handicapped. Kuwait's traditional values look askance on unveiled women. A political poster can help a female candidate raise her name recognition with the electorate. In some neighborhoods, however, that same poster will earn her the label of "wanton woman." In conservative Kuwaiti society, even today, a "good" woman simply will not flaunt her physical appearance.

Similarly, in Kuwait's form of democracy, most of the preelection campaigning takes place in the country's *diwaniyat* (the plural of *diwaniyah*). This means that Kuwaiti women are handicapped. A female candidate simply is not allowed to roll up her sleeves and interact with members of the very powerful and all-male diwaniyat of Kuwait. Thus, while women now make up 57 percent of Kuwait's electorate of approximately 340,000, none of the 27 women candidates (out of 249 total candidates) were elected in the 2006 election for the National Assembly.

International observers continue to report that Kuwait's elections are fair and meet international norms. Nevertheless, during the elections held in 2006 for the National Assembly, many complaints of corruption and mismanagement were expressed. While the emir voiced concern over the criticism, the government took no steps to officially limit dissension, steps that were occasionally taken in the past. Government plans to cut Kuwait's electoral precincts from 25 to 10 drew the harshest reaction from the people. Reformers in the National Assembly wanted the redrawn precincts to number only five, to minimize the possibility of buying and trading votes among traditional tribal and religious constituencies, something that has happened before. The issue was taken up in Kuwait's diwaniyat, and popular emotion swelled. Thousands of liberal young Kuwaitis soon took to the streets in vocal but peaceful support of the reformers in the opposition groups.

Several large public demonstrations in downtown Kuwait City spurred the emir to dissolve the National Assembly, by then at loggerheads over the redistricting issue, and call for early elections to seat a new National Assembly. Turnout for the election was estimated at 80 percent. Once the votes were counted, reform candidates held 36 seats in the new assembly, while Islamic candidates and tribal affiliates, traditionally powerful, showed marked decline in seats held. It appears clear that, as long as Kuwait's women are allowed to continue to participate fully in the political process, the trend is toward increased democratization in Kuwait and less authoritarian rule, however benevolent, by the Al-Sabah family.

The Kuwaiti government continues to occasionally constrain freedom of assembly. For example, public demonstrations require advance approval. Though political dialogue takes place in virtually every diwaniyah in Kuwait, whenever a group of five or more Kuwaitis issues statements for the public, government approval must again be obtained. This restriction is mitigated in part by the fact that Kuwait's politicians, cabinet ministers, and even members of the ruling family take pains to visit a wide sampling of the diwaniyat every year. The annual popular access that this provides to Kuwait's highest political echelon is incredible when viewed for the first time. The opportunity afforded to a typical Kuwaiti man, but not to a woman, to speak his opinion directly in the ear of a key government figure means Kuwait enjoys an aspect of democracy not available in any of the world's key democratic nations. While an all-female diwaniyah is uncommon, it is not unheard of. It will be interesting to see if more of these all-woman groups spring up to provide Kuwait's women voters the same opportunities enjoyed by their male counterparts.

The Ministry of the Interior oversees Kuwait's state security and criminal investigation functions. Kuwait's national guard component is responsible for border protection, serves as a reserve for the army, and sometimes augments the police force when ordered. In general, Kuwait's laws are effectively and fairly enforced by these highly bureaucratic organizations. Overall, the level of crime in Kuwait is generally low. Drug offenders make up more than two-thirds of the prison population. Some prisoners still in custody were originally convicted of collaboration with the Iraqis during the occupation. A handful of prisoners have been convicted recently of terrorism or terrorist-related activities. Several members of a domestic terrorist cell centered on Kuwait City were sentenced to long prison terms when the group was uncovered in 2000.

Kuwait's justice system has essentially been rebuilt following the Iraqi invasion and liberation. The reconstituted system of courts has replaced the courts martial that dispensed justice with a heavy hand immediately following liberation, as well as the Courts of Special State Security, which replaced military law during reconstruction, until abolished in 1995. By international standards, Kuwait's justice system is now considered fair and balanced, with occasional noteworthy lapses. While Amnesty International has been highly critical of Kuwait, most of the complaints stem from martial law and the special security courts of the early to mid-1990s.

On paper, Kuwait's judiciary is independent, but since the emir appoints judges, there is always the possibility of partiality. Judges who are Kuwaiti citizens hold lifetime appointments. Interestingly, most of Kuwait's judges are non-nationals, appointed for one- to three-year terms. Torture is banned under the constitution, but there have been reports of abuse, especially in cases of state security. A higher rate of complaints has come from Kuwaiti Shiites, as well. Criminal and civil law are adjudicated in the same court system. Family court, however, is broken down along religious lines, with separate courts and judges for Sunni and Shiite petitioners. The high court of appeals gives Kuwaitis the opportunity, according to law, to appeal any judgment against them. An appellate court for Shiites was established in 2000, largely to defuse criticism from Kuwait's Shiites that the judicial system favored Sunnis, Kuwait's majority sect.

Though often overcrowded, Kuwait's prisons generally meet or exceed international standards. Most of the death sentences handed down after liberation, which resulted in heavy international criticism at the time, were eventually commuted to life in prison. One example is the case of Alaa Hussein, the figurehead of the provisional government during the Iraqi occupation. Hussein had been sentenced to death by hanging in 1993, but his sentence was commuted in 2000 due to his timely expression of remorse for his wartime infractions. According to the constitution, the emir also has extra-judicial power to pardon or commute the sentences awarded by Kuwait's multitiered court system.

Kuwaiti citizens do not enjoy the many civil rights taken for granted in the United States and elsewhere. Kuwait's press law prohibits pieces that criticize the emir, criticize Islam, are immoral, or can in any way be construed as spreading dissension among the people or religious groups of Kuwait. The government has not imposed official censorship for years because Kuwaiti

journalists, knowing the consequences should they fail to do so, wisely cen-
sor themselves. This negates the fact that Kuwait's newspapers are privately
owned. Kuwaiti journalists are quick to rein themselves in when the government suggests that the press is going too far in its opposition to government
actions or policies. Foreign correspondents, however, are generally given unhindered access to report from Kuwait.

Government control of television and radio in effect imposes media restrictions on the political opposition. Kuwait's Ministry of Information reviews in
advance all books, films, and imported materials, censoring or banning those
found to be inappropriate. Internet service providers operate under a very
restrictive government protocol. This prevents Kuwait's many Internet users
from access to sites deemed by government censors to be either immoral or
unacceptably political in content. Moreover, operators of Internet cafés, which
are increasingly popular in both urban and suburban Kuwait, are required to
maintain records of users—data that are then provided to the government.

When charged with crimes for which punishment of three years or more is
possible, all suspects, Kuwaiti or non-Kuwaiti, are provided with legal representation. For lesser crimes, the cost of legal representation is borne by the
individual. Suspects in cases of common crimes must be charged within four
days and either tried or released within three weeks. In terrorism cases and
other cases of state security, suspects can be held indefinitely. Such cases, as
well as cases referred directly by the cabinet, are tried before a special security
court, generally in closed session, though records are usually released to the
public shortly thereafter. The U.S. Department of State considers these courts
to meet the standards of fairness held by the international community.

CONTINUING REGIONAL INSTABILITY

While not the only Arab country to support the U.S.-led coalition that invaded Iraq to topple Saddam Hussein, Kuwait was one of the few Arab countries to do so publicly. As a staging area and secure storage depot, Kuwait was
a valuable contribution to the coalition. The logistical support that Kuwait
later provided to the efforts of the British military forces to stabilize the Iraqi
region of Basrah was equally critical to success. That Kuwait was so open in
its cooperation is primarily a measure of how threatened the Kuwaitis were
as long as Saddam was in power. Secondarily, it is a sign of how important
regional stability is to the future of Kuwait's oil-based economy. The sooner
the Arabian Gulf is stabilized, the better for Kuwait's people and its petroleum industry. Thus, the government continues to actively support the United
States in spite of vocal criticism from many in the Muslim world. Kuwait's
pro-American policies could also lead to internal political and social turmoil if
the domestic situation was allowed to get out of hand.

Kuwait continues to watch Iran with wariness. Iran's fomenting of sectarian violence inside Iraq is troublesome to the Kuwaiti government, even when Iranian terrorism is exported somewhere other than Kuwait. Kuwaitis know that if Iran can foster civil war in Iraq with the hope of carving out an independent Shiite state, then oil-rich Kuwait is probably next on Iran's list of easy targets. Kuwaitis also fear Iran's concerted research efforts to develop long-range missiles and nuclear weapons. The Kuwaiti government believes that Iran hopes to establish hegemony over the entire Arabian Gulf, a traditional objective as far back as the Persian Empire. The Kuwaitis are loath to see that occur, but they are also fearful that preemptive American or Israeli military strikes to prevent Iran from getting a nuclear weapon might further destabilize the region. Western strikes on Iran could possibly inflame the entire Muslim world, and the Al-Sabah family understandably wishes to avoid any incendiary events. Knowing they have no control over decisions made in Teheran, Washington, and Tel Aviv, Kuwaiti military strategists and diplomats continue to focus on their own military readiness and the strength of Kuwait's key defensive alliances with the United States, Great Britain, and the GCC.

CONCLUSION

As the new century begins, Kuwait remains a unique nation. In some respects, the country has changed very little over the past two and a half centuries. It is a tradition-minded, religiously conservative Muslim country. If a time traveler from the eighteenth century walked into a Kuwaiti home today, this individual would be unlikely to notice any differences whatsoever. Contemporary Kuwaitis still embody the strong Islamic values and powerful sense of hospitality that has marked them since their Bedouin days. At the same time, Kuwait is years, perhaps decades, ahead of its neighbors in democratization and liberalization. The average Kuwaiti citizen has an increasing say in governance, and there is no reason to expect the trend to reverse itself, though it may slow. Moreover, Kuwaiti women in many respects are setting an example of the progress that remains to be seen elsewhere across the Arab and Muslim worlds.

Thus, Kuwait is a paradox, and for that reason alone it is worthy of our detailed study. Adding to the importance of understanding Kuwait, second in the world in known oil reserves, is the fact that it is located in the heart of the world's most volatile and valuable real estate. The tiny nation of Kuwait is intricately and irrevocably linked to world events, from oil prices to terrorism perpetrated by Islamist radicals. It is time that this small but critically important Arab nation receive the close attention that its colorful history and promising future merit.

Notable People in the History of Kuwait

Al-Ibrahim, Yusuf (ca. 1830–1906). Merchant and trusted financial advisor to Mohamed. He plotted to overthrow Mubarak the Great. Between 1897 and 1906, he mounted several expeditions to invade Kuwait, but was repeatedly deterred or repulsed by British military protection.

Al-Sabah, Abdullah (1740–1814). Known as Abdullah I, he was Kuwait's second ruler, 1762–1814.

Al-Sabah, Abdullah (1814–1892). Known as Abdullah II, he was Kuwait's fifth ruler, 1866–1892.

Al-Sabah, Abdullah Al Salem (1895–1965). Known as Abdullah III, he was Kuwait's eleventh ruler, 1950–1965. He oversaw Kuwait's independence from Great Britain in 1961 and signed Kuwait's first constitution.

Al-Sabah, Ahmad Al Jaber (1885–1950). He was Kuwait's tenth ruler, 1921–1950. After the discovery of oil, he oversaw the development of modern Kuwait as a welfare state.

Al-Sabah, Jaber (1770–1859). Known as Jaber I, he was Kuwait's third ruler, 1814–1859.

Al-Sabah, Jaber (1860–1917). Known as Jaber II, he was Kuwait's eighth ruler, 1915–1917.

Al-Sabah, Jaber Al Ahmad Al Jaber (1926–2006). Known as Jaber III, he was Kuwait's thirteenth ruler, 1977–2006. He was exiled by the Iraqi invasion in 1990 and returned to his throne in 1991 following Operation Desert Storm to oversee Kuwait's massive reconstruction efforts.

Al-Sabah, Jarrah bin Sabah bin Jaber (1834–1896). Brother of Mohamed and Mubarak, he was assassinated by Mubarak.

Al-Sabah, Mohamed (1831–1896). He was Kuwait's sixth ruler, 1892–1896, until assassinated by his brother Mubarak Al-Sabah.

Al-Sabah, Mubarak (1837–1915). Known as "Mubarak al-Kabir," or "Mubarak the Great," he was Kuwait's seventh ruler, 1896–1915. He assassinated his brothers Mohamed and Jarrah, severed ties with the Ottoman Empire, and made Kuwait a protectorate of the British Empire.

Al-Sabah, Saad Al Abdullah Al Salem (1930–). In 2006, he was Kuwait's fourteenth ruler, but ill health drove him to abdicate after only 9 days and the National Assembly simultaneously voted to depose him.

Al-Sabah, Sabah (ca. 1810–1866). Known as Sabah II, he was Kuwait's fourth ruler, 1859–1866.

Al-Sabah, Sabah Al Ahmad Al Jaber (1929–). Known as Sabah IV, he is Kuwait's fifteenth ruler, ruling since 2006.

Al-Sabah, Sabah Al Salem (1913–1977). Known as Sabah III, he was Kuwait's twelfth ruler, 1965–1977.

Al-Sabah, Sabah bin Jaber (ca. 1700–1762). Known as Sabah I, he founded the Al-Sabah dynasty and ruled from ca. 1756–1762.

Al-Sabah, Salem Al Mubarak (1864–1921). He was Kuwait's ninth ruler, 1917–1921.

Al-Saud, Abd Al Aziz (ca. 1876–1953). First king of Saudi Arabia, often referred to as Ibn Saud. After years in exile in Kuwait, he later launched an unsuccessful Wahhabi-inspired assault by the Ikhwan to overthrow the Al-Sabah in Kuwait.

Al-Saud, Khalid ibn Sultan ibn Abd al Aziz (1949–). Saudi Arabian general and deputy commander of coalition military forces that defeated Iraq and liberated Kuwait.

Alexander the Great (356–323 B.C.E.). Greek (Macedonian) military leader whose conquests included the Arabian Gulf region. Kuwait's Faylakha Island was once a trading post and military outpost in Alexander's empire.

Barrak bin Ghuraif (ca. 1625–1682). From 1669 to 1682, sheikh of the Bani Khalid tribe, which ruled eastern Arabia. In either 1672 or 1680, he built a small fort in what is present-day Kuwait, around which the city would grow.

Bush, George H. W. (1924–). President of the United States who, along with Britain's prime minister Margaret Thatcher, formed and led a coalition to defeat Iraq and liberate Kuwait in 1991.

Bush, George W. (1946–). President of the United States who ordered the invasion of Iraq in 2003, which led to the subsequent removal of Saddam Hussein as well as the ongoing insurgency inside Iraq.

Cox, Percy Zachariah (1864–1937). British high commissioner who imposed the Uqair Protocol on Kuwait in 1922.

Hussein, Saddam (1937–2006). Dictator of Iraq who ordered the Iraqi invasion of Kuwait in 1990. Operation Desert Storm liberated Kuwait but did not remove him from power. He continued to threaten Kuwait militarily until he was forcibly removed, and later arrested, by United States military forces, which invaded Iraq in 2003. He was convicted under Iraqi law of crimes against humanity and executed by hanging.

Khomeini, Ruhollah Musavi (1900–1989). Shiite fundamentalist cleric who inspired the 1979 revolution in Iran and established theocratic rule. Subsequent Iranian military and terrorist activities continue to pose a significant threat to the Sunni Al-Sabah rulers of Kuwait.

Meade, Malcolm C. (1854–1933). British colonel and resident political agent who negotiated Kuwait's historic defense pact with Sheikh Mubarak the Great.

Midhat Pasha (1822–1883). Ottoman governor who attempted to reform the imperial educational and legal systems. He strengthened, but never cemented, the informal ties between Kuwait and the Ottoman Empire.

Mohamed (570–632). Prophet who founded the Muslim religion, the state religion of Kuwait. His militant ideals inspired the Wahhabi movement of Central Arabia, which threatened Kuwait's existence for over three hundred years.

Schwarzkopf, H. Norman (1934–). American general who commanded the coalition of Western and Arab nations that defeated Iraq and liberated Kuwait.

Glossary

Anglo-Ottoman Convention: Treaty between Great Britain and the Ottoman Empire that identified Kuwait as a sovereign sheikhdom under Ottoman suzerainty.

Baath Party: Iraq's Socialist Arab Rebirth Party, which was the only political party allowed in Kuwait under Iraqi occupation.

Bani Utub: Literally "people who wandered"; the name assumed by Bedouin migrants who founded Kuwait.

Bedouin: An Arab of the desert.

Bidun: Literally "without"; the Kuwaiti name for a temporary Arab worker without citizenship papers from another country.

Black rain: The ash-laden precipitation over Kuwait from the many oil fires set by retreating Iraqi troops.

Dinar: The official currency of Kuwait.

Divided Zone: Formerly the "Neutral Zone." An area between Kuwait and Saudi Arabia claimed by both; since 1966, the oil revenues have been equally divided.

Diwaniyah: Literally "the room in which guests are entertained"; in modern times, a diwaniyah is a social custom in which Kuwaiti males get together on a weekly basis to informally discuss, among other things, politics.

Emir: Prince; at independence in 1961, Kuwait went from sheikhdom to emirate, and Kuwait's leaders became emirs rather than sheikhs.

Environmental terrorism: A newly created category of war crime; the deliberate destruction of oil facilities by retreating Iraqis that resulted in toxic spills and environmental damage that will last for decades.

Gulf Cooperation Council (GCC): The defensive alliance formed in 1981 by the Arabian Gulf states of Kuwait, Saudi Arabia, Bahrain, Oman, Qatar, and the United Arab Emirates to deter aggression by Iran and, later, Iraq.

Icaros: Greek name for Kuwait's Faylakha Island in ancient times.

Ikhwan: Literally "brotherhood"; a Wahhabi military force sent by Saudi Arabia's king, Ibn Saud, to invade Kuwait in 1920.

Islam: The Muslim religion, founded by the prophet Mohamed.

Madrassahs: Islamic school, generally just for boys.

Majlis: Literally "council," from the reception room in which a council is held; Kuwait's National Assembly is the Majlis al-Umma.

Majlis Movement: The 1938 movement to increase popular participation in Kuwait's government through creation of the National Assembly.

Muslim: An Islamic follower of the prophet Mohamed.

Najd: Literally "plateau"; the name of Arabia's central highlands, the original homeland of the Bani Utub, who settled Kuwait.

Qadha: A subprovince under the Ottoman Empire; Kuwait was once considered a subprovince of the Ottoman province of Basrah.

Qadi: An Islamic judge.

Qurain: From *qarn*, or "hill," the early European name, sometimes written as Grane, for the fishing village once located at the site of present-day Kuwait.

Qur'an: The holy book of the Muslim religion.

Shariah: Religious law of Islam; a source of Kuwait's modern legal code.

Sharif: "Honorable" or "noble"; Arab tribes and families that can trace their lineage back to the time of the prophet Mohamed.

Shatt al Arab: The "River of the Arabs," near Kuwait in southern Iraq.

Sheikh: Head of an Arab tribe or family; prior to independence in 1961, Kuwait was a sheikhdom and the ruler was a sheikh from the Al-Sabah family.

Shiite: The smaller of the two main branches of Islam; Shiites are a minority in Kuwait.

Shura: "Consultation"; Kuwait's rulers have a tradition of consultation and collaboration with the other top merchant families of the emirate.

Souk: Marketplace or bazaar; the Souk al Manakh, Kuwait's unofficial stock market, crashed in 1982, creating a financial and political crisis.

Sunni: The larger of the two main branches of Islam; Sunnis are the majority in Kuwait.

Tanzimat: Bureaucratic, educational, and legal measures enacted in the nineteenth century to reform the Ottoman Empire.

Uqair Protocol: An agreement imposed by the British Empire in 1922 that gave two-thirds of the territory claimed by Kuwait to Saudi Arabia.

Wahhabi: Islamic fundamentalist movement in Arabia that periodically invaded Kuwait in the 1700s and 1800s.

Bibliographic Essay

Some informative texts on Kuwait's general history include Ahmad Mustafa Abu-Hakima, *The Modern History of Kuwait: 1750–1965* (London: Luzac and Company Limited, 1983); Frank Clements, *Kuwait* (Oxford: Clio Press, 1985); William Facey and Gillian Grant, *Kuwait by the First Photographers* (New York: I.B. Tauris, 1998); and David Clayton, ed., *Kuwait's Natural History: An Introduction* (Kuwait City: Kuwait Oil Company, 1983). For readers interested in Kuwait under the Ottoman Empire, see Frederick F. Anscombe, *The Ottoman Gulf: The Creation of Kuwait, Saudi Arabia, and Qatar* (New York: Columbia University Press, 1997). For detailed history of the Al-Sabah family, see Alan Rush, *Al-Sabah: Genealogy and History of Kuwait's Ruling Family, 1752–1986* (New Jersey: Ithaca Press, 1987).

Although the following selections are dated and less objective than some other modern references on Kuwaiti history, readers will definitely enjoy exploring Harold Richard Patrick Dickson, *Kuwait and Her Neighbours* (London: George Allen & Ruskin, 1956) and *The Arab of the Desert: A Glimpse into Badawin Life in Kuwait and Sau'di Arabia* (London: Allen & Unwin, 1967). Other Dickson family members also recorded their own firsthand experiences of life in Kuwait. These include Violet Dickson, *Forty Years in Kuwait* (London: Allen & Unwin, 1971), and Xahra Dickson Freeth, *A New Look at Kuwait* (London: Allen & Unwin, 1972).

For detailed discussion of Kuwait's economy and petroleum industry during the twentieth century, see Jill Crystal, *Kuwait: The Transformation of an Oil State* (Boulder, CO: Westview Press, 1992); Jill Crystal, *Oil and Politics in the Gulf: Rulers and Merchants in Kuwait and Qatar* (New York: Cambridge University Press, 1995); Mary Ann Tetreault, *The Kuwait Petroleum Corporation and the Economics of the New World Order* (Westport, CT: Quorum Books, 1995); Fida Darwiche, *The Gulf Stock Exchange Crash: The Rise and Fall of the Souq al-Manakh* (London: Croom Helm, 1986); Abdulrasool Al-Moosa, *Immigrant Labor in Kuwait* (London: Croom Helm, 1985); and Shamlan Alessa, *The Manpower Problem in Kuwait* (London: Kegan Paul, 1981).

Modern Kuwait's political, social, and foreign policy developments are covered in Jacqueline Ismael, *Kuwait: Social Change in Historical Perspective* (Syracuse, NY: Syracuse University Press, 1982); Helen Mary Rizzo, *Islam, Democracy, and the Status of Women: The Case of Kuwait* (New York: Routledge, 2005); Miriam Joyce, *Kuwait, 1956–1996: An Anglo-American Perspective* (Portland, OR: Frank Cass, 1998); Abdul-Reda Assiri, *Kuwait's Foreign Policy: City-State in World Politics* (Boulder, CO: Westview Press, 1990); and Ali Akbar Mahdi, *Teen Life in the Middle East* (Westport, CT: Greenwood Press, 2003).

The historic border dispute that was a contributory cause of the war is examined in David H. Finnie, *Shifting Lines in the Sand: Kuwait's Elusive Frontier with Iraq* (New York: I.B. Tauris, 1992). For the liberation of Kuwait during the First Gulf War, see Anthony H. Cordesman, *The Iraq War: Strategy, Tactics, and Military Lessons* (Westport, CT: Praeger, 2003); John Keegan, *The Iraq War* (New York: Knopf, 2004); Norman Friedman, *Desert Victory: The War for Kuwait* (Annapolis, MD: Naval Institute Press, 1991); Harry G. Summers Jr., *On Strategy II: A Critical Analysis of the Gulf War* (New York: Dell Publishing, 1992); James Blackwell, *Thunder in the Desert: The Strategy and Tactics of the Persian Gulf War* (New York: Bantam, 1991).

For a harrowing picture of Kuwaiti civilian life under Iraqi occupation, consult John Levins, *Days of Fear: The Inside Story of the Iraqi Invasion and Occupation of Kuwait* (London: Macmillan House, 1997); Jean P. Sasson, *The Rape of Kuwait: The True Story of Iraqi Atrocities against a Civilian Population* (New York: Knightsbridge Publishing, 1991): Jehan S. Rajab, *Invasion Kuwait: An English Woman's Tale* (New York: I.B. Tauris, 1996). The environmental effects of the war are summarized and discussed in T. M. Hawley, *Against the Fires of Hell: The Environmental Disaster of the Gulf War* (New York: Harcourt Brace Jovanovich, 1992) and Angus M. Gunn, *Unnatural Disasters: Case Studies of Human-Induced Environmental Catastrophes* (Westport, CT: Greenwood Press, 2003).

For the invasion of Iraq, the toppling of Saddam Hussein, and the subsequent U.S. occupation, see Michael R. Gordon and Bernard E. Trainor, *Cobra II: The Inside Story of the Invasion and Occupation of Iraq* (New York: Pantheon, 2006) and Thomas E. Ricks, *Fiasco: The American Military Adventure in Iraq* (New York: Penguin, 2006).

Background history on the region, early civilizations, and Bedouin life can be found in Hans J. Nissen, *The Early History of the Ancient Near East 9000–2000 BCE* (Chicago: University of Chicago Press, 1983); Harriet E. W. Crawford, *Dilmun and Its Gulf Neighbours* (New York: Cambridge University Press, 1998); Alan Keohane, *Bedouin: Nomads of the Desert* (London: Trafalgar Square Publishing, 1999); and Carl Raswan, *The Black Tents of Arabia* (London: Kegan Paul, 2000).

For readers interested in Kuwait under the Ottoman Empire, see Frederick F. Anscombe, *The Ottoman Gulf: The Creation of Kuwait, Saudi Arabia, and Qatar* (New York: Columbia University Press, 1997). For a general overview of the Ottomans and their empire, see Jason Goodwin, *Lords of the Horizons: A History of the Ottoman Empire* (New York: Henry Holt, 1998); Andrew Wheatcroft, *The Ottomans: Dissolving Images* (New York: Penguin Books, 1995); Norman Itzkowitz, *Ottoman Empire and Islamic Tradition* (Chicago: University of Chicago Press, 1972); Lord Kinross, *The Ottoman Centuries: The Rise and Fall of the Turkish Empire* (New York: Morrow Quill, 1977); and Colin Imber, *The Ottoman Empire* (New York: Palgrave, 2002).

For in-depth coverage of Ottoman, Arabic, and Islamic men-at-arms over the centuries, along with their weapons and uniforms, beautifully complemented by color illustrations, see David Nicolle, *Armies of the Ottoman Turks 1300–1774* (London: Osprey Books, 1983); *Armies of the Muslim Conquest* (London: Osprey Books, 1993); *The Armies of Islam: 7th–11th Centuries* (London: Osprey Books, 1982); *Rome's Enemies: The Desert Frontier* (London: Osprey Books, 1991); *The Janissaries* (London: Osprey Books, 1995); and Peter Wilcox, *Rome's Enemies 3: Parthians and Sassanid Persians* (London: Osprey Books, 1986).

For discussion of historical, political, and social developments around the Arabian Gulf region, consult Ahmad Anani and Ken Whittingham, *The Early History of the Gulf Arabs* (London: Longman, 1986); Erik Peterson, *The Gulf Cooperation Council: Search for Unity in a Dynamic Region* (Boulder, CO: Westview Press, 1988); Alvin Cottrell, ed., *The Persian Gulf States: A General Survey* (Baltimore: Johns Hopkins University Press, 1980); Anthony H. Cordesman, *The Gulf and the West: Strategic Relations and Military Realities* (Boulder, CO: Westview Press, 1988); Federal Research Division, *Persian Gulf States: Country Studies*, 3rd ed. (Washington, DC: Library of Congress, 1994); Milton Viorst, *Sandcastles: The Arabs in Search of the Modern World* (New York: Alfred Knopf, 1994); and Sheikha al-Misnad, *The Development of Modern Education in the Gulf* (London: Ithaca Press, 1985).

For Islamic history, beliefs, and politics, consult Seyyed Hossein Nasr, *Islam, Religion, History, and Civilization* (New York: HarperCollins, 2003); Karen Armstrong, *Islam: A Short History* (New York: Random House, 2002); John

Esposito, ed., *The Oxford History of Islam* (Oxford: Oxford University Press, 1999); Ira M. Lapidus, *A History of Islamic Societies* (Cambridge: Cambridge University Press, 2002); Marshall Hodgson, *The Venture of Islam* (Chicago: University of Chicago Press, 1974); and P. M. Holt, Ann K. S. Lambton, and Bernard Lewis, eds., *Cambridge History of Islam, 1: The Central Islamic Lands* and *History of Islam, 2: The Further Islamic Lands, Islamic Society, and Civilization* (New York: Cambridge University Press, 1970). For a controversial global context within which to view modern Islam, consider Robin Wright, *Sacred Rage: The Wrath of Militant Islam* (New York: Touchstone, 2001); and Efrain Karsh, *Islamic Imperialism: A History* (New Haven, CT: Yale University Press, 2006).

The following Internet sites generally provide very accurate, detailed information relevant to modern-day Kuwait and are regularly updated: United States Library of Congress, "Kuwait: A Country Study," http://memory.loc.gov/frd/cs/kwtoc.html; United States Central Intelligence Agency, "World Fact Book," https://www.cia.gov/cia/publications/factbook/index.html; United States Department of State Human Rights Report, http://www.state.gov/g/drl/rls/hrrpt/; United Nations Homepage, http://www.un.org; Amnesty International Homepage, http://www.amnesty.org; and Human Rights Watch Homepage, http://www.hrw.org.

Index

Agriculture, 7, 58, 61, 77, 130–31
Ahmadiyyah School, 63
Airborne Warning and Control
    System (AWACS), 83
Air Force, 12, 83, 91, 107, 115, 127
Alexander the Great, 16–17
Al-Ghanim. *See* Al-Zayid
Ali-al-Salem air base, 91
Al-Ibrahim, Yusuf ibn
    Abdullah, 44–45
Al-Jaber air base, 91
Al-Jalahima, 23, 26–27, 32–33, 35
Al-Khalifa, 23, 26–27, 32–35, 40
Al-Majid, Ali Hasan ("Chemical
    Ali"), 94
Al-Nassar, 32–34
Al-Nisf. *See* Al-Jalahima
Al-Sabah: Abdullah I, 30, 32–33,
    35–39, 41; Abdullah II, 41–44;
    Abdullah III, 49, 60, 64, 66, 68–69;

Ahmad, 49, 56–57, 59–60, 63;
    assumption of sheikhdom, 26–27;
    Fahd al-Ahmad, 89; independence,
    65, 72; Jaber I, 39, 41; Jaber II,
    44, 49, 50–53, 58–59, 62, 68, 69;
    Jaber III, 68, 73, 93, 111–12, 114,
    122, 126, 136; Jarrah, 44; Mariam,
    32–34; migration, 1, 11, 21, 23–24;
    Mohamed, 44; Mubarak, 44–46,
    49–53, 58, 62, 69, 86; recent
    dynasties, 49, 68; Saad, 136; Sabah I,
    28–32; Sabah II, 41; Sabah III, 68;
    Sabah IV, 135–36; Salem, 44, 49,
    53–56, 58; Salim 33–34
Al-Saleh, 24
Al-Saud: family, 40–41, 52–53;
    Fahd bin Abdul Aziz, 92; "Ibn
    Saud", 52–57; Khalid ibn Sultan
    Abd al Aziz, 104
Al-Shamlan, 24

Al-Zayid, 24

American Independent Oil
    Company (Aminoil), 59–60, 75

Amnesty International, 94, 96, 113

Anglo-Ottoman Convention,
    51–52, 86

Anglo-Persian Oil Company
    (APOC), 58–59

Arabian Oil Company (AOC), 60, 75

Arabic language, 8, 132

Arab League, 12, 67, 68, 86, 87, 111

Arab nationalism. *See* Pan-Arabism

Arab Satellite Communications
    Organization (Arabsat), 109,
    120, 131

Ash Shuaybah industrial zone,
    75, 76–77

Ash Shuwaykh ocean terminal,
    6, 76–77

Baath Party, 94, 102

Bahrain: Al-Khalifa conquest
    of, 33; ancient settlement, 16;
    constitution, 69; liberation of
    Kuwait, 104, 106; member of
    GCC, 80, 103; Ottoman vassal, 23;
    pearl banks, 26, 32; Trucial Coast,
    40; telecommunications, 131

Bani Kaab, 32–34

Bani Khalid, 2, 19, 22–23, 26,
    31–32, 37

Bani Utub, 19, 24, 26–27, 32

Basrah: during Bani Utub migration,
    23, 26; incorporation of northern
    Kuwait, 85; Ottoman province,
    27, 31, 35, 37, 42–45, 48–50, 68,
    86; plague, 35, 36; threat from, 22,
    23, 32; trade, 30–31, 35–36, 39, 50;
    under British occupation, 140

Battle of Red Fort, 55

Battle of Riqqah, 34

Bedouin, 17–23, 25–27, 31, 137, 141

Bidun, 10, 82–83, 90, 99, 127, 134–35

Black rain, 108

British East India Company, 35–37

British Petroleum Company (BP).
    See Anglo-Persian Oil Company
    (APOC)

Bubiyan Island, 6, 51, 58, 79, 85

Burgan oil field, 48

Bush, George H. W., 92, 101–2,
    106, 115

Bush, George W., 129

Cabinet, 72, 135–36

Camel caravans, 30–31

Cement industry, 61, 120

Censorship, 70, 98, 123, 139–40

Central Bank, 7, 61, 76, 120, 125

Central Command, 101

Cheney, Dick, 92

Civil Reserve Air Fleet (CRAF), 102

Constitution, 68–71, 134

Constitution Movement, 73–74,
    79, 122

Count Kapnist, 45

Cox, Sir Percy, 55–56

Cradle of civilization, 15

Credit and Savings Bank, 76

Cuneiform, 16

Damascus Agreement, 113

Dasman Palace, 89

Democratic Forum, 122–23, 124

Desalinization plant. *See* Distillation
    plant

Difficult Credit Facilities
    Resettlement Program, 78

Dilmun, 16

Dinar, 7, 65, 76, 130

Distillation plant, 5, 60, 76, 131

Divided Zone, 79

Dutch Reformed American
    Church, 62–63

Education system, 63–64, 74, 125, 131–32

Egypt: liberation of Kuwait, 102, 104, 128; Ottoman province, 38; recipient of foreign aid, 71, 93; workers from, 10, 63, 71, 82

Elections, 72, 74, 136–38

Emiri Guard, 89

Emiri Hospital, 63

Environmental terrorism, 108–9, 133

Extrajudicial execution, 97, 99

Fauna, 4

Faylakha Island, 6, 15–17, 51

Fayruz, Ibn, 30

Fertile Crescent, 4, 17

First World War, 52

Fishing industry, 7–8, 9, 77, 108, 131

Flora, 4

Foreign aid, 80, 81

France: colonial competition, 43, 44; liberation of Kuwait, 103; military assistance, 82–83, 114, 126; trade partner, 8, 130; war with Great Britain, 31, 36–37

General Headquarters, 89–90

General Reserve Fund, 122

General Treaty of Peace, 42

Geography, 4–5, 6–7

Germany: colonial competition, 44, 50–51; military assistance, 82–83, 114, 127; trade partner, 8, 130

Ghuraif, Barrak bin, 2, 19, 22–23, 26, 31–32, 37

Glaspie, April, 87–88

Government in exile, 93, 98, 120

Governorates, 11

Grane. See Qurain

Great Arab Revolt, 52

Great Britain: control over Arabian Gulf, 31, 34, 38–39, 40–42; early contact with Kuwait, 35–38, 40–42; Kuwait as protectorate of, 2, 11–13, 45–46, 49–56; Kuwait's independence from, 65–68, 79–80, 82–83; liberation of Kuwait, 92, 99, 102–3, 105–6, 108, 110, 112–15; post-war relations, 126, 128, 140–41

Greeks, 16–17

Gross Domestic Product (GDP), 7, 129

Gulf Cooperation Council (GCC), 12, 80, 93, 103–4, 113, 128, 135, 141

Gulf Oil Company, 59

Gulf War Syndrome, 108

Hammurabi, 16

Harvard University School of Public Health, 133

Hawk missiles, 127

Health care, 74, 110, 132–33

High Court of Appeal, 11

Hornet fighter-bombers, 127

Human Rights Watch, 94, 96, 97

Human shields, 95

Hussein, Alaa, 94, 139

Hussein, Saddam: invasion of Kuwait, 2, 56, 81, 87–88, 91–92; liberation of Kuwait, 102–5, 109; occupation of Kuwait, 95, 98, 125; post-liberation period, 13, 117, 128, 129, 140

Hydroponics, 130

Ibn Fayruz, 30

Icaros, 16–17

Ikhwan, 54–55, 111

Industrial Bank of Kuwait, 76

Industrial Development Committee, 76

International Atomic Energy Agency (IAEA), 12

International Committee of the Red
  Cross, 96, 111
International Day for Preventing
  the Use of the Environment in
  Military Conflicts, 109
International Marine Satellite
  System (Inmarsat). 131
International Telecommunications
  Satellite Organization (Intelsat),
  109, 120, 131
INTERPOL, 12
Investment Bank of Kuwait, 76
Iran: domestic interference inside
  Kuwait, 9–10, 79, 80, 128, 141;
  empire, 15–16, 58–59; historic
  threat to Kuwait, 1, 6, 32, 40, 66;
  member of OPEC, 62; modern
  threat to Kuwait, 73, 77, 79, 87, 93,
  113; revolution, 73, 79; workers
  from, 10, 132
Iran-Iraq War, 77, 80–82, 83
Iraq: argument for war, 67–68, 81,
  86–88; occupation of Kuwait, 9,
  94–99; relations with Kuwait, 1, 2,
  56–58, 62, 66–68, 76, 79–83, 140
Islam, 9, 17, 20–21, 69, 134, 139
Islamic Constitutional Movement,
  122, 124
Islamic Parliamentarian Alliance,
  122–23, 124

Joint Forces Command East
  (JFCE), 104, 105, 106
Joint Forces Command North
  (JFCN), 104, 105, 106

Kadhima, 85
Khalid Division, 104, 106
Khomeini, Ayatollah Ruhollah, 73, 79
King Fahd. *See* Al-Saud, Fahd bin
  Abdul Aziz
King Hussein. *See* Talal, Hussein bin

Koran. *See* Qur'an
Kuwait Bay, 2, 15, 39, 50–51
Kuwait City: attacks on, 37–38, 55;
  development of, 6, 19, 22, 43, 47, 51,
  61, 63; liberation of, 101, 103–6; port
  operations, 29, 35, 36, 53; domestic
  problems in, 73, 78, 138, 139;
  reconstruction, 110, 120, 126; under
  occupation, 85, 88–89, 94, 96–97, 99
Kuwait Foreign Petroleum
  Exploration Company, 76
Kuwait Fund for Arab Economic
  Development (KFAED), 81
Kuwaiti Institute for Scientific
  Research (KISR), 110
Kuwait International Airport, 89,
  110, 119, 131
Kuwait National Petroleum
  Company (KNPC), 75–76, 130
Kuwait News Agency (KUNA), 123
Kuwait Oil Company (KOC), 59,
  75, 130
Kuwait Oil Tanker Company, 75
Kuwait Petroleum Corporation
  (KPC), 76, 130
Kuwait University, 74

Land Force, 12
Landmines, 109
League of Nations, 56
Liberation Brigade, 107

Majlis Movement, 57–58, 66
Maritime Treaty, 42
Martial law, 73, 112–13, 122, 139
Martyrs' Brigade, 91, 106, 107
Meade, Malcolm C., 45–46
Mecca, 20, 38
Medina, 38
Mesopotamia, 16, 18
Midhat Pasha, 41, 42, 43
Mina al Ahmadi oil terminal, 76

Ministry of Information, 123, 140
Ministry of the Interior, 138
Ministry of Social Affairs and
    Labor, 130
Mohamed (prophet), 8–9, 18, 20, 134
Mubarak, Hosni, 87
Mubarakiyyah School, 63
Mutla'a Ridge, 90

Najd, 17, 19, 23–24, 26, 55, 57
National Assembly (Majlis
    al-Umma), 11, 67–69, 71–74,
    79, 123–26, 135–38
National Committee for the Missing
    and POW Affairs (NCMPA), 111
National Council, 73–74
National Guard, 12
National Islamic Coalition, 123, 124
Naval Force, 12, 83, 90, 107, 115, 127
Neutral Zone, 56, 59–60, 79
Non-Aligned Movement, 12
Numan, Aziz Salih, 94

Office of Military Cooperation, 126
Oil industry: exploration, 58–60, 76;
    fires, 107–9, 117–18; production,
    60, 76, 107, 118–19; reserves, 7,
    118–19, 130; revenue, 62, 76, 78, 87
Oil Producing and Exporting
    Countries (OPEC), 12, 62, 76, 87,
    119, 130
Oman, 27, 38, 40, 80, 103, 113
Operation Desert Shield, 92–93, 99
Operation Desert Storm, 93, 99, 101–7
Organization of the Islamic
    Conference, 12
Ottoman empire, 11, 23, 27–32,
    34–38, 40–45, 50–54, 86

Palestine Liberation Organization
    (PLO), 81, 90, 92
Palestinian Authority, 92, 128

Palestinian workers, 82, 90, 92, 96,
    112–13, 124–25, 134
Pan-Arabism, 8, 69
Parthian empire, 17
Patriot missile, 106, 127
Pearling industry, 7, 9, 26, 39, 42, 48,
    57–58
Peninsula Shield defense force, 80
Persian empire, 17, 18, 34, 66, 141
Petrochemicals Industries Company
    (PIC), 75, 130
Petroleum. *See* Oil
Plague, 35–36
Post-Traumatic Stress Disorder
    (PTSD), 110, 133
Prime minister, 11, 135–36

Qatar, 22–24, 32, 40, 80, 103–4,
    106, 131
Qawasim, 34, 38
Q8, 75
Qurain, 2, 22–23
Qur'an, 9, 20, 30, 63, 134

Ras al Kadhima, 50
Ratqa oil field, 85, 87
Real Estate Bank, 76
Republican Guard, 102–3, 115
Reserve Fund for Future
    Generations, 78, 122
Resistance movement, 98–99
Rumaylah oil field, 86–87, 112

Safe houses, 98
Safwan, 106
Sassanid empire, 17
Saudi Arabia: Bedouin roots, 21;
    borders, 1, 6, 55–56, 58, 60, 78, 89;
    defense of 92–93, 103; designs on
    Kuwait, 1, 54, 66, 73; exile location,
    89–91, 93, 111, 120, 122; liberation of
    Kuwait, 83, 87–88, 92, 98–99, 102–6;

member of GCC, 80; member of
OPEC, 62; telecommunications,
131, trade partner, 8, 57, 130;
workers from, 134
Schwarzkopf, Norman, 104, 106
Scud missile, 105–6
Second of August Movement, 114
Second World War, 59, 61, 67
Seleucid empire, 17
Sevres Treaty, 86
Shariah, 11, 20, 30, 69, 70, 124, 134, 137
Shatt al-Arab, 23, 27, 39, 42, 47, 50,
53, 85
Show prisoners, 96
Shura, 29, 58
Siege of al-Qatif, 42
Slant drilling, 86–87
Slavery, 26, 39–40, 48
Smallpox epidemic, 63
Socialist Arab Rebirth Party.
   See Baath Party
Souk al Manakh crash, 73, 78, 120–21
Special State Security Court, 112–13,
125, 139
Suez, 31
Suez Canal, 36, 39, 50
Suffrage, 12, 70
Sulubba, 25
Summary execution.
   See Extrajudicial execution
Susa, 16
Syria: liberation of Kuwait, 102–4,
113, 128; Ottoman province, 53;
recipient of foreign aid, 81, 102;
trade, 26, 30–31, 53; workers
from, 10, 112, 134

Taif, 93
Talal, Hussein bin, 87
Tanzimat, 43
Taurus System, 50–51
Tectonic movement, 3

Telecommunications, 8, 97, 107, 109,
119–20, 131
Territorial limit, 6
Terrorism, 73, 79, 139, 140
Tigris-Euphrates river system, 3
Tomahawk missile, 103, 104
Torture, 69, 96, 113, 125
Trade partners, 7–8, 26, 30–31,
35–36, 75, 119, 130
Treaty of Lausanne, 55–56, 86
Trucial Coast, 40

Umm Qasr naval base, 112
United Arab Emirates (UAE), 38, 40,
80, 103, 131
United Nations (UN), 12, 67, 68, 74,
86, 91–94, 97, 111
United Nations Compensation
Committee 133
United Nation Security Council,
91–92, 95, 102–3, 112, 128
United States (U.S.): defense
agreements with Kuwait, 12,
79–81, 83, 87–88; economic
interest in Kuwait, 59–60, 67;
liberation of Kuwait, 92–94,
101–6; post-liberation relations, 2,
12, 113–15, 118, 126–28, 140–41
Uqair Protocol, 55–56
Uruk, 16

Wahhabis, 20, 26, 32, 34, 37–38,
40–41, 54–55, 58
Warbah Island, 51, 58, 79, 85
Weapons of Mass Destruction
(WMD), 102, 105, 115
Welfare system, 10, 41, 61, 70, 72
Women's rights, 9, 10, 11, 137, 141
Workforce, 10, 66, 126, 130, 134
World Health Organization
(WHO), 12
World Trade Organization (WTO), 12

About the Author

MICHAEL S. CASEY is Professor of the Humanities at Graceland University in Iowa. He holds a doctorate in philosophy and writes extensively on military history. He is coauthor of *Teaching the Korean War: An Instructor's Handbook.* As a member of the Kuwait-United States Defense Review Group, he helped plan the rebuilding of Kuwait's postwar national defense, during which time he lived in Kuwait and worked with the top echelons of Kuwait's defense establishment.

Other Titles in the Greenwood Histories of the Modern Nations
Frank W. Thackeray and John E. Findling, Series Editors

The History of Argentina
Daniel K. Lewis

The History of Australia
Frank G. Clarke

The History of the Baltic States
Kevin O'Connor

The History of Brazil
Robert M. Levine

The History of Canada
Scott W. See

The History of Central America
Thomas Pearcy

The History of Chile
John L. Rector

The History of China
David C. Wright

The History of Congo
Didier Gondola

The History of Cuba
Clifford L. Staten

The History of Egypt
Glenn E. Perry

The History of Ethiopia
Saheed Adejumobi

The History of Finland
Jason Lavery

The History of France
W. Scott Haine

The History of Germany
Eleanor L. Turk

The History of Ghana
Roger S. Gocking

The History of Great Britain
Anne Baltz Rodrick

The History of Holland
Mark T. Hooker

The History of India
John McLeod

The History of Indonesia
Steven Drakeley

The History of Iran
Elton L. Daniel

The History of Iraq
Courtney Hunt

The History of Ireland
Daniel Webster Hollis III

The History of Israel
Arnold Blumberg

The History of Italy
Charles L. Killinger

The History of Japan
Louis G. Perez

The History of Korea
Djun Kil Kim

The History of Mexico
Burton Kirkwood

The History of New Zealand
Tom Brooking

The History of Nigeria
Toyin Falola

The History of Panama
Robert C. Harding

The History of Poland
M.B. Biskupski

The History of Portugal
James M. Anderson

The History of Russia
Charles E. Ziegler

The History of Serbia
John K. Cox

The History of South Africa
Roger B. Beck

The History of Spain
Peter Pierson

The History of Sri Lanka
Patrick Peebles

The History of Sweden
Byron J. Nordstrom

The History of Turkey
Douglas A. Howard

The History of Venezuela
H. Micheal Tarver and Julia C. Frederick